BEGINNING C#
GAME PROGRAMMING

THOMSON
™
COURSE TECHNOLOGY
Professional ■ Technical ■ Reference

ISBN: 1-59200-517-9

Library of Congress Catalog Card Number: 2004107745

Printed in the United States of America

06 07 08 PH 10 9 8 7 6 5 4 3 2

SVP, Thomson Course Technology PTR:
Andy Shafran

Publisher:
Stacy L. Hiquet

Senior Marketing Manager:
Sarah O'Donnell

Marketing Manager:
Heather Hurley

Manager of Editorial Services:
Heather Talbot

Senior Acquisitions Editor:
Emi Smith

Senior Editor:
Mark Garvey

Associate Marketing Manager:
Kristin Eisenzopf

Marketing Coordinator:
Jordan Casey

Project Editor/Copy Editor:
Estelle Manticas

Technical Reviewer:
Brian Lich

PTR Editorial Services Coordinator:
Elizabeth Furbish

Interior Layout Tech:
Shawn Morningstar

Cover Designer:
Mike Tanamachi

CD-ROM Producer:
Brandon Penticuff

Indexer:
Katherine Stimson

Proofreader:
Nancy Sixsmith

THOMSON

COURSE TECHNOLOGY

Professional ■ Technical ■ Reference

Thomson Course Technology PTR,
a division of Thomson Course Technology
25 Thomson Place
Boston, MA 02210
http://www.courseptr.com

BEGINNING C#
GAME PROGRAMMING

RON PENTON

THOMSON

™

COURSE TECHNOLOGY

Professional ■ Technical ■ Reference

ACKNOWLEDGMENTS

I would first like to thank my family for supporting me through this, my third book. It's been a long three years, hasn't it?

I would also like to thank all of my friends for their encouragement and friendship, especially Jim, Andrew, Dan, James, Scott, Tracy, Jenny, Josefina, Brett, Kristy, Wendy, Lisa, Marla, Irina, Yelena, Tina, Jordi, and Liz.

I would also like to thank everyone at work.

Finally, I would like to thank everyone I know in the game development scene, specifically (and in no particular order): Dave Astle, Kevin Hawkins, Trent Polack, Evan Pipho, April Gould, Joseph Fernald, Andrew Vehlies, Andrew Nguyen, John Hattan, Ken Kinnison, Seth Robinson, Ernest Pazera, Denis Lukianov, Sean Kent, Nicholas Cooper, Ian Overgard, Greg Rosenblatt, Yannick Loitière, Henrik Stuart, Chris Hargrove, Richard Benson, Mat Noguchi, Richard "Superpig" Fine, Anthony Casteel, Danny McCue, Tyler "Acoustica" Roehmholdt (socialite extraordinaire), Mike Stedman, Pouya Larjani, "They Call Me Fred" Fred, Mark "SteelGolem" Yorke, Jesse Towner, Jean McGuire, Andrew Russell, Thomas Cowell, Matthew "Programmer One" Varga, Dillon Cower, Matthew Daley, Jack McCormack, Patrick van der Willik, and Kent "_dot_" Lai Shiaw San.

ABOUT THE AUTHOR

RON PENTON has always tinkered around with video games. From the age of 11, when his parents bought him his first game-programming book on how to make adventure games, Ron has always striven to learn the most about how games work and how to create them.

Ron holds a bachelor's degree in Computer Science and a minor in Mathematics from The State University of New York at Buffalo. He has written two other books, *Data Structures for Game Programmers*, and *MUD Game Programming*. Ron has also contributed to Bruno de Sousa's book *Game Programming All in One*.

Contents at a Glance

Introduction xvi

Part I: Learning C#   1

Chapter 1 The History of C# 3

Chapter 2 The Basics 13

Chapter 3 A Brief Introduction to Classes 35

Chapter 4 Advanced C# 63

Chapter 5 One More C# Chapter 87

Part II: Game Programming in C#   121

Chapter 6 Setting Up a Framework 123

Chapter 7 Direct3D 145

Chapter 8 DirectInput 197

Chapter 9 DirectSound 219

Chapter 10 Putting Together a Game 227

Conclusion 283

Part III: Appendixes   285

Appendix A Answers to Review Questions 287

Appendix B Setting Up DirectX and .NET 303

Index 307

CONTENTS

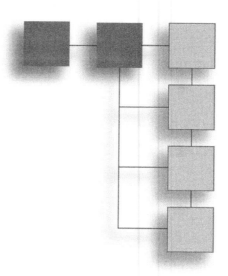

Introduction xvi

PART I: LEARNING C#   1

Chapter 1   **The History of C#** 3
A Brief History of Computers 3
     Machine and Assembly Languages 4
     Portability. 4
     High-Level Languages Save the Day 5
     Portability with Virtual Machines. 6
.NET to the Rescue 7
     Just In Time Compilation. 8
     Reduction Theory 9
     The Future 10
Summary 10
     What You Learned. 11
     Review Questions 11
     On Your Own. 11

Chapter 2 **The Basics** **13**

Why You Should Read This Chapter 13

Your First C# Program 14

    Classes. 14

    The Entry Point 14

    Hello, C#!! 15

    Compiling and Running 15

The Basics 16

    Basic Data Types. 16

    Operators 17

    Variables. 20

    Constants 21

    Typecasts. 21

Branching 23

    if Statements 24

    Switch Statements. 25

    Short-Circuit Evaluation 26

Looping 27

    while Loops 28

    for Loops 28

    do-while Loops 29

    Break and Continue. 29

Scoping 30

Summary 31

    What You Learned. 31

    Review Questions 32

    On Your Own. 34

Chapter 3 **A Brief Introduction to Classes** **35**

Values versus References 36

    Value Types. 36

    Reference Types. 36

Basics of Structures and Classes 39

    Creating Classes and Structures 40

    Differences between Structures and Classes 40

    Putting Functions in Your Classes and Structures 41

    Constructors. 45

    Destructors. 46

More Advanced Class Tricks 48

    The Basics of Inheritance 48

    Static Members 53

    Properties 55

Enumerations 57

Summary 59

    What You Learned 59

    Review Questions 59

    On Your Own 61

Chapter 4   **Advanced C#** **63**

Namespaces 64

    Creating Namespaces 65

    Using Namespaces 66

    Namespace Aliasing 66

Polymorphism 67

    Basic Polymorphism 67

    Virtual Functions 68

    Abstraction 71

    Polymorphism and Functions 72

    Objects 73

Arrays 74

    A Basic Array Example 74

    What Is an Array? 75

    Inline Initialization 76

    References versus Values 76

    Inheritance and Arrays 77

    Multidimensional Arrays 77

    Another Kind of Loop 81

Strings 82

Summary 84

    What You Learned 84

    Review Questions 85

Chapter 5   **One More C# Chapter** **87**

Interfaces 88

    Interfaces versus Abstract Classes 89

    Multiple Inheritance 91

    Extending and Combining Interfaces 93

Exceptions 94
    Exception Basics 94
    Advanced Exception Topics 98
Delegates 100
    Creating a Delegate 100
    Chaining Delegates 102
Collections 102
    The Array List 103
    Hash Tables 105
    Stacks and Queues 106
    Other Collections 107
File Access 107
    Streams 107
    Readers and Writers 109
    File Streams 112
Random Numbers 114
    Seeds 114
    Generating Numbers 115
    Other Generation Techniques 115
Above and Beyond 116
    The Preprocessor 116
    Operator Overloading 116
    Variable Parameter Lists 117
    Unsafe Code 117
    C# 2.0 Features 117
Summary 117
    What You Learned 117
    Review Questions 118
    On Your Own 119

PART II: GAME PROGRAMMING IN C#   121

Chapter 6   Setting Up a Framework 123
             Creating a Project 123
                 SharpDevelop 124
                 Visual C# 132
                 Visual C#'s D3D Framework 133

The Advanced Framework 134
   Have You Got the Time?. 134
   Problems with the Timer. 137
   Changes to the Framework 138
Summary 142
   What You Learned. 143
   Review Questions 143
   On Your Own. 143

Chapter 7   Direct3D **145**
DirectX Versions 146
One Device to Rule Them All 146
   It's All about Presentation 146
   Buffers and Buffer Swapping 146
   Creating a Device. 149
   The Manager 151
Updating the Framework 154
   Setting Up a Device. 155
   Handling Multi-Tasking. 157
Actually Drawing Stuff 159
   Vertexes 160
   Defining Some Vertexes 161
   Final Touches 162
Colors and Alpha 163
   Playing with Colors 164
   Playing with Alpha 164
   Another Demo. 167
Texturing and Other Shapes 169
   Texturing 170
   Other Forms of Geometry. 173
   Demo 7.4 175
Sprites 177
   The Sprite Class 177
   Making the Code Better 179
   Demo 7.5 185
Fonts 190
   Creating a System Font. 190
   Drawing Text 191
   Demo 7.6 191

Summary 193
   What You Learned. 194
   Review Questions 194
   On Your Own 195

Chapter 8   **DirectInput** **197**
Keyboards 197
   Creating a Device. 198
   Gathering Input by Polling 199
Mice 200
   Creating a Mouse 200
   Polling a Mouse. 200
Game Devices 201
   Finding a Game Device 202
   Creating a Game Device 202
   Getting Joystick Axis Data 203
   Modifying Axis Attributes. 204
   More Joystick Data 206
   Demo 8.3: Joysticks 207
Force Feedback 210
   The Effect Editor 210
   Loading Effects 211
   Playing Effects 212
   Stopping Effects. 213
   Demo 8.4 213
Summary 216
   What You Learned. 216
   Review Questions 217
   On Your Own 217

Chapter 9   **DirectSound** **219**
The Sound Device 219
Sound Buffers 220
   Playing Buffers. 220
   Buffer Descriptions 221
   Demo 9.1 222
Sound Effects 222
Sound in 3D 223
   3D Buffers. 223
   Additional 3D Topics 223

Summary 224
   What You Learned. 224
   Review Questions 224
   On Your Own. 225

Chapter 10   Putting Together a Game **227**
Setting Up a Design 227
The Game Genre 228
Deciding How the Game Works 228
   The Universe 229
   The Actors 229
The Data. 229
   Spaceships 229
   Weapons. 230
   Projectiles. 230
   Powerups 230
   Common Attributes. 230
A New Framework 231
   Setting Up 232
   Device Options. 232
   Device Blocks 233
   Input Checkers 233
Joysticks 235
   Game States. 235
   State Changes 237
   A Sample State. 239
   The Game Class 240
Generic Space Shooter 3000 244
   Game Objects. 244
   The States for GSS3K 256
   The Help State 260
   The Game State 260
   Playing GSS3K 277
The Future 279
   3D Worlds. 279
   Advanced Collision Detection. 279
   Artificial Intelligence. 279
   Networking 280
   Advanced Storage 280

Summary 280
 What You Learned. 280
 Review Questions 281
 On Your Own. 281

Conclusion **283**

Part III: Appendixes   285

Appendix A Answers to Review Questions **287**
 Chapter 1: The History of C# 287
 Chapter 2: The Basics 288
 Chapter 3: A Brief Introduction to Classes 291
 Chapter 4: Advanced C# 294
 Chapter 5: One More C# Chapter .296
 Chapter 6: Setting Up a Framework 298
 Chapter 7: Direct3D 299
 Chapter 8: DirectInput 300
 Chapter 9: DirectSound 301
 Chapter 10: Putting Together a Game 301

Appendix B Setting Up DirectX and .NET **303**
 The .NET Framework 303
 The .NET SDK 303
 Integrated Development Environments 304
 Managed DirectX 304
 Setting Up References 304

Index **307**

INTRODUCTION

Only a few short years ago, everyone programmed games in C. There was no question about it—if you wanted to program cutting-edge games, you did so in C. Sure, C++ was around, but it was too "slow." The advanced features that C++ offered took off too much processing power, and that was simply unacceptable to a game programmer.

Over time, computers got faster and faster and video games got bigger and bigger. Soon, people realized that games were just getting too big to write in C. When programs were small, C was a great language to use because there was no real need for a lot of management in your code. One person could write a program and easily understand what everything did. But C becomes a problem when programs get bigger; it's just too hard to manage a large program written in C. I'm not going to get into why here—if you've ever used C, then you know why.

C++ fixed a lot of problems with C, but maintaining backwards-compatibility was a major problem, and as a result, C++ ended up being one of the biggest language mutations in existence. It's also a great language, but it has a mighty long list of flaws associated with it.

It used to be that your computer was outdated almost the minute you walked out the computer-store door with it. I found myself upgrading my video card once a year, easily; true die-hard gamers would upgrade twice or even three times a year! Things aren't like that anymore. My computer has been sitting here for a year and a half, and I haven't touched the inside of it except to add a new hard drive.

Computers have gotten to a point where they are fast enough to handle most of what you need them to in a reasonable amount of time, and there's really no huge benefit to upgrading your computer to run the newest games because the newest games are so close to reaching photorealistic quality that huge advances just aren't being made anymore.

It's no wonder that "slow" languages like C# and everything else that's part of .NET are now becoming popular again. Managed languages like C# take a lot more overhead than older languages, but they offer so much more in terms of protection that statistically, you're much less likely to make bugs in your programs, just because of the way the language is designed. Sure, these languages take more processing power to do more checking for you, but people are realizing that it's worth it in the end because they allow you to make games in less time, without worrying about tiny little nuances.

Who This Book Is For

This book is for anyone who wants to learn how to program in C# and DirectX 9. You are not required to have *any* knowledge of C# at all in order to read this book, but some programming background (in any language) would be helpful.

Additionally, you don't have to go out and buy any tools in order to dig into C# programming because everything you need to program in C# is available for free! Look into Appendix B for more information on getting set up to program in C#.

This book will not be a complete comprehensive guide to C#, DirectX, or game programming in general. It is simply intended to give you a jumpstart into the topic. It would be impossible to offer a complete guide to any of those topics in a book of this size (and it would be impossible to offer a complete guide to game programming in a book of *any* size), so I've gone through C# and DirectX and picked out the fundamental topics to cover, as well as other topics that are especially important to game programming.

Book Layout

This book is broken into three different parts. Each part and chapter is previewed in the next sections.

Part I: Learning C#

This section of the book is intended to give you a good look at how to start programming in C#.

Chapter 1: The History of C#

You can't get a good grasp of any concept without understanding how it came to be, so this chapter tells you why C# and .NET were created and how they work.

Chapter 2: The Basics

This chapter will give you a look at your very first C# program and will introduce you to some basic language concepts, including data types, mathematical operators, variables, constants, type conversions, conditional logic, and looping logic.

Chapter 3: A Brief Introduction to Classes

Classes are the basic building blocks of any object-oriented language. This chapter will go over how to create classes, the differences between value and reference types, garbage collection, structures, functions, constructors, inheritance, enumerated types, and properties.

Chapter 4: Advanced C#

Once you know all the basics of C# programming, this chapter will take you deeper into the jungle, introducing you to the concepts of namespaces, polymorphism, abstraction, and basic data structures.

Chapter 5: One More C# Chapter

This chapter goes over all the important topics that weren't covered in the previous chapters, such as interfaces, exceptions, delegates, file access, random numbers, and more advanced data structures.

Part II: Game Programming in C#

Now that you've gotten all the basic C# stuff out of the way, this section of the book will introduce you to the basics of accessing DirectX and making a computer game using the various video, input, and sound components.

Chapter 6: Setting Up a Framework

There's a lot of setup necessary when you're initializing the various components of a game; this chapter goes over how to create a basic framework with which to start your game projects.

Chapter 7: Direct3D

Graphics programming is one of the most complex parts of games these days, so it's no surprise that this is one of the longest chapters in the book. It goes over what you need to know in order to create a Direct3D device, back buffers, and display formats, as well as how to handle multi-tasking and how to draw triangles. It also covers color shading, blending, textures, sprites, and text.

Chapter 8: DirectInput

Getting user input is an essential part of game programming, and this chapter covers it all, from keyboards to mice and every game device in between. This chapter also covers force feedback programming.

Chapter 9: DirectSound

Sound is the final major media component of a game. In this chapter, you will learn how to load and play sounds from disk, and you'll get to play around with some of the neat effects programming and 3D sound programming features that DirectSound offers as well.

Chapter 10: Putting Together a Game

In this final chapter, you will learn how to combine the knowledge you gained in all of the previous chapters and program an actual game, *Generic Space Shooter 3000*.

Appendixes

There are two appendixes in this book.

Appendix A: Answers to Review Questions

Every chapter has review questions at the end of it, and this appendix contains the answers to these questions.

Appendix B: Setting Up DirectX and .NET

This appendix goes over how to set up the various components you'll need in order to start programming your games in C#.

Here We Go!

You're ready to start reading (and programming in C#!). If you have any questions I'd be glad to answer them; just send me an e-mail at CSBook@ronpenton.net. Please be patient when waiting for a reply—I have many e-mails to answer on a daily basis, and I don't always have time to get to them in a timely manner.

Are you ready? You'd better be! Here we go!

PART I

LEARNING C#

CHAPTER 1
The History of C# 3

CHAPTER 2
The Basics 13

CHAPTER 3
A Brief Introduction to Classes 35

CHAPTER 4
Advanced C# 63

CHAPTER 5
One More C# Chapter 87

In this first part of the book, you will learn almost everything you need to know about C# in order to start programming your own games. Obviously, a book this size cannot possibly cover every C# topic, but all the important stuff is explained.

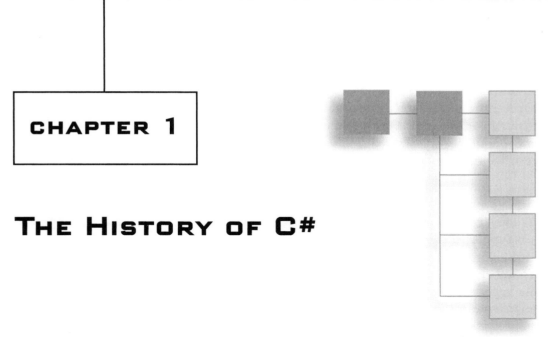

CHAPTER 1

THE HISTORY OF C#

History has always been a favorite subject of mine. I find it incredibly useful to know how and why events happened in the past. Knowledge of history helps to explain why things are the way they are now, and it gives you an idea of where things are going in the future. This is why whenever I'm learning a new technology, I try to find out about the history of that technology first; doing so gives me an idea of what problems it was designed to solve, as well as what problems it cannot solve. In this chapter, you will learn:

- That machine languages tell a computer what to do.
- That assembly languages tell a computer what to do in readable, human-like terms.
- How high-level programming languages allow you to abstract your programs away from low-level machine language and describe them in an easier fashion.
- How virtual machines translate imaginary machine code into actual machine code.
- How virtual machines can help port programs to many platforms easily.
- That all programs can be reduced into machine language formats.
- That .NET speeds up the VM process by translating the code only the first time it is run.

A Brief History of Computers

Once upon a time, in a mystical land far, far away, some crazy people decided to invent mathematics. Of course, back in those times, there were no such things as calculators or computers, so people did mathematics by hand, on paper. As anyone who has taken school math classes without a calculator can attest, this is not fun at all. Besides actually having to use your brain (the horror!), your hand could quite easily cramp up after a few hundred calculations. Where's the fun in that?

To solve the problem, some enterprising folks came up with the brilliant idea of making a machine that could do mathematical calculations for you, without all of the bothersome thinking and writing. Man created computer, and saw that it was good. Now we didn't have to wait for some poor soul to perform a few hundred calculations on paper; instead, we had a machine that could do it in far less time, and with completely accurate results.

Machine and Assembly Languages

In those ancient times, computer programs were simple. Some of the earliest computers only supported eight different commands, total, and could only execute a few dozen of them before a new program had to be created. Basically, a programmer made out a list of numbers, fed it into a computer, and ran it; the numbers would represent the commands. In a hypothetical example, the number 0 would represent an addition command, and 1 would represent a multiplication command. Programs written like this are said to be written in *machine language*.

With simple machines like the early computers, one could quite easily remember what number meant what command—after all, there were only eight commands or so. Eventually, however, computers became more complex. People started adding more and more commands, so that soon you had a few dozen, or maybe even over a hundred or so commands available. Very few people can remember that many commands, and looking them up in a manual all the time would be very tedious, so assembly languages were invented. An *assembly language* is essentially a language that directly translates word-based commands into machine language. For example, in the hypothetical machine mentioned previously, the machine language code to multiply 6 times 7 would look something like this:

```
1 6 7
```

where the 1 represents the command and the two numbers following it represent the data. Of course, looking at printouts of hundreds of lines of numbers can hurt your eyes and your brain, so an assembly language command might look something like this:

```
MUL 6, 7
```

Ah, now that's prettier to the eye! At least now you can tell right away that you want to multiply 6 times 7. Computers have programs called *assemblers*, which would take assembly language code and translate it directly into machine language code. Assemblers are very simple programs; basically, all they do is find the name of the command and replace it with the number representing the command.

Portability

Now let's talk about portability. The term *portability* refers to the ability of a program to be moved onto another computer. Portability, until recently, was pretty much a huge pain in the butt. You see, there were many people making computers in the bad old days, and almost none of the computers worked together. So you'd have one machine that understood the command 1 to mean *multiply*, but another machine would foolishly use, say, 2 to indicate *multiply* instead.

Assembly languages helped solve some of these problems. You could pretty much assume that most machines had the basic add, subtract, multiply, and divide commands, so basically all you needed was an assembler for Machine A to translate "MUL" into 1, and an assembler for Machine B to translate "MUL" into 2.

Theoretically, you could *port* an assembly program to many different machines, assuming each of those machines had an assembler program that understood the assembly language grammar you were using.

But things got ugly fast. See, computers became quite complex, and all the computer companies decided that they wanted to throw as many commands onto a processor as they could. But none of the companies could ever agree as to *what* commands they should use! Some computers had commands to perform floating-point mathematics, others didn't. Some could perform binary-coded decimal (BCD) calculations and others couldn't. Still others gave you a dozen different ways to access memory, and others would give you only one!

note

Don't worry about what BCD calculations are; they're not really used much in game programming.

Houston, we have a problem. Assemblers could no longer port programs from one platform to another because the platforms were becoming a jumbled mess. So, rather than try to make programs for all machines, most programmers learned how to use one machine, and made their programs just for that machine. Want to run a program that was made for Machine A on Machine B? Tough luck; it wasn't going to happen.

High-Level Languages Save the Day

Enter *high level programming languages*, stage right. These were highly complex languages that described how to perform mathematical calculations, but didn't go into all of the messy details of how to actually do them. You could say something like this:

```
int i = 6 * 7;
```

In a language like C (one of the earliest and most popular high-level programming languages), a program called a *compiler* would take that text and translate it into machine language for you. You really don't need to know how it happens—all you know is that you created a number that stores the result of 6 times 7.

Unfortunately, high-level languages have failed to create perfectly portable programs. The problem is that every compiler is different, and does things differently. Every operating system has a different *Application Programming Interface (API)* that other machines can't use. If you make a Windows program, you'll deal with the WIN32 API, but good luck trying to get that to work on a Macintosh.

Portability with Virtual Machines

Then someone had the brilliant idea to invent a *virtual machine (VM)*. A virtual machine is a computer processor that is simulated in software. For example, let's say you create your own machine language. That's great, but if you don't have your own processor to execute the language, it's kind of useless. So you go ahead and create a piece of software that will be your virtual machine. This software will read in instructions from your own machine language and translate them to instructions for the computer it's running on. Figure 1.1 shows this process.

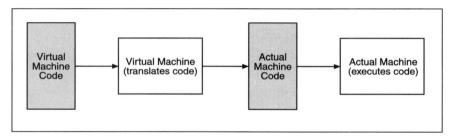

Figure 1.1 A virtual machine translates instructions to be run on an actual machine.

So what is the point of this? Why not just write your program in the actual machine language in the first place? The answer is portability. Imagine if you could go out and make VMs for ten different platforms. Now you could create just one program in your VM language, and run it on ten completely different machines! Figure 1.2 shows how this works.

One of the most popular virtual machines to hit the computer industry was the Java Virtual Machine (JVM), invented to go along with the Java programming language. The idea was to create a computer language that would run on *any* computer *anywhere*—100 percent portability. This would allow developers to create one program and sell it on any computer that had a JVM, without having to spend many hours and lots of money trying to make it work on another platform. The immediate upside to this is that developers instantly had access to a much larger target audience. Not only would your programs work on Windows machines, but they would also work also on Macintoshes and Linux machines, with no extra effort on your part.

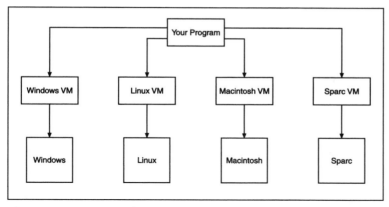

Figure 1.2 You can take one program and execute it on many different platforms using different virtual machines (VMs).

While all of this sounds excellent in theory and Java did become a very popular language, it failed to take hold of the game industry in any way. The first problem, of course, is speed. A virtual machine has overhead, which means that everything has to go through the virtual machine before it can be executed on the actual machine. Game programming, however, has almost always been concerned with speed: everybody to the limit! You want to take what you have and just push it as far as you can go.

Having a virtual machine in the way was a big problem; why would you program a game in Java that will be half as fast as a game you could do in C++? Obviously, for small games, and especially for Web-based games, speed isn't really a big concern (and Java really took off with Web-based applications and games) but for anything really big, Java wasn't even a consideration.

A single language is not the answer to every problem. There are times when you want to program a game in a language like Java, but at other times Java just doesn't have what it takes. I'm not going to go too far in depth on this, but entire languages exist out there that use completely different programming paradigms and are able to solve problems much more easily (for example, *functional programming languages* like LISP are quite often used for artificial intelligence programming) than Java can. It's simply not a good idea to tie a language to a virtual machine because you're forcing people to program in a language that people just may not like (and believe me, there are a ton of people out there who cannot stand Java).

.NET to the Rescue

So along comes .NET. Microsoft paid good attention to the mistakes that Sun made with Java and tried to fix them in .NET. They didn't get them all, but on the whole, .NET is a vast improvement on Java, and accomplishes a lot of what Java failed to deliver.

The Microsoft .NET platform is essentially a very complex web of tools that encompasses everything from security to Web deployment. The most interesting part of .NET, however, is the Common Language Runtime (CLR), which is a pseudo-virtual machine that executes Microsoft Interpreted Language (MSIL) code. I'll get to the meaning of that in a little bit.

.NET is not tied to any particular language. Microsoft officially supports four different .NET languages:

- Managed C++
- C# (pronounced *see-sharp*)
- Visual Basic.NET
- J# (pronounced *jay-sharp)*

Unofficially, there are literally dozens more languages that have compilers that generate MSIL code. These languages include LISP, PERL, Python, and even (gasp) COBOL.

caution

As there are many languages that can be compiled into .NET, and .NET has access to DirectX, it is theoretically possible to program games in COBOL. But this is something only qualified professionals should attempt; in other words, don't try this at home, kids. You might hurt someone.

The very best part of .NET, however, is the fact that everything in .NET shares a similar layout, called the *Common Type System*. Basically, if you create a class in one language (such as Visual Basic), give it two integers, and compile it, then you can create the same class in C# with the same data and it should theoretically compile into the same MSIL code.

Anything that is compiled into .NET can access other .NET modules as well, which has the interesting side effect of allowing many different languages to talk to each other. For example, if you're using C#, you can actually tell it to use classes that were created in Visual Basic.NET. Even better, you can inherit from them and expand their capabilities, meaning you can have classes that were created using more than one language! The .NET system is unbelievably flexible for this reason alone; never has a system been developed that allows you to integrate so many paradigms so easily.

Just In Time Compilation

All virtual machines have an overhead, as I mentioned previously. The .NET system isn't exactly a pure virtual machine, however. The .NET system does something really clever: it uses a method called *Just In Time* (JIT) compilation to speed up execution of code. The JIT system keeps track of your MSIL code, and whenever you run a module for the first time, it takes your MSIL code and converts that into the native code of your machine. So when you run a .NET module on your Windows machine for the first time, the JIT loads in the MSIL code, translates it directly into x86 code, and then saves that code. From that point on, whenever your module is run, the computer executes the native x86 code and completely bypasses any use of the virtual machine at all, so it's almost as if you've compiled a program directly from a high-level language into machine language—but not quite. Figure 1.3 shows this process.

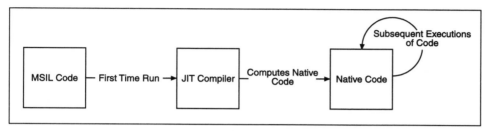

Figure 1.3 Your MSIL modules are translated into native code when they are first executed, thus preventing the translation penalty every time your code is executed.

Reduction Theory

The idea behind .NET and virtual machines in general is that programs in high-level languages can always be "downsized" or "reduced." Take, for example, the idea of printing out words to your monitor. In a language like C#, this is accomplished by one line of code:

```
System.Console.WriteLine( "I like pies" );
```

But what does that do, really? Internally, the computer basically just moves some memory around and tells the input/output bus to send some data to the screen. In theory, any complex command in any language can be reduced down into a bunch of simpler commands.

Here's a real-world analogy: When you turn the ignition key in a car, the car starts up; that's like a high-level language. Inside the engine of the car, a sequence of events occurs:

1. The battery starts turning the pistons.
2. The battery ignites the spark plug.
3. The spark plug explodes the gas in the cylinders.
4. The exploding gas starts turning the pistons even faster.

Each large command (like starting a car engine) can be broken down into a specific set of small commands (such as those listed above). There are only a few different types of small commands, and these are what virtual machines rely on. You can create some super complex language that has functions such as MakeSuperCoolGameNow(), but in the end, the computer reduces it down into a sequence of commands that do math calculations and move memory around. In reality, that's all a computer does anyway—perform math calculations and move memory around.

So if all a virtual machine needs to know is how to perform math calculations and move memory around, that means they can be very simple to make and easy to port to different platforms.

note

An entire area of computer science exists that is dedicated to the idea of reducing problems into a simpler form. There is actually a whole class of computer problems, called *NP-Complete* problems, wherein every single problem can be reduced down into one problem that describes *every* NP-Complete problem in the world.

The Future

C# is Microsoft's flagship for the .NET platform. The company wanted to take C++ and fix what's wrong with it; that's a pretty hefty goal, but if anyone has enough resources to tackle that problem, it's Microsoft.

As of this writing, no major game studios are publicly developing with C#, but that's understandable. The language is still in its infancy, and a big company doesn't want to blow millions of dollars on a project that they aren't 100 percent sure about. In time, however, that will change. In fact, the single greatest plus about a system like .NET is the portability it can provide. Right now, if you want to write a game for the PC and a game console, you practically have to write two games because chances are that the systems don't have anything in common. This is a tremendous problem for companies that are cash-strapped and cannot afford to write two games, so they're probably going to have to settle for writing the game for the PC or a particular console. In the future, consoles like the XBox 2 are likely to support .NET, so it should be possible to write one game and have it work perfectly on the PC and a console at the same time! Just as high-level languages introduced a whole new level of semi-portability to the computer world, .NET is poised to make an even greater impact.

Summary

This chapter acquainted you with the ideas behind Microsoft's .NET platform and gave you an idea of what portable computing is all about. While you technically didn't have to learn about any of this, I still feel that it is a very important area you should be familiar with if you're ever going to get deep into .NET game programming.

What You Learned

The main concepts that you should have picked up from this chapter are:

- Machine languages tell a computer what to do.
- Assembly languages tell a computer what to do in readable human-like terms.
- High-level programming languages allow you to abstract your programs away from low-level machine language and allow you to describe them in an easier fashion.
- Virtual machines translate imaginary machine code into actual machine code.
- Virtual machines can help port programs to many platforms easily.
- All programs can be reduced into machine language formats.
- .NET speeds up the VM process by translating the code only the first time it is run.

Review Questions

These review questions test your knowledge of the important concepts explained in this chapter. The answers can be found in Appendix A.

1.1. Why does a virtual machine slow down programs?

1.2. How does JIT compilation speed up VM execution?

1.3. What languages does Microsoft officially support for .NET?

1.4. Can other languages support .NET as well?

On Your Own

If you have any favorite programming languages, try to find a project that will compile your language into .NET. For example, search the Internet for Ironpython if you're interested in running Python programs on .NET.

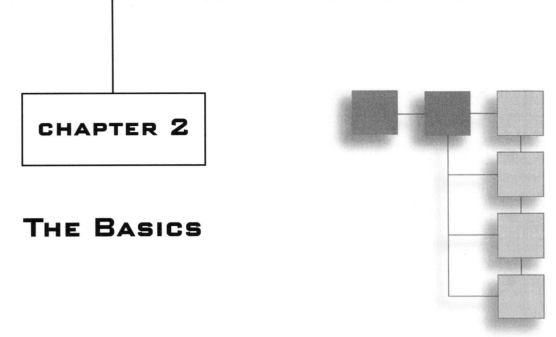

CHAPTER 2

THE BASICS

Chapter 1 showed you some history on why .NET and C# were created. Now it's time to dive deep into the abyss and learn just how to use C#. In this chapter, I will show you:

- How to compile and run a C# program.
- What a class is.
- What an entry point is.
- The basic data types.
- The basic mathematical and bitwise operators.
- How to declare variables and constants.
- How to perform basic typecasts.
- How to create program branches using if and switch statements.
- How to create loops using while, for, and do-while statements.
- How scoping works.

Why You Should Read This Chapter

If you already know a language like C/C++ or Java, then this chapter is going to be a breeze for you. In fact, you may even be tempted to skip over this chapter. After all, the basics of most programming languages are pretty much the same within the C family of languages. Unfortunately, though, even though the syntaxes of all of the languages are close to identical, the behavior of each language is different. There's actually quite a bit about C# that is different from other languages, so it's in your best interest to go ahead and read this chapter.

Your First C# Program

There is an ancient tradition (okay it's not that old) in computer programming that says that your first program in any language should be a "Hello World" program, a program that simply prints out a welcome message on your computer.

On the CD for this book you will find a demo entitled "HelloCSharp." You can find it in the /Demos/Chapter02/01-HelloCSharp/ directory. The HelloCSharp.cs file in that directory contains the code for the program; you can open it up in any text editor or Visual Studio and view it. The code should look like this:

```
class HelloCSharp
{
    static void Main( string[] args )
    {
        System.Console.WriteLine( "Hello, C#!!" );
    }
}
```

At first glance, you can see that this is about four or five lines longer than you could write it in C or C++; that's because C# is a more complicated language.

Classes

C# is an *object-oriented* programming language, which may not mean anything to you at this point. I will go over the concepts in much more detail in Chapter 3, "A Brief Introduction to Classes," but for now, all you need to know is that C# represents its programs as objects.

The idea is to separate your programs into nouns and verbs, where every noun can be represented as an object. For example, if you make a game that has spaceships flying around, you can think of the spaceships as *objects*.

A *class* in a C# program describes a noun; it tells the computer what kind of data your objects will have and what kind of actions can be done on them. A spaceship class might tell the computer about how many people are in it, how much fuel it has left, and how fast it is going.

In C#, your entire program is actually a class. In Demo 2.1, you have the HelloCSharp class, which is the name of the program.

The Entry Point

Every program has an *entry point*, the place in the code where the computer will start execution. In older languages like C and C++, the entry point was typically a global function called main, but in C# it's a little different. C# doesn't allow you to have global functions, but rather it forces you to put your functions into classes, so you obviously cannot use the same method for a C# entry point. C# is like Java in this respect; the entry point for every C# program is a *static function* called Main inside a class, like the one you saw defined in Demo 2-1. I'll cover functions and static functions in a lot more detail in Chapter 3, so just bear with me for now.

Every C# program must have a class that has a static Main function; if it doesn't, then the computer won't know where to start running the program. Furthermore, you can only have one Main function defined in your program; if you have more than one, then the computer won't know which one to start with.

note

> Technically, you can have more than one Main function in your program, but that just makes things messy. If you include more than one Main, then you need to tell your C# compiler which class contains the entry point—that's really a lot of trouble you can live without.

Hello, C#!!

The part of the program that performs the printing is this line:

```
System.Console.WriteLine( "Hello, C#!!" );
```

This line gets the System.Console class—which is built into the .NET framework—and tells it to print out "Hello, C#!!" using its WriteLine function.

Compiling and Running

There are a few ways you can compile this program and run it. The easiest way would be to open up a console window, find your way to the demo directory, and use the command-line C# compiler to compile the file, like this:

```
csc HelloCSharp.cs
```

The other way you could compile this program would be to load up the 01-HelloCSharp.cmbx project file in SharpDevelop or the 01-HelloCSharp.sln file in Visual Studio.NET, depending on which IDE you're using. You can find more detailed instructions on how to do this in Appendix B.

Now, when you run the program, you should get a simple output on your screen:

```
Hello, C#!!
```

Ta-da! You now have your very first C# program, which spits out some text to your screen!

The Basics

Almost every programming language has common properties. For one thing, programming languages generally know how to store data. They must also operate on that data by moving it around and performing calculations on it.

Basic Data Types

Like most programming languages, C# has a large number of built-in data types, mostly representing numbers of various formats. These are shown in Table 2.1.

note

C# is an *extendible* language, which means that you can create your own data types later on if you want. I'll go into much more detail on this in Chapter 3.

Table 2.1 C# Built-in Data types

Type	Size (bytes)	Values
bool	1	true or false
byte	1	0 to 255
sbyte	1	-128 to 127
char	2	Alphanumeric characters (in Unicode)
short	2	-32,768 to 32,767
ushort	2	0 to 65,535
int	4	-2,147,483,648 to 2,147,483,647
uint	4	0 to 4,294,967,295
*float	4	-3.402823×10^{38} to 3.402823×10^{38}
long	8	-9,223,372,036,854,775,808 to 9,223,372,036,854,775,807
ulong	8	0 to 18,446,744,073,709,551,615
*double	8	$-1.79769313486232 \times 10^{308}$ to $1.79769313486232 \times 10^{308}$
**decimal	16	-79,228,162,514,264,337,593,543,950,335 to 79,228,162,514,264,337,593,543,950,335

* - These are *floating-point* formats, which can represent inexact decimal values

* - This is a fixed-point format, which represents exact decimal values with up to 28 digits

The integer-based types (byte, short, int, long, and so on) can only store whole numbers, such as 0, 1, 2, and so on; they cannot hold decimal numbers, such as 1.5 or 3.14159.

In order to hold decimal numbers, you need to switch to either a *floating-point* or a *fixed-point* format. The exact details on how these kinds of numbers are stored is beyond the scope of this book, but there is a subtle difference that will affect scientists and mathematicians (but probably not game programmers).

note

Basically, floating-point numbers cannot hold precise numbers; they can only approximate decimal numbers within a certain amount of error. For example, using floats, you can represent the numbers 1.0 and 1.00000012, but you can't represent any number in between. So, if you set a float to be equal to 1.00000007, then the computer will automatically round that up to 1.00000012. Doubles are the same way, but have more precision (up to 15 digits). Decimals are encoded in a different way, and even though the .NET documentation calls them *fixed-point* numbers, they are still technically *floating-point* numbers, and they have a precision of up to 28 digits.

Operators

Operators are symbols that appear in a computer language; they tell the computer to perform certain calculations on data. Operators are commonly used in math equations, so I'm sure this concept will be very familiar to you.

The C# language has a number of built-in operators in the language, and if you've ever used C++ or Java, then you probably already know most of them.

Mathematical Operators

C# has five basic mathematical operations built into the language, as shown in Table 2.2.

Table 2.2 Basic Mathematical Operators in C#

Operator	Symbol	Example	Result
Addition	+	5 + 6	11
Subtraction	-	6 - 5	1
Multiplication	*	6 * 7	42
Division	/	8 / 4	2
Modulus	%	9 % 3	0
Increment	++	10++	11
Decrement	—	10—	9

The first four operators are no-brainers, or at least they ought to be. The fifth operator may be new to you if you haven't done a lot of programming before. Modulus is sometimes known as "the remainder operator" or "the clock operator." Basically, the result from a modulus operation is the same as the remainder if you took the first number and divided it by the second. In the example given in Table 2.2, 3 divides into 9 evenly, so the remainder is 0. If you took 10 % 3, the result would be 1, as the remainder of 10/3 is 1.

note

Modulus is often called the clock operator because you can easily calculate the result using a clock. For example, take the calculation 13 % 12. Imagine you have the hand of a clock starting at 12, and you move it forward one hour every time you count up by 1. So when you count to 1, the hand will be at 1, and when you count to 2, the hand will be at 2, and so on. Eventually, when you get to 12, the hand will be at 12 again, and when you count to 13, the hand moves back to 1. So the result of 13 % 12 is 1.

note

The increment and decrement operators actually each have two different versions: the post- and pre- versions. For example, ++x is the pre-increment version, and x++ is the post-increment version. The difference is when the operators actually perform their calculations. For example, if x is 10 and you write y = x++, then the computer first puts the value of x into y and then increments x, leaving y equal to 10 and x equal to 11 when the code is done. On the other hand, y = ++x performs the increment first and performs the assignment later, leaving both x and y equal to 11. This is another holdover from C, and can make it ugly and difficult to read, so I don't really recommend using these operators too much.

You should note that all mathematical operators have alternate versions that allow you to directly modify a variable (see more about variables later on in this chapter). For example, if you wanted to add 10 to x, you could do this:

```
x = x + 10;
```

But that's somewhat clunky and redundant. Instead, you can write this:

```
x += 10;
```

All of the other math operators have similar versions:

```
x *= 10;    // multiply by 10
x /= 10;    // divide by 10
x -= 10;    // subtract 10
x %= 10;    // modulus by 10
x >>= 2;    // shift down by 2
x <<= 2;    // shift up by 2
```

Bitwise Math Operators

In addition to the standard math operators, there are also bitwise math operators, which perform binary math operations on numbers. The basic bitwise operators in C# are listed in Table 2.3.

Table 2.3 Basic Bitwise Operators in C#

Operator	Symbol	Example	Result
Binary And	&	6 & 10	2
Binary Or			6	10	14
Binary Xor	^	6 ^ 10	12
Binary Not	~	~7*	248

* - this example is performed on a byte

Bitwise math operators have alternate versions as well:

```
x &= 10;   // and by 10
x |= 10;   // or by 10
x ^= 10;   // xor by 10
```

Shifting Operators

There are two shifting operators, $\ll$ and $\gg$. These operators shift the bits in a number up or down, resulting in the following equations:

- - x $\ll$ y is the same as $x * 2^y$
- - x $\gg$ y is the same as $x / 2^y$

So 5 $\ll$ 3 is the same as 5 * 8, or 40, and 40 $\gg$ 3 is the same as 40 / 8, or 5.

note

Bitshifting is a lot faster than straight multiplication or division, but it's rarely used anymore. The speed savings just aren't that spectacular, and it makes your programs harder to read, anyway.

Logical Operators

There are a few common logical operators that perform comparisons on things and return the Boolean values true or false, depending on the outcome. Table 2.4 lists the logical operators.

Table 2.4 Logical Operators in C#

Operator	Symbol	Example	Result
Equals	==	1 == 2	false
Des Not Equal	!=	1 != 2	true
Less Than	<	1 < 2	true
Greater Than	>	1 > 2	false
Less Than or Equal To	<=	1 <= 2	true
Greater Than or Equal To	>=	1 >= 2	false
Logical And	&&	true && false	false
Logical Or	||	true || false	true
Logical Not	!	!true	false

* - This example is performed on a `byte`

Variables

In C#, as in almost any other language, you can create instances of the basic data types, called *variables*, and perform mathematical operations on them.

Declaring a piece of data in your program is an easy thing to do. All you need to do is put in the name of the type of data, then the name of the variable you want to create after that, and then (optionally) initialize the data with a value. Here's an example:

```
int x = 10;
float y = 3.14159;
decimal z;
```

caution

Note that if you try using a variable before initializing it (if you try using z from the previous code sample, for example), then you will get a compiler error in C#. Older languages, such as C and C++, would allow you to use a variable without giving it a value, which could cause a lot of errors because you never know what was in the variable if you never set it!

Here's an example using variables with the mathematical functions:

```
int x = 10 + 5;         // 15
int y = 20 * x;         // 300
int z = x / 8;          // 1
float a = (float)x / 8.0;  // 1.875
x = (int)a;             // 1
```

Pay particular attention to the last two lines. These lines show you how to use *typecasts* in your program. An explanation of typecasts is coming soon.

Constants

You can declare *constants*, pseudo-variables that cannot be changed, in your code. This is just another safety feature that's been around in computer languages for years now. For example:

```
const float pi = 3.14159;
```

Now you can use pi in your calculations, but you can't change its value (because changing the value of pi to 3.0 makes absolutely no sense!). This will cause a compiler error:

```
pi = 3.0;    // ERROR!
```

tip

Constants improve the readability of your programs by eliminating magic numbers. *Magic numbers* are numbers in your program that have no immediate meaning to whomever is reading it. For example, you can write x = 103; somewhere, but no one really knows what 103 means. It could mean the number of bullets in an ammo clip, or something else completely. Instead, you can use constants to show exactly what you mean, by defining a constant, called const int BulletsInClip = 103;, earlier in your program and then later using the constant x = BulletsInClip;. See how much more readable that is?

Typecasts

Check out this code:

```
float a =  1.875;
int x = (int)a;                 // 1
```

Look at the last line: the value of a is 1.875, a fractional number, and the last line of code is trying to put the value of a into x, which is an integer. Obviously, you can't just transfer the contents of a into x, so you need to lose some precision. Older languages, such as C/C++, would do this for you automatically, and chop 1.875 down to 1 in order to fit it into the integer (the process is called *truncation*). If you tried typing this line into a C# program, however, you would get a compiler error:

```
x = a;    // error!  Cannot implicitly convert type 'float' to 'int'
```

Of course, this code works perfectly well in older languages, so a lot of people will automatically dismiss C# as "difficult to use." I can hear them now: "Can't you just automatically convert the float to the integer, you stupid compiler?"

Well, the compiler isn't actually stupid; it's trying to save you some time debugging. You may not realize it, but a common source of bugs in programs is accidental truncation. You might forget that one type is an integer and some important data may get lost in the translation somewhere. So C# requires you to explicitly tell it when you want to truncate data. Tables 2.5 and 2.6 list which conversions require explicit and implicit conversions.

Table 2.5 Explicit/Implicit Conversions, Part 1

From	byte	sbyte	short	ushort	int	uint
byte	I	E	I	I	I	I
sbyte	E	I	I	E	I	E
short	E	E	I	E	I	E
ushort	E	E	E	I	I	I
int	E	E	E	E	I	E
uint	E	E	E	E	E	I
long	E	E	E	E	E	E
ulong	E	E	E	E	E	E
float	E	E	E	E	E	E
double	E	E	E	E	E	E
decimal	E	E	E	E	E	E

Table 2.6 Explicit/Implicit Conversions, Part 2

From	long	ulong	float	double	decimal
byte	I	I	I	I	I
sbyte	I	E	I	I	I
short	I	E	I	I	I
ushort	I	I	I	I	I
int	I	E	I	I	I
uint	I	I	I	I	I
long	I	E	I	I	I
ulong	E	I	I	I	I
float	E	E	I	I	E
double	E	E	E	I	E
decimal	E	E	E	E	I

The charts may look confusing at first, but they are actually quite simple. For example, if you want to convert from an int to a double, look at Table 2.2, find "int" on the left and find "double" on the top. In that position is an I, meaning you can perform an implicit conversion:

```
int a = 10;
double b = a;  // ok
```

Now say you want to convert a double to an int. Look at Table 2.1, find "double" on the left and "int" at the top. There is an E at that place, which means you need to perform an explicit conversion:

```
double a = 10.0;
// int b = a    <--- ERROR
int b = (int)a;  // ok
```

note

Converting from a float or a double to a decimal requires an explicit cast. This is because decimals encode data in a different way than do floats or doubles, so there is a distinct possibility of losing some data when performing the conversion. It's probably nothing that we game programmers should be concerned with, but you should be aware of it.

Branching

If you've really studied programming languages, then you know that there are three different traits that a language must have to be considered a true programming language. They are

- Sequencing
- Branching
- Repetition

You've already seen the first trait, sequencing, in action in Demo 2.1. *Sequencing* essentially means that the language must be able to execute commands in a given sequence.

Now I want to cover conditional statements, the use of which is known as *branching*. Essentially, branching allows a computer program to look at a given set of variables and decide whether it should continue executing or should *branch* to a different part of the program.

C# has a few conditional statements built in to the language; all of them were inherited from C, so you may be familiar with them.

if Statements

Quite often in a program, you will want to test to see if a condition is true or not, and then take action depending on the outcome. For example, if you wanted to perform an action if a condition evaluates to true, then you would write some code like this:

```
if( x == 10 )
{
    // do something
}
```

The code checks to see if some variable named x has the value of 10, and then executes the code inside the brackets if, and only if, x is 10. This is called an if statement.

You can also add on an else clause at the end, in order to execute code in any case where x is *not* 10:

```
if( x == 10 )
{
    // do something
}
else
{
    // do something
}
```

So the computer executes everything in the first block when x is 10, and executes anything in the second block when x is anything but 10.

Furthermore, you can chain elseif statements to the end, to perform multiple inquiries:

```
if( x < 10 )
{
    // do stuff if x < 10
}
else if( x < 20 )
{
    // do stuff if 10 <= x < 20
}
else if( x < 30 )
{
    // do stuff if 20 <= x < 30
}
```

note

If you're used to a language like C++, then you know you can use numbers inside of a conditional to produce code like this: if(x), where x is an integer. In older languages, the computer treats 0 as false and anything else as being true, meaning that if x is 0, then the if block won't execute, but it will for anything else. C# isn't like this, however, and it actually requires you to use a Boolean inside all conditional expressions. So the code will give you a compiler error in its current form. When you think about it, the old way isn't really safe anyway, because it doesn't explain exactly what you are testing. C# makes your programs safer and more readable.

Switch Statements

Using switch statements is a handy way to compare multiple outcomes of a single variable quickly. For example, if you have a variable, x, that variable can hold the values of 1, 2, 3 and 4, and your program will take a different course of action for each value. You can code a switch statement to do this:

```
switch( x )
{
case 1:
    // do something if 1
case 2:
    // do something if 2
case 3:
    // do something if 3
case 4:
    // do something if 4
default:
    // do something if something else
}
```

So if x is 2, then the code will jump to the case 2 block, and so on.

There is a catch, however. In the current state of the code in the previous block, if x is 2, then the code will jump right to block 2, but it will also continue on and execute the code in every block below it. This means that the code will execute code block 3, 4, and default as well. Sometimes you may want this behavior, but most of the time you won't, so you need to use the break keyword to break out of the switch after each block:

```
switch( x )
{
case 1:
    // do stuff
    break;  // jump out of switch
```

```
case 2:
    // do stuff
    break;  // jump out of switch
default:
    // do stuff
    break;  // optional here
}
```

tip

The break in the last block of the switch statement is optional, of course, because there is no code below it. But it's always a good idea to include the break anyway—just in case you end up adding more blocks later on and forget to add in the last break.

Short-Circuit Evaluation

Let me go off on a tangent here and go over a topic that is fairly important when evaluating conditional statements.

All C-based languages support something called *short-circuit evaluation*. This is a very helpful performance tool, but it can cause some problems for you if you want to perform some fancy code tricks.

If you know your binary math rules, then you know that with an and statement, if either one of the operands is false, then the entire thing is false. Table 2.7 lists the logical and and logical or result tables.

Table 2.7 Logical and/Logical or result tables

x	y	x and y	x or y
true	true	true	true
true	false	false	true
false	true	false	true
false	false	false	false

Look at the table, specifically the two lines where x is false. For the operation "x and y," it doesn't matter what y is because the result is always going to be false. Likewise, if you look at the first two lines, you'll notice that whenever x is true, the operation "x or y" is true, no matter what y is.

So if you have code that looks like this:

```
if( x && y )
```

the computer will evaluate x, and if x is false, then it won't even bother to evaluate y.

Likewise:

```
if( x || y )
```

If x turns out to be true, then y isn't even evaluated. This is a small optimization that can speed up your programs greatly in the right circumstances. For example:

```
if( x || ( ( a && b ) && ( c || d ) ) )
```

If this code executes and finds out that x is true, then the whole mess on the right side will never be calculated at all.

This can be a very tricky source of bugs, but only if you write tricky-looking code. Look at this line, for example:

```
if( x || ( ( y = z ) == 10 ) )
```

If your first reaction to seeing this code is "What the hell is going on here?" then you deserve a cookie. This code is unbelievably ugly, and you can't tell what the author intended to do with it. But unfortunately, this is perfectly legal C# code, and someone somewhere will think they're hot enough to write stuff like this and get away with it.

Anyway, if x is true, then the computer ignores the second half of the code. But if x is false, then whatever is in z is assigned to y, then the result is compared to 10, giving this code the same structure as this more readable version:

```
if( x == false )
    y = z;
if( x || ( y == 10 ) )
```

The second version looks almost nothing like the first, so you can see how trying to do some clever tricks will get you into loads of trouble one day.

Looping

The third trait a computer language has is *repetition*, or *looping*. Essentially, looping allows you to perform one specific task over and over again. C# has four looping mechanisms built-in; the three I'll cover in this section are inherited from the C programming language. I won't get to the fourth one until Chapter 4, "Advanced C#."

while Loops

The first and easiest loop structure is the `while` loop. Here's an example:

```
while( x < 10 )
{
    // do stuff
}
```

Whatever is inside the brackets will be executed over and over until the value of x is less than 10. If x never gets to be equal or above 10, then the loop will loop infinitely.

for Loops

Another popular loop is the `for` loop, which is just a different way to perform a `while` loop. The basic syntax of a `for` loop is as follows:

```
for( initialization; condition; action )
```

The initialization part of the code is executed only once, when the `for` loop is entered. This allows you to set up any variables you might need to use.

The condition part is evaluated at the beginning of each loop; and if it returns false, then the loop exits.

The action part is executed at the end of every loop.

Generally, you use `for` loops to create a loop that will go through a range of numbers for a particular variable. For example, if you want to perform 10 calculations on x, where x ranges from 0 to 9, you would create a loop like this:

```
for( int x = 0; x < 10; x++ )
{
    // do stuff
}
```

The first time the loop executes, x is 0, and then the next time it is 1, and so on, until it reaches 9.

You can also do some other fancy stuff, like initialize multiple variables or perform multiple actions:

```
for( int x = 0, int y = 0; x < 10; x++, y += 2 )
```

This loop creates two variables, x and y, where x loops from 0 to 9, and y loops from 0 to 18 by skipping every other number.

do-while Loops

Sometimes in programming, a situation will arise in which you want to make absolutely certain that a loop executes at least once. Look at this code, for example:

```
int x = 0;
while( x > 0 )
{
    // this loop never gets executed
}
```

With `for` loops and `while` loops, there's always a chance that, if the condition evaluates to false, the code inside the loop will never be executed. Instead of a `for` loop or a `while` loop, you can use the `do-while` loop, which executes everything and checks the condition after the loop is executed. Here's an example:

```
do
{
    // loop code here
} while( condition );
```

Break and Continue

`break` and `continue` are two useful keywords that you can use when doing stuff inside of loops to alter their flow.

Break

The first is the `break` keyword, which you've already seen used inside of switch blocks. Basically, putting in a break will cause the program to jump to the end of the loop and exit. Here's an example:

```
for( int x = 0; x < 10; x++ )
{
    if( x == 3 )
        break;
}
```

This loop will make x go through values 0, 1, 2, and 3, and then quit out when x is 3.

Continue

The other loop modifier is the `continue` keyword. This keyword causes the loop to stop executing and go back up to the top and start over. Here's an example:

```
for( int x = 0; x < 10; x++ )
{
    FunctionA();
```

```
    if( x == 3 )
        continue;      // jump back up to top, skip anything below
    FunctionB();
}
```

Pretend that FunctionA and FunctionB actually exist for a moment. This loop will make x go through every number from 0 to 9. On every single iteration, FunctionA will be executed, but when x is 3, the code will skip FunctionB() and jump right up to the top of the loop again.

Scoping

The term *scope*, when dealing with a computer program, refers to the place in a program where a variable is valid. For example, say you have this code in a program:

```
class ScopeDemo
{
    static void Main( string[] args )
    {   // bracket A
        int x = 10;
    }   // bracket B

    static void blah()
    {
//      x = 20;    <-- YOU CAN'T DO THIS!
    }
}
```

The variable x is said to have a scope between brackets A and B. If you tried referencing x outside of those brackets, the C# compiler will give you a strange look and ask you what the hell you're talking about.

Seems simple enough, doesn't it? Here's another example:

```
static void Main(string[] args)
{
    if( 2 == 2 )
    {   // bracket A
        int y;
    }   // bracket B
//  y = 10;    <-- YOU CAN'T DO THIS!
}
```

The if block in this code will always execute because 2 is, obviously, always equal to 2; but that's beside the point. Inside of brackets A and B, a new variable, y, is created, and then the if block ends. But y only has a scope in between those two brackets, meaning that nothing outside of the brackets can access it; so if you try using y outside of the if block, the computer will barf error messages all over you because it has no idea what y actually is.

There's still one more example I'd like to show you:

```
static void Main(string[] args)
{
    for( int x = 0; x < 10; x++ )
    {
        // do something here
    }
    // x = 10;     <-- YOU CAN'T DO THIS!
}
```

In this final example, you've created a new variable x *inside* the for statement, and you can access x anywhere inside the parentheses or the for block, but nowhere outside of it.

Summary

Computer languages are very complex, and no one can ever fully understand an entire language anymore—they're just far too complex nowadays. Luckily, you won't need many of the features in a language, so you don't have to be a versed expert in the language in order to use it—that's what reference manuals are for.

This chapter is enough to get you started on making some simple C# programs, but you really can't do anything really complex yet. But that's okay; you're only two chapters into the book!

This chapter has shown you how to create your very first C# program and compile it, and has introduced you to the very basic concepts of the language, such as the basic data types, mathematical operators, conditional statements, and looping statements. In the next chapter you'll go on to even more advanced topics.

What You Learned

The main concepts that you should have picked up from this chapter are:

- How to compile and run a C# program.
- Every program has a main class that defines an entry point, where program execution starts.
- There are many built-in numeric data types in C#.
- Short-circuit evaluation can be used to speed up your programs, but may introduce unforeseen flaws.
- Constants make your programs easier to read.

- Typecasts are strict in C# when compared to C/C++, because you might accidentally lose data if you're not paying close enough attention.
- Scoping allows you to manage your variables in an efficient manner.

Review Questions

These review questions test your knowledge of the important concepts explained in this chapter. The answers can be found in Appendix A.

2.1. Every C# program requires at least one main static class. (True/False)

2.2. Booleans are only 1 bit in size. (True/False)

2.3. Unsigned integers can hold numbers up to around 4 billion. (True/False)

2.4. Floating point numbers hold exact representations of numbers. (True/False)

2.5. Why can't you use variables before they have been assigned a value?

2.6. Why do constants make your programs easier to read?

2.7. Is the following code valid?

```
int x = 10;
float y = 20;
x = y;
```

(Yes/No)

2.8. What is the value of x after this code is done?

```
int x = 10;
if( x == 10 )
    x = 20;
```

2.9. Assume that c is 0. What are the values of the variables after this code is done, and why?

```
int w = 0, x = 0, y = 0, z = 0;
switch( c )
{
case 0:
    w = 10;
case 1:
    x = 10;
case 2:
    y = 10;
    break;
case 3:
    z = 10;
    break;
}
```

2.10. Now assume that c is 2 and the code from Question 2.9 is run again. What are the values of the variables w, x, y, and z?

2.11. Does the computer compare the value of x and 10 in this example?

```
int x = 10, y = 20;
if( y == 20 && x == 10 )
    x = 20;
```

2.12. Does the computer compare the value of x and 10 in this example?

```
int x = 10, y = 20;
if( y == 20 || x == 10 )
    x = 20;
```

2.13. When this code is completed, what is the value of x?

```
int x = 0;
while( x < 10 )
    x++;
```

2.14. For each loop, does the value of x increase before FunctionA executes or after it executes?

```
for( int x = 0; x < 10; x++ )
{
    FunctionA();
}
```

2.15. Rewrite the code in Question 2.14 using a while loop instead.

2.16. How many times is FunctionA executed?

```
int x = 0;
do
{
    FunctionA();
} while( x == 1 );
```

2.17. What is the value of x after the following code is done?

```
int x = 0;
for( int y = 0; y < 10; y += 2 )
{
    if( y == 4 )
        break;
    x++;
}
```

2.18. What is the value of x after the following code is done?

```
int x = 0;
for( int y = 0; y < 10; y += 2 )
```

```
    {
        if( y == 4 )
            continue;
        x++;
    }
```

2.19. Is this code valid? (Assume that FunctionA exists.)

```
    for( int y = 0; y < 10; y++ )
    {
        FunctionA();
    }
    y = 0;
```

On Your Own

Play around with the looping structures to find out what they do exactly. Sometimes they can be a little bit difficult to pick up for an absolute beginner, and it's very important that you learn exactly how they operate before you start making serious code.

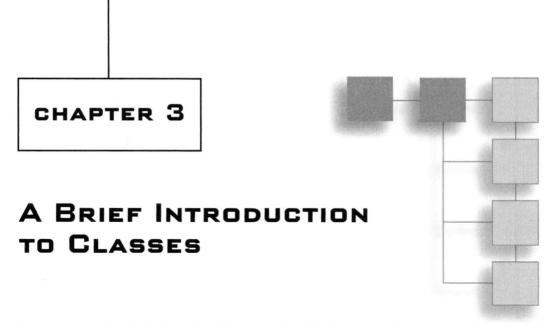

CHAPTER 3

A BRIEF INTRODUCTION TO CLASSES

By now, you should feel comfortable enough with C# to pound out a very simple program. You really don't know how to use any of the more powerful features of C# yet, though, so this chapter will to show you how. I'm not going to go over everything in the language—I'd need to write a much larger book to do that, and I still wouldn't have any room to get into the game programming stuff. Right now, I'm mostly going to go over things that will be important to game programming.

In this chapter, you will learn:

- The primary differences between value types and reference types.
- How garbage collection works and makes your programs safer.
- The basics of structures and classes.
- The differences between structures and classes.
- How functions, parameters, and return values work.
- How constructors and destructors work.
- How inheritance and data hiding works.
- How static members work.
- How accessors and properties make your programs safer.
- How enumerated types make your programs easier to read.

Values versus References

There are different ways for a compiler to talk about data, and C# has two different ways to do so. All datatypes in C# fall into one of two categories:

- Value types
- Reference types

I'll explain each of these different kinds of types in the following sections.

Value Types

A value type is typically a small piece of data that the system spends very little time managing. You have already used value types in Chapter 2 with all of the built-in numeric data types. Everything listed in Table 2.1—such as ints, floats, and so on—is a value type.

note

> Value types are created on the *system stack*. You don't necessarily need to know what that is, but if you're interested, I strongly urge you to research it on your own. This topic goes beyond the scope of this book, so I don't have enough room to explain it here, but it greatly helps you understand exactly how computers work, which will in turn make your programs faster and more efficient.

Value types are fairly simple and straightforward to use, as you can see in this code:

```
int x = 10, y = 20;
x = y;    // value of y is copied into x
y = 10;   // y is set to 10
```

Along with the built-in data types, structures are value types as well, which I explore in much more detail later in this chapter.

Reference Types

Reference types are completely different from value types. Classes, unlike structures, are always reference types. Reference types, rather than storing the data directly, store an address inside of them, and that address points to the actual data in the computer somewhere. Check out Figure 3.1.

Declaring a Reference Type

One of the biggest differences between values and references lies in the way you declare them. A reference type must be created using the new keyword (pretend we have a class named Foo):

```
Foo x = new Foo();
```

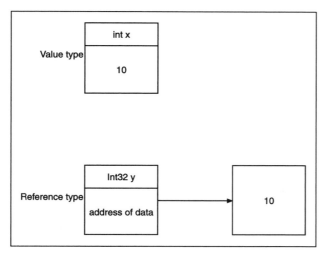

Figure 3.1 Value types are stored directly, whereas reference types store an address pointing to the actual data.

That may look like a lot of work at first, but you'll get used to it. Basically, the code is performing two tasks. It is:

1. creating a new reference type named x, and

2. creating a new Foo object on the heap and making x point to it.

note

The *heap* is another part of the computer that stores memory. I don't have enough room to explain it here; this is something else you should research on your own if you're interested.

Of course, you don't have to do that all at once. You could easily split it up like this:

```
Foo x;
x = new Foo();
```

It's up to you.

Playing with References

Now it's time to play around with references, which is something you haven't done before. Unfortunately for you, references don't exactly work the same way as value types, and this can be kind of confusing at first.

This is where references tend to get a bit tricky. You absolutely *must* remember at all times that you are using references, or else you will end up with programs that don't act the way you want them to act. For example, try to guess what this code does:

```
Foo x = new Foo();
Foo y = new Foo();
y = x;
// perform some operation that changes y here
```

You'd think that after this code executes, x would be in its original state and y would be changed, right? Wrong! They're both changed. Bear with me—it's a little difficult to see at first, but it makes sense. A diagram may help; see Figure 3.2.

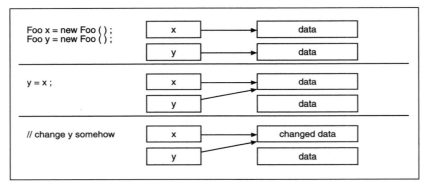

Figure 3.2 Assigning x to y makes y point to x's data, and doesn't actually copy the value as you would expect.

Basically, the line that really messes everything up is the following:

```
y = x;
```

What does that actually accomplish? You probably wanted to copy the data from x into y, but that didn't happen. Instead, as they are both reference types, the computer makes y point to the same data that x is pointing to. So x and y are now pointing to the same data in memory, and performing any operation on y will do the same to x.

note

If you really wanted to copy a reference type into a new reference type rather than just making two references point to the same data, you need to use a built-in C# function to perform a clone of the class. You can see this done with the GameObject class in Chapter 10.

Garbage Collection

In the example shown in Figure 3.2, you may have noticed that y was given some memory, which it then ignored once it was assigned to x. What happens to that memory that y was pointing to?

In older languages, like C, the memory would be lost forever. You would be creating what is called a *dangling pointer* (pointers are like references); the computer knows that the memory is being used, but your program forgot where it was, and you'll never be able to reclaim that memory until you shut down the program.

C# solves this problem using *garbage collection*. Every time you create a new piece of data in C#, the .NET runtime keeps track of how many times your program is pointing at that data, and if that number ever goes down to 0, then the garbage collector will detect it and release that memory for something else to use.

It is impossible to create memory leaks in C#.

note

> Okay, it *is* possible to create memory leaks in C#. But I'm not going to show you how. Nya Nya. You don't want to know anyway, believe me.

null

There's a special value that you can use with reference types; it's called null. The null value essentially means "nothing." If you set a reference to null, then you're telling the computer that the reference is pointing to nothing at all. Older languages used the value 0 to denote this, but null is more readable.

Basics of Structures and Classes

In the olden days of computer programming, programming languages were quite simple, and you could create only a limited number of variables. This, obviously, made programs very limited and quite ugly, to boot. For example, you would be creating programs like the following in an older language:

```
int SpaceshipArmor;
int SpaceshipPower;
int SpaceshipFuel;
int EnemyArmor;
int EnemyPower;
int EnemyFuel;
```

As you can imagine, this gets to be a tangled mess rather quickly, and makes it very difficult to manage your code.

Using classes and structures makes your life easier by encapsulating data into an easy-to use packet of data.

Creating Classes and Structures

Basically, the idea behind classes and structures is to create your very own kind of object using pieces of what was already in the language. A *structure* is essentially a data type that can hold other pieces of data inside of it, allowing you to build your own types of data; it is sort of like a building block. For example, here's a structure describing a simple space-ship object in C#:

```
struct Spaceship
{
    public int fuel;
    public int armor;
    public int power;
}
```

note

The keyword public tells the compiler that any function anywhere can access the data inside of a structure. You don't have to worry about this right now; I'll go more into depth on this later on in the chapter. If the word *public* is left out, then the computer assumes you don't want things out-side of the class accessing it.

note

To create a class, simply replace the struct keyword with class in the previous example.

Now, inside of your programs you can create your very own spaceship variables:

```
Spaceship player;
Spaceship enemy;
player.fuel = 100;
enemy.fuel = 100;
```

That was pretty easy, wasn't it?

Differences between Structures and Classes

In C#, there are a few fundamental differences between classes and structures. Structures are meant to be lightweight constructions, meaning they're usually very simple and don't have a lot of complex features in them. Structures are also usually smaller than classes, so C# will always create structures as value types (meaning they will always be created on the stack).

Classes, unlike structures, are always reference types, and thus are always created on the heap, rather than on the stack. Classes have many features that that structures do not have, but instead of throwing them all at you now, I'll explain these features as we come across them.

Putting Functions in Your Classes and Structures

Classes and structures not only have the ability to store data, but they can perform certain operations as well, if you give them the ability to do so. For example, you might want to make it easy to quickly reset all of the data in a spaceship to 100; without a function, this would look like the following:

```
player.fuel = 100;
player.armor = 100;
player.power = 100;
```

Obviously, this isn't something that you want to be doing all over the place, so why not put it inside a function instead, thus making the Spaceship class look like this (the new part is in bold):

```
struct Spaceship
{
    public int fuel;
    public int armor;
    public int power;

    public void Recharge()
    {
        fuel = 100;
        armor = 100;
        power = 100;
    }
}
```

Now you can just call the Recharge function on a spaceship whenever you want to have all of its variables recharged:

```
player.Recharge();
```

Return Values

Functions not only perform tasks, but they can return values, as well. For example, say you have a spaceship; you know how much fuel and power it has, but you're not really sure how much longer the power supplies will last. To calculate this, you make up a formula—

let's say you get two hours of time from each power unit; in order to find out how much time you have left on your current power level, you would do something like this:

```
int hoursleft = player.power * 2;
```

Well, that's one way to solve the problem, but it isn't really a great solution. Later on in the game, you may decide that each power unit supplies three hours instead of two. To make this change, you'd have to go through all of your code and find all the places where you used 2 and change them to 3. Not fun.

So make this process into a function!

```
int HoursofPowerLeft()
{
    return power * 2;
}
```

Ta-da! The int in front of the function name tells the compiler what type is being returned from the function, and you use the return keyword to return a value. If you don't want to return anything, then just use void, as you saw previously.

You should note that the return statement causes the function to exit immediately. If you look at the following code, you'll see that some of it will never execute:

```
int Function()
{
    return 0;
    int x = 10;    // this never executes
}
```

note

You should note that the C# compiler is smart enough to realize that the code won't execute, and it yells at you for writing code like that.

You're also allowed to have multiple return statements in your code:

```
int Function()
{
    if( something )
        return 0;
    return 1;
}
```

In this code, if something is true (assuming it exists, of course), then 0 is returned; other-wise, 1 is returned.

Parameters

You're also allowed to give a function some parameters to work with. My example of calculating the amount of time left with your available power level is a very simple calculation that doesn't use any parameters, but I can change this and make it more flexible.

What if the power drain on a spaceship depends on some external factor, like how much radiation is in the system (bear with me—I'm just making this up)? Let's say that the lower the radiation level in the system, the less power drain there is. So, if you rewrite the previous function with this in mind, you get:

```
int HoursofPowerLeft( int radiationlevel )
{
    return (power * 2) / radiationlevel;
}
```

If the radiation level was 1 (I'm using completely fictitious data measurements here; just pretend it makes sense) and your power is 100, then the number of hours left is 200. If the radiation level is 2, then you have 100 hours left; and if it's 3, you have 66 hours left.

You would call the function like this:

```
int hoursleft = player.HoursofPowerLeft( 1 );
```

Multiple Parameters

There will be times when you're going to want to pass in more than one parameter, and C# allows you to do that:

```
int Function1( int parameter1, float parameter2, double parameter3 )
```

Value Parameters versus Reference Parameters

This is where things can get a little tricky. Let's say you have a class with two functions that looks like this:

```
class MyClass
{
    public void Function1( int parameter )
    {
        parameter = 10;
    }

    public void Function2()
    {
        int x = 0;
        Function1( x );
```

```
        // what is x?
    }
}
```

So what is x after this code completes? Is it 0 or is it 10? The answer is 0 because you passed x in *by-value*. This means that the computer took the value of x, copied it, and placed it into a new variable named parameter; now, when parameter is changed, nothing happens to x.

So how do you make it pass by reference? Just do two things. First, change the declaration of Function1:

```
public void Function1( ref int parameter )
```

Second, change the function call to look like this:

```
Function1( ref x );
```

Now you'll pass a reference to x, and the value of x will be changed.

You should note that classes are always passed by reference. For example:

```
public void Function1( Int32 parameter )
```

In this function, any Int32 (a fictional class that I just made up) you pass into it will always be passed by reference, not by value.

Function Overloading

You can have a class or a structure with several functions that have the same name. This may sound silly at first, but it works out pretty well in real life. For example, let's say you have two different methods of calculating the distance a spaceship can travel, given its current fuel reserves; one method takes into account the amount of cargo the spaceship is currently carrying, and another method just ignores the cargo and gives you a "best case scenario" result. You could make the functions look like this:

```
public int DistanceLeft( int cargoweight )    // with cargo
{
    // do calculations here
}
public int DistanceLeft()                     // optimal, no cargo
{
    // do calculations here
}
```

so that later on in your code you could call them like this:

```
int distance;
distance = player.DistanceLeft( 100 );
distance = player.DistanceLeft();
```

You can overload functions as many times as you want; the only restriction is that each overloaded function must have a different signature. The signature is defined by the parameters that you pass in, not by the return value.

So you can do this:

```
void Function1();
void Function1( int p1 );
void Function1( float p1, int p2 );
```

And you can do this, too:

```
int Function1();
void Function1( int p1 );
float Function2( float p1, int p2 );
```

But you absolutely *cannot* do this:

```
int Function1();
float Function1();    // same signature! ERROR!
```

Constructors

Constructors are a really helpful feature of most modern programming languages. They allow you to automatically initialize your classes and structures.

Back in the bad old days, when you created a new structure or class, you really had no idea what was in it. You see, the computer doesn't erase memory, so when you stopped using a piece of memory, the computer just marks that it isn't being used anymore, and then dishes it out to the first thing who needs it, with the same data still sitting in it from whatever was using it before. This meant that you would often have structures full of junk data that made no sense, and this could cause lots of problems if you just started using the structure without first making sure it had valid values.

Constructors are just basically functions that C# calls automatically when you create a new class.

Default Constructors

Let me show you a simple example of a constructor on a class to start off with:

```
class Spaceship
{
    public int fuel;

    public Spaceship()     // default constructor
    {
        fuel = 100;
```

```
    }
}
```

The bolded code is what is called a *default constructor*. Whenever you create a new space-ship, the function Spaceship (note that it has the same name as the class) is automatically called.

This code creates a spaceship with 100 for its fuel:

```
Spaceship s = new Spaceship();
```

Non-Default Constructors

Like regular functions, constructors can also have overloaded versions, which is useful when you need to provide extra data when creating a class. Here's an example showing how to create a non-default constructor that takes in a variable amount of fuel to assign to a spaceship:

```
public Spaceship( int p_fuel )
{
    fuel = p_fuel;
}
```

Now when you create a new spaceship, you can call this new constructor like this:

```
Spaceship s = new Spaceship( 50 );  // create a ship with 50% fuel
```

You can create as many constructors as you want, as long as they each have a different signature.

Structures and Constructors

Structures can have constructors too, but there's one catch: Structures cannot have default constructors. Microsoft claims that this was done in the interest of efficiency because structures are supposed to be lightweight. So structures can have non-default constructors, but not default constructors.

Destructors

If constructors are called whenever a class is created, then destructors are called whenever a class is destroyed. In older languages such as C++, destructors were very important because you always had to free the memory you were not using anymore. But since the advent of garbage collection, destructors have mostly gone the way of the dinosaurs. They're really not needed much anymore, but are still included in the language just in case.

A Basic Example

This is what a destructor looks like:

```
class MyClass
{
    ~MyClass()
    {
        // code here
    }
}
```

In a language like C++, this is where you would make the class automatically clean up any memory it has requested. But as the .NET runtime takes care of all the memory stuff for you, you really don't need to do that here.

tip

> The most useful purpose for a destructor in C# is for *instance counting*, where you want to know how many instances of a particular class you have created at any given moment. Basically, the idea is to add one to the count every time the constructor is called, and subtract one from the count every time the destructor is called. So if you have no instances of a class, then the instance count would be 0.

Delayed Destruction

Another fact about destructors is that they are not called immediately. Look at this code, for example:

```
Spaceship s = new Spaceship();     // new spaceship
s = null;                          // reference to spaceship is lost
```

In this code, a new spaceship is created and a reference to it is assigned to s. On the very next line, however, the reference is set to null, so now you have a spaceship on your system somewhere, but you have no idea how to get to it.

That's not a really big deal for you, because you know the garbage collector will find it later on and destroy it. But it can cause some problems that you might not think about immediately.

The thing is, in C#, you really have no idea when a class instance is going to be destructed. You can set all references to it to null, but the system may keep the instance around for a long time after you've set the references.

Hence, the main problem with destructors is that you really don't know when they'll be called. You cannot count on a class being destructed immediately, so don't assume that it will be destructed when you clear all references.

There are ways around this, but as you probably won't use destructors much anyway, I won't bother telling you how.

note

Structures do not have destructors because they're supposed to be really lightweight constructs.

More Advanced Class Tricks

You should feel safe enough with classes now that you could create a simple one to perform small tasks such as storing data and performing simple calculations. Classes have many more features than what you've seen so far, however.

The Basics of Inheritance

One of the biggest advantages of an object-oriented programming language is *inheritance*. I'm not going to go heavily into the more advanced inheritance topics, but you should be able to understand and use inheritance after reading this book.

Inheritance allows you to model your programs in a realistic manner, by defining hierarchies of capabilities, allowing your classes to resemble real-world objects. The easiest way to think about inheritance is to think about the scientific classification of animals.

An Example of Inheritance

If you remember your high school biology, then you know that mammals all have certain features in common, like giving live birth and a four-chambered heart. In a computer program, you could create your mammal class and give it those characteristics.

But even though all mammals share some characteristics, they do not share all of the same characteristics. Humans have two legs, cows have four—obviously, you cannot use one mammal class to represent both humans and cows.

At the same time, it's stupid to create two completely different classes to represent both humans and cows. The code you write to represent features in common between a human and a cow would have to be duplicated between the two classes, and you'll just end up with a design that's prone to errors. Figure 3.3 shows this situation.

caution

Duplicating code is always a bad idea. Someday, you will need to change a piece of code you've written, and if you have that code in different places, I guarantee you that you will forget where some of it is and end up with two different versions of code running around.

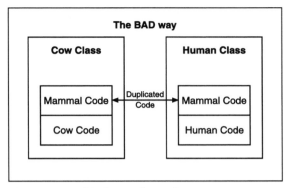

Figure 3.3 This figure shows the wrong way to model a cow/human system.

This is where inheritance comes into play. Inheritance allows you to create a new class and have it automatically use all of the features of another class. This is called the *is-a* relationship (a cow *is a* mammal). Figure 3.4 shows how inheritance is used.

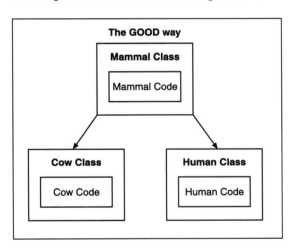

Figure 3.4 You can use inheritance to properly share common code among classes.

Using Inheritance

Inheritance is pretty easy to use in C#. First you need to create a *base class*, which goes at the top of your inheritance hierarchy (the mammal class in the previous section, for example).

Say you want to create a base spaceship class, a class that will describe the common characteristics of *all* spaceships in existence. Since all spaceships have fuel in them, you can create that in your base class:

```
class Spaceship
{
    public int fuel;
};
```

note

> Keep in mind that these examples are extremely simplistic, with the code kept to a minimum in order to demonstrate a point. I'm trying not to confuse the heck out of you.

So now you have a spaceship, but all it has is fuel. Now maybe you want to create a warship, which has weapons on it:

```
class Warship : Spaceship
{
    public int weapons;
};
```

You tell the compiler that a warship *is a* spaceship by putting a colon after the class name and the name of the class you're inheriting from.

For example, you can create a cargo ship, as well:

```
class Cargoship : Spaceship
{
    public int storage;
};
```

Now you can use the features you've added and the features of the base class, as well:

```
Warship w = new Warship();
w.weapons = 100;     // new feature
w.fuel = 100;        // inherited feature from Spaceship
Cargoship c = new Cargoship();
c.storage = 100;     // new feature
c.fuel = 100;        // inherited feature from Spaceship
```

And that's pretty much all there is to basic inheritance.

Access Levels and Data Hiding

Up until now, you've seen the word *public* in the code examples, but I haven't yet explained what it means or why it's there. Basically, when you say something is *public*, you're telling the compiler that everything can access it. If you give a class a public integer, then anything can read the integer or change it. This is pretty much the way all computer languages worked until the idea of *data hiding* came about.

The Idea Behind Data Hiding

Data hiding is a concept that allows you to essentially hide data from other parts of your program. You may be wondering why in the heck you would want to hide data. Well, the answer to that takes a little explaining.

You don't want to let just anyone touch your data; you don't know if someone is going to do something harmful to it. Take a spaceship, for example. In a spaceship, when the fuel goes down to 0, then the engines should shut off. Now imagine all of the places in your code where you would have functions modifying the fuel of your spaceship. Maybe your ship will leak some fuel if it gets hit by shrapnel. Or maybe you get an extra fuel pod to add some fuel to your tank. There are a million possibilities.

There are tons of places that change the fuel, and all of them need to turn off the engines if the fuel drops to 0, which is a bad thing. Furthermore, someone might try putting more fuel into your tanks than they can actually hold, which you don't want happening. Essentially, if you let any function to modify your data, those functions might accidentally (or even purposefully) mess it up, and that's definitely not a good thing.

Take a look at Figure 3.5.

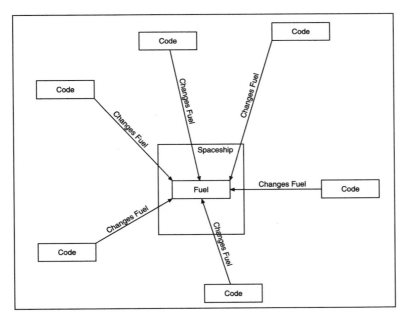

Figure 3.5 This figure shows how crazy your code can get if you let everyone access your data.

In the figure, there are six different pieces of code that modify your fuel, which could present a problem because each piece of code needs to take care of some housekeeping tasks. For example, each piece of code would need to check if the fuel goes to 0, and if so, it needs to turn the engines off. Or the code needs to check to make sure that the fuel doesn't go over the maximum amount, so that it doesn't overflow your tanks.

Either way, that's a lot of code to duplicate all over the place, and it'll only get worse as your program gets more complex. So basically it's a bad idea to let all the other parts of your program touch your data.

Another question you need to ask is whether the rest of your code really needs to know about all your data in the first place. Your spaceship may monitor the temperature of Weebul Capacitor Influx Gasket #43, but does any class besides the spaceship even need to know that spaceships have Weebul Capacitor Influx Gaskets? You can probably safely assume that nothing else cares except the spaceship, and therefore, anything that tries to care about something like that is probably going to be a bad thing. It's better to hide this data, so you don't accidentally mess things up later on.

Access Levels

C# has several defined access levels. You've already seen one of them, public. As you can guess, public means that anyone can access the feature.

The other two popular access levels are *protected* and *private*.

note

> There are two more access levels, *internal* and *protected internal*, but they're not nearly as common as the other three, and you'll probably not need them unless you're making some really complex programs.

Private access means that no other parts of your code can access the feature except the class itself. Not even inherited classes. Examine the following code:

```
class Spaceship
{
    private int fuel;
};
class Warship : Spaceship
{
    public void SomeFunction()
    {
        fuel = 10;    // ERROR! Cannot see "fuel"!!
    }
};
```

```
Spaceship s = new Spaceship();
s.fuel = 10;    // ERROR! Cannot see "fuel"!!
```

Inside the warship, the function SomeFunction tries to access fuel. Previously, you had no problem doing this; after all, a warship is a spaceship, and therefore has fuel and can be modified.

But now that the fuel is private, the warship cannot access it anymore. The fuel is still there, of course, but the warship isn't allowed to touch it.

Other code isn't allowed to touch the fuel in regular spaceships, either; the data is hidden.

note

If you forget to put in an access level to a function or a variable, then the C# compiler will automatically assume that it's using *private* access.

The *protected* access level is similar to private, with one minor difference: Anything that is protected is still hidden to code outside of the class, but classes that inherit from the base class can still see the features. Look at this example:

```
class Spaceship
{
    protected int fuel;
};
class Warship : Spaceship
{
    public void SomeFunction()
    {
        fuel = 10;    //  This is ok now, because it's protected
    }
};
Spaceship s = new Spaceship();
s.fuel = 10;    // ERROR! Cannot see "fuel"!!
```

This example is very similar to the previous one, but this time the fuel is protected and the warship can access it just fine.

Static Members

Up until now, all you've seen inside of classes are instance members. An *instance member* is a part of a class that exists within a single instance of that class. If you have two spaceships, and spaceships have an integer representing fuel, then you'll have two integers, one for each ship.

On the other hand, you can also have static members. A *static member* is a piece of data (or a function) that is shared among all instances of a class, rather than being duplicated for each instance. See Figure 3.6 for an example.

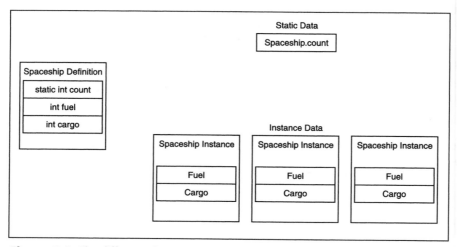

Figure 3.6 The difference between static data and instance data

Static Data

Look at the following code segment:

```
class Spaceship
{
    public static int count;
    public int fuel;
    public int cargo;
};
```

This creates a class definition for a spaceship, where each spaceship will have fuel and cargo, and the class definition will keep track of an integer called count. You can access this integer at any time by invoking the following code (or anything similar):

```
Spaceship.count = 10;
```

You don't need to have any spaceship instances in order to use this variable; it always exists. It doesn't belong to any specific spaceship either; anyone can use it. Statics are an easy way to get the same functionality offered by global variables in languages like C or C++; plus they are neater, from a design perspective.

Static Functions

Functions can also be static. Basically, a static function can be called without needing a specific instance to operate on. For example:

```
class Spaceship
{
    public static void FunctionA()
    {
        // do something
    }
};
```

Now you can call this function at a later time just by invoking it like so:

```
Spaceship.FunctionA();
```

You don't need any spaceship instances to call the function.

caution

Static functions cannot operate on instance data without an actual instance to operate upon. It seems obvious when you think about it, but some people don't get this concept right away.

Properties

I told you previously that data hiding is a good thing. In fact, I've been naughty and have been using some bad tricks to make the examples in this book seem less confusing. Generally speaking, you should *never* have public data in your classes. The temptation to allow direct access to your data is just too strong sometimes, and sooner or later you're going to run into the problems I told you about previously. And when you start getting bugs from out of nowhere, I don't want you to come crying to me.

Accessors

Generally, in the past, the preferred method for making data accessible without making it public has been to use *accessor* functions. To do so, you make two functions for each variable: one to get the value, and one to set the value. Like so:

```
class Spaceship
{
    protected int fuel;
    public int GetFuel() { return fuel; }
    public void SetFuel( int p_fuel ) { fuel = p_fuel; }
};
```

And you'd access the fuel like this:

```
Spaceship s = new Spaceship();
s.SetFuel( 10 );
int f = s.GetFuel();
```

note

> This method is considered safe because you can change how the fuel is accessed later without messing up any of your other code. For example, if you decide one day that you don't want people to be able to set the fuel below 0, you can change the SetFuel function so that it takes care of that automatically.

This, from an engineering perspective, is very safe. From an I've-been-typing-for-hours-and-I-just-want-to-go-home perspective, however, this solution sucks. That's a lot of extra coding just to make your program "safer."

C#'s Solution: Properties

To fix the "way too much typing" problem that existed in earlier languages, C# introduces a new concept called *properties*. A property allows you to use less code to make your variables more accessible, while still maintaining the protections of accessor functions. Here's an example:

```
class Spaceship
{
    protected int fuel;
    public int Fuel {
        get { return fuel; }
        set { fuel = value; }
    }
};
```

The code in bold is the property field. Basically I've created a property named Fuel (capital F), which will act exactly like a piece of data on the outside:

```
Spaceship s = new Spaceship();
s.Fuel = 10;
int f = s.Fuel;
```

What is actually happening underneath the scene, however, is that the property functions get and set are being called, and are executing their code.

You can do anything you want in either property function, but most of the time you're probably going to be doing most code work inside the set function. For example, you can make sure that no one ever sets the fuel of a spaceship below 0 by changing the `Fuel.set` function like this:

```
public int Fuel {
    get { return fuel; }
    set {
        if( value < 0 )
            fuel = 0;
        else
            fuel = value;
    }
}
```

So now, if you perform this code:

```
s.Fuel = -10;
```

the `set` function will automatically set the fuel to 0 instead of -10.

caution

> Properties don't have infinite recursion detection, which can be a pain in the butt sometimes. For example, if you accidentally typed `Fuel = value` rather than `fuel = value` inside of the `set` function, the computer would automatically call the `set` function again, and would keep doing so until the program crashes. Watch out for that.

Enumerations

One feature of C# (and other languages) that makes your life easier is the concept of *enumerated types*, or *enumerations*. How many times do you find yourself writing a program where you have some kind of data that isn't a number, but doesn't call for a custom data type, either?

Picture this: You're making a simple system wherein each spaceship in your game will know what state it is in—whether it is moving around, stopped, or in a fierce battle with some evil pirates. You could decide to use an integer, like this:

```
class Spaceship
{
    int state;
    // other code here
};
```

Okay, so state 0 is moving, state 1 is stopped, and state 2 is battle. Sounds fair enough, right? No! This is *evil*. Don't *ever* do this! It's ugly, and you won't be able to remember what each code means.

C#'s solution is enumerations. An enumerated type encapsulates a grouping of names into one type that is easily referenced and readable. Here's an enumerated type representing the spaceship states:

```
enum SpaceshipState
{
    moving,
    stopped,
    battle
};
```

This code creates an enumerated type named Spaceshipstate, which has a total of three different values: moving, stopped, or battle. You can use it like this:

```
SpaceshipState s;
s = SpaceshipState.moving;
if( s == SpaceshipState.battle )
    // code here
// and so on
```

Enumerations are essentially integers underneath; you don't necessarily need to think of them that way, but you can if you want to. Typically, the first enumeration is given a value of 0, and the rest are incremented by 1.

```
int i;
i = (int)SpaceshipState.moving;    // 0
i = (int)SpaceshipState.stopped;   // 1
i = (int)SpaceshipState.battle;    // 2
```

If you don't like the default values, you can change them, like this:

```
enum SpaceshipState
{
    moving = 10,
    stopped = 12,
    battle              // this is automatically 13
};
```

So now moving has a value of 10, stopped has a value of 12, and battle, as it isn't explicitly defined, takes the value of the previous enumeration and adds one to it, making it 13.

Summary

I think that about sums it up for all of the basic ideas behind classes. This is by no means a complete comprehensive look at C#'s capabilities with classes, but by now you should be well-versed enough in classes to make your own.

I'm not kidding when I say this: C# is one of the most complex languages ever made. There is so much to it that there's simply no way I can fit everything into this book. The C# reference manual, written by Anders Hejlsberg, is over 600 pages long, and it doesn't even attempt to cover any actual programming applications—that gives you an idea of just how complex the language is. Naturally, I can't go over every detail of C#, so I'll briefly touch on some more advanced topics in the next chapter and then we'll get busy with some actual game programming! Yeah!

What You Learned

The main concepts that you should have picked up from this chapter are:

- The primary differences between value types and reference types.
- How garbage collection works and makes your programs safer.
- The basics of structures and classes.
- The differences between structures and classes.
- How functions, parameters, and return values work.
- How constructors and destructors work.
- How inheritance and data hiding works.
- How static members work.
- How accessors and properties make your programs safer.
- How enumerated types make your programs easier to read.

Review Questions

These review questions test your knowledge on the important concepts in this chapter. The answers can be found in Appendix A.

3.1. Are basic types created as values or as references?

3.2. Are classes created as values or references?

3.3. Are structures created as values or references?

3.4. What is the value of x after the following code is executed?

```
int x = 10;
int y = x;
y = 20;
```

3.5. Is the data in x and y the same after the following code is executed (assume class Foo exists and has a function named change which changes data)?

```
Foo x = new Foo();
Foo y = new Foo();
y = x;
y.change();
```

3.6. Where does the old data of y go when you execute the following line of code?

```
Foo x = new Foo();
Foo y = new Foo();
y = x;
```

3.7. What parts of the following function definition are "the signature?"

```
int function1( int x, int y )
```

3.8. Can a class have the following two functions at the same time?

```
int function1( int x, int y )
float function1( int x, int y )
```

3.9. Why is it a good idea to create constructors?

3.10. Are destructors really needed in C#? Why or why not?

3.11. When a class contains data, that is called the *has-a relationship*. A class has a float, and so on. When a class inherits from another class, what is the relationship called?

3.12. What is the primary reason for using inheritance?

3.13. Why would you want to hide your data?

3.14. What can access x from the following class?

```
class foo {
    public int x;
}
```

3.15. What can access x from the following class?

```
class foo {
    protected int x;
}
```

3.16. What can access x from the following class?

```
class foo {
    private int x;
}
```

3.17. When you don't specify an access level (protected, private, public), what is the default level?

3.18. Why are accessors and properties a good thing?

3.19. How do enumerations make your code cleaner?

On Your Own

Play around and create your own classes. You should be able to create multiple constructors, functions, hidden data, and properties. Try modeling an object from a game you want to make—a spaceship from a space shooter, for example.

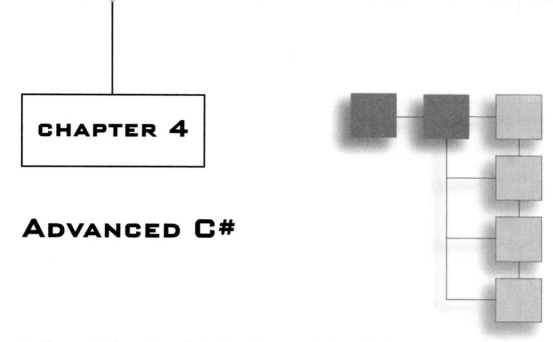

CHAPTER 4

ADVANCED C#

In Chapter 3, I showed you the basics of classes and other related topics. That's some pretty heavy stuff for a beginner to learn, but now it's time for something even more complex.

Fortunately, the most complex features in C# aren't really general-purpose. You'll probably use some of them only rarely, so I'm not going to bother covering some topics. I'll list the important topics that I've skipped at the end of Chapter 5, however.

This chapter will give you a brief introduction to some of the more complex ideas used in C#, such as polymorphism, namespaces, and data storage techniques. In this chapter, you will learn:

- How namespaces segment your programs.
- How to create namespaces.
- How to alias namespaces.
- How polymorphism makes your programs more flexible.
- How to use virtual functions and overriding.
- How to use abstraction.
- How to use objects to box and unbox value-types.
- How to use arrays.
- How to use multidimensional arrays.
- How to use the foreach loop on collections.
- How to use strings.

Namespaces

Namespaces are a relatively new concept in computer languages, but they are very useful, and some might argue that their existence is essential these days.

One of the biggest problems in programming is *name overlapping*. Say you create a bunch of classes for your program, and then you decide to import someone else's library to help your program. What happens if some of that person's classes have the same names as yours, but do different things? It happens quite a lot, unfortunately.

For example, both Direct3D and DirectSound have classes called `Device`, and you obviously can't have two classes with the same name. Namespaces makes it easy, so you can refer to the different devices as `Direct3D.Device` and `DirectSound.Device`.

You can think of a namespace sort of like a city. If you tell someone merely that you live on Main Street, you aren't telling him much, as there are thousands of Main Streets across the country. In order to really pinpoint where you live, you need to tell that person what city you live in, too. Creating a namespace is like specifying your city and street in that you can place a certain class (street) inside a specific namespace (city), therefore neatly segmenting your programs.

You can put almost anything into a namespace, including a class, a struct, an enumeration, and even another namespace! Figure 4.1 shows an example of namespaces.

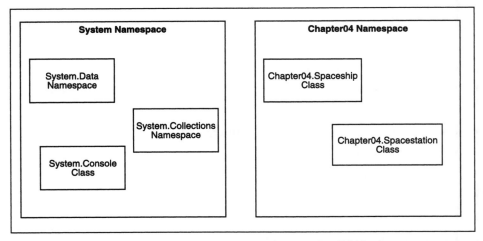

Figure 4.1 Here are two namespaces, `System` and `Chapter04`. Within the namespaces are sub-namespaces and classes.

Namespaces are cool because you can *nest* them—you can put more namespaces inside existing namespaces. For example, the .NET framework comes with the `System` namespace, and within this namespace are other namespaces, such as `System.Data` and `System.Collections`.

To expand upon the previous analogy, nested namespaces allow you to create even larger hierarchies, like the United States exists inside North America, California exists within the United States, Los Angeles exists within California, and Main Street exists within Los Angeles.

Creating Namespaces

Here's some code demonstrating the use of a namespace:

```
namespace Chapter04
{
    class Spaceship
    {
        // real code would go here
    };

    class Spacestation
    {
        // real code would go here
    };
}
```

And then, outside of the namespace, you would access those classes like this:

```
Chapter04.Spaceship s = new Chapter04.Spaceship();
```

Another great feature of namespaces is that they can be split up into multiple sections. For example, you can have this in one file:

```
namespace Chapter04
{
    class Spaceship
    // blah blah
}
```

and then put the space station in a different file:

```
namespace Chapter04
{
    class Spacestation
    // blah blah
}
```

The C# compiler will automatically join the namespaces for you, so you don't have to put everything into one large file.

Using Namespaces

When you are within a namespace, you can use anything in that namespace without having to qualify it. If you were to access the spaceship class inside of the spacestation class in the example I showed you before, you could just type in **Spaceship** and C# would assume you were talking about Chapter04.Spaceship because you're in the same namespace.

If you're outside of the namespace, however, you must qualify the namespace by putting in Chapter04. first.

Of course, typing Chapter04.Spaceship over and over can get annoying after a while, especially if you know that you're only going to be using spaceships from Chapter 4 and nowhere else. Luckily, you're allowed to tell your C# compiler, using the using keyword, that you want to use everything within a specific namespace. It looks like this:

```
// at the top of the source file:
using Chapter04;

// later on in the file:
Spaceship s = new Spaceship();
```

note

The using keyword can be placed only in certain places. The keyword cannot be placed inside of classes, structs, or enums, but it can be placed almost anywhere else. It's usually good practice to place your using statements at the top of your source code files, so that you know immediately what other libraries your file needs.

Namespace Aliasing

Nested namespaces can be a large pain in the butt. You haven't seen them yet, but when you come across them while hot and heavy into DirectX, you will be screaming, "Damn you, Microsoft!" at the top of your lungs...that is, unless you know about namespace aliasing.

Everything related to Direct3D is inside the Microsoft.DirectX.Direct3D namespace. So if you want to access a Direct3D device, you would have to type **Microsoft.DirectX.Direct3D.Device**. Ugh, right? Luckily, namespace aliasing makes it all better! Basically, you can take one namespace and tell C# to use an alias for it.

Here is an alias for the Direct3D namespace:

```
using D3D = Microsoft.DirectX.Direct3D;
D3D.Device d;  // instead of: Microsoft.DirectX.Direct3D.Device d;
```

See how much easier namespace aliasing makes things?

Polymorphism

The topic of *polymorphism* is large and complex—universities offer entire courses on the topic. I can only give you a limited glimpse into the subject in this modest book. But you don't need to learn any of the really complex parts of polymorphism, anyway.

Literally, the word *polymorphism* means "many forms." In computer programming, polymorphism allows you to interact with many different objects without worrying about what those objects really are.

For a real-world example of polymorphism in the computer-programming sense, think of a car. You can get into a car, turn it on, and hit the gas, and you know what's going to happen: The car is going to move! Now get out of the car, get into a totally different car, and do the same thing: That car is going to move, too! Both cars have the same *interface*, and you really don't care how the engines work underneath. Whether you're riding in a four-cylinder dorkmobile, an eight-cylinder racing beast, or a politically correct electric car, you know that when you press on the gas, the car is going to go. This is polymorphism at its best. The computer tells an object to work, and the object, no matter what it is, goes to work.

Let's look at polymorphism in a gaming situation. Let's say you're programming a simple shooter-type game—you're in a spaceship and you're flying around, shooting lasers at everything. Whenever a laser blast hits something, the object reacts somehow, right? In a polymorphic system, it would make sense for each object to know how it should react when it gets hit. A computer-controlled spaceship would sustain some damage, and tell its AI to attack whoever shot the laser. A player-controlled spaceship would sustain damage and maybe send some force-feedback signals to the player's joystick. An asteroid would split into many pieces. The point is that the actual game engine really doesn't care how objects react when they get hit by lasers—all it needs to do is tell the object that it got hit in the first place, and let the object take care of the details. I'll expand on this concept a bit more later on.

Basic Polymorphism

Say you have a very basic inheritance tree: one root and two leaves. The root is a Spaceship and the leaves are CombatShip and CargoShip, as seen in Figure 4.2.

You can play around with them as usual:

```
Spaceship s = new Spaceship();
CargoShip c = new CargoShip();
```

This is nothing new, of course. But the fact that a CargoShip *is* a Spaceship allows you to perform some neat tricks. Look at this line of code, for example:

```
Spaceship s = new CargoShip();
```

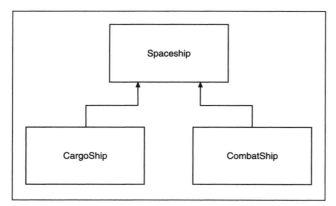

Figure 4.2 A simple inheritance tree

That code is perfectly legal. A CargoShip is a Spaceship, after all, so it would make sense to be able to make a Spaceship reference point to a CargoShip, right?

There is one downside to this: The Spaceship reference is not allowed to access any specific parts of the CargoShip class that it didn't inherit from the Spaceship. Assume that Spaceships have a Refuel function, and CargoShips add a LoadCargo function, and then look at this code example:

```
Spaceship s = new CargoShip();
s.Refuel();        // ok
// s.LoadCargo();   // COMPILER ERROR. Spaceships can't load cargo.
CargoShip c = (CargoShip)s;  // so turn it into a cargo ship
c.LoadCargo();     // ok
```

Whenever you have a reference to a class, you can only access the features of that specific class, even if the object it's really pointing to supports more features.

note

Note that you can't use polymorphism the other way around. If you tried writing CargoShip c = new Spaceship();, you would get a compiler error. A Spaceship is *not* a CargoShip.

Virtual Functions

One of the most important aspects of polymorphism is the idea of a virtual function. A *virtual function* basically allows you to define a function in a base class and then change it later on. Say that by default, all spaceships handle getting hit by lasers one way, so you define that behavior inside a base Spaceship class. Then, later on, you decide that combat ships should handle getting hit differently because they have better armor.

Virtual functions allow you to handle this situation easily, which you'll see in the next few sections.

Without Virtual Functions

Here is some code that will make clear what would happen in my example without a virtual function:

```
class Spaceship
{
    public void LaserHit()
    {
        // lots of damage
    }
}

class CombatShip : Spaceship
{
    public void LaserHit()
    {
        // less damage
    }
}
```

What I've done here is create a Spaceship class that, by default, causes the ship to sustain a lot of damage when it's hit by lasers. I wanted the CombatShip it to sustain less damage because it's more armored, so I created a new LaserHit function that sustains less damage.

This code does exactly what you think it does:

```
Spaceship s = new Spaceship();
CombatShip c = new CombatShip();
s.LaserHit();    // lots of damage
c.LaserHit();    // less damage
```

No tricks there. But what about the following code?

```
Spaceship s = new Spaceship();
Spaceship c = new CombatShip();
s.LaserHit();    // lots of damage
c.LaserHit();    // lots of damage... why?
```

What's the difference? Instead of using a CombatShip reference like in the first example, I used a Spaceship reference instead, so why would the combat ship take damage just like a regular space ship? The reason is that the spaceship's LaserHit function never disappeared —it's still there. When you say c.LaserHit(), it calls Spaceship.LaserHit() because it knows c is a Spaceship. Why is the compiler too dumb to realize that c is actually a CombatShip in disguise? It turns out that this is the way the compiler is supposed to work, and that making it work the way you really want it to requires using *virtualism*.

Welcome to Virtualism

Virtual functions are a great invention. They're not even really complicated, either. Before I get into explaining them, let me change the class definitions for Spaceship and CombatShip from the previous section, to add a few keywords in the function declarations:

```
class Spaceship
{
    virtual public void LaserHit()
    {
        // lots of damage
    }
}

class CombatShip : Spaceship
{
    override public void LaserHit()
    {
        // less damage
    }
}
```

Two little things have been changed: the word virtual has been added to the Spaceship.LaserHit function, and override has been added to CombatShip.LaserHit. Now, if you run this code, it will do exactly what you want it to do:

```
Spaceship s = new Spaceship();
Spaceship c = new CombatShip();
s.LaserHit();    // lots of damage
c.LaserHit();    // less damage now. Hooray!
```

Why does this work? Declaring a function virtual tells the compiler that the function might be replaced with a different version in a child class later on. It says, "Hey, this laser hit function works for all spaceships, but some spaceships later on may want to change it."

Likewise, declaring a function to be override tells the compiler that this function is overriding an earlier version. It says, "Hey, I know this function was declared earlier, but this version is better so use it instead."

note

If you don't use the override keyword when declaring CombatShip.LaserHit, then you'll run into the same problem you had before. All combat ships, when treated as spaceships, will use SpaceShip. LaserHit instead of the function you want it to. You must explicitly declare that a function is overriding an older version. Languages such as C++ and Java don't require this, so it may be a bit confusing to you at first.

note

The opposite of the override keyword is the new keyword. To revert to the original behavior, you would write **new public void LaserHit()** rather than **override public void LaserHit()**. This prevents the Spaceship.LaserHit function from being replaced with the new version; the old version will be called whenever you're working on a Spaceship reference, and the new version will be called whenever you're working on a CombatShip reference.

Abstraction

You're occasionally going to have a situation in which you don't know what the default behavior for a base class is going to be. Maybe you'll realize that saying "all spaceships will get hit by lasers in this particular way" is kind of stupid because every spaceship is different and you're just going to end up overriding the LaserHit function in every child class, anyway.

So why define a Spaceship.LaserHit function in the first place? In this case, you want to use a feature called *abstraction*. The Spaceship.LaserHit function is abstract—you don't know how ships are going to get by lasers, but you still know that every ship *can* get hit by lasers.

If you simply remove the LaserHit function from the Spaceship class, you'll make things a pain in the butt:

```
Spaceship s = new CargoShip();
s.LaserHit();  // ERROR! Spaceships don't know how to get hit by lasers.
```

Luckily, C# gives you a way of saying, "All spaceships know how to get hit by lasers, but I'm not sure how, yet." Here's a redefined Spaceship class:

```
abstract class Spaceship
{
    abstract public void LaserHit();
}
```

Now you have a Spaceship class, and you know that all spaceships can get hit by lasers, even if you have no idea how at this point in time. How does this affect things, though? Is the following code valid?

```
Spaceship s = new Spaceship();  // ERROR!
```

Oops. You can't create SpaceShips anymore. That's okay, though, because you probably don't want to be doing that anyway—you probably want to create CombatShips or CargoShips instead:

```
Spaceship s1 = new CargoShip();
Spaceship s2 = new CombatShip();
s1.LaserHit();
s2.LaserHit();
```

note

You cannot instantiate abstract classes. Furthermore, if you have any abstract functions in the class, the class must be declared abstract as well.

note

Any function that is declared to be abstract must be declared as an override in child classes. If you don't do this, you'll get a compiler error.

Polymorphism and Functions

I thought I'd add a small note on using polymorphism with function parameters, in case the concept still isn't quite clear to you.

Let's say you create a function that works on all kinds of spaceships. Something like this:

```
class Foo
{
    static void ProcessSpaceship( Spaceship s )
    {
        // some code
        s.LaserHit();
    }
}
```

You can pass cargo ships or combat ships into the function and it won't mind—as long as you're passing in some kind of spaceship:

```
CargoShip cargo = new CargoShip();
CombatShip combat = new CombatShip();
Foo.ProcessSpaceship( cargo );
Foo.ProcessSpaceship( combat );
```

The Foo.ProcessSpaceship function doesn't care what kind of spaceship you use because all spaceships have the same basic capabilities. This is the power of polymorphism.

Objects

In C#, there's a class called `object`, from which everything inherits automatically. This allows you to store objects in containers easily (you'll see this later in the chapter).

Look at this code, for example:

```
object o = new CargoShip();
o = new int();
o = new float();
o = new WeebulCapacitorInfluxGasket();
```

Objects can hold *anything*.

Using the `object` class is an easy way of turning value-types—such as the built-in numerics and your own structures—into reference types. That's because `object`s can be used to box value-types. Whenever you put a value-type into an `object`, the object immediately allocates memory for that value-type and points itself at the new memory.

Figure 4.3 shows this process.

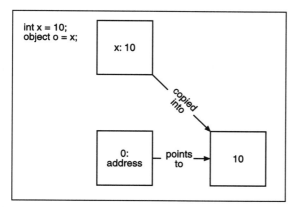

Figure 4.3 This shows how you can use an `object` class to box a value-type and make it a reference-type.

Look at this code:

```
int x = 10;
object o = x;   // o is now a reference to a copy of the integer 10
x = 20;         // change x; o shouldn't change since it was copied
x = (int)o;     // unbox o, x is now 10 again
```

That code shows you how to perform basic boxing and unboxing.

note

Whenever you unbox an object, you must *explicitly* cast it back to its original type (or some related type, as long as it's compatible). Implicit conversion is not possible.

Arrays

You know, I really can't believe it's taken me this long to get to arrays. What can I say—C# is one hell of a complex language.

Arrays are containers that allow you to store many objects in them. Basically, you need some way to store lots of data, and using plain variables to store all your game objects becomes very tedious, very quickly:

```
Spaceship s1;     // ok
Spaceship s2;     // meh
Spaceship s3;     // ok this is getting annoying
...
Spaceship s20;    // my fingers hurt
...
Spaceship s42;    // DEAR LORD MAKE IT STOP
```

That's a terrible way of storing your game data. Don't do that. Ever. Or I will send a rabid squirrel to your house to chew the power cable of your coding computer right before you hit Save after you spent the past 10 hours coding in a Mountain Dew-inspired frenzy. I mean it.

Instead of doing all that stupid typing, create an array, which is a chunk of data that you can access by number.

A Basic Array Example

Here is an example of using array:

```
int[] array = new int[10];
array[0] = 0;     // first item is 0
array[1] = 10;    // second item is 10
...
array[9] = 90;    // last item is 90
```

Now you have ten integers, and you can access them easily by using the bracket notation after the name of the array.

Arrays use *zero-based* indexing, meaning that the first object in any array has an index of 0 rather than 1, as many would suspect. This means that the array in the previous example has valid indexes of 0 through 9, and 10 is invalid.

What Is an Array?

An array, like I said before, is just a chunk of data. When you write the following code, it says that you're creating a variable named a, which is a reference to an array of integers:

```
int[] a;
```

All arrays are reference types, which means you *must* use the new keyword to actually create an array:

```
a = new int[8];
```

That line of code creates a new array of eight integers, as shown in Figure 4.4.

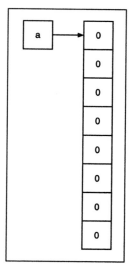

Figure 4.4 This shows an array of eight integers.

For all intents and purposes, you can treat a just like any other reference type. Here's some code showing you how you can use arrays:

```
int[] a = new int[10];
int[] b = a;        // b points to the same array now
```

```
b[0] = 10;        // changing b also changes a
int i = a[0];     // i is now 10
b = null;         // b doesn't point to anything anymore
a = new int[20];  // the old array is lost, to be garbage-collected later
object c = a;     // you can even make it an "object" type
```

Arrays are pretty easy to use, as you can see.

Inline Initialization

You can initialize the values of an array directly when you create it, by using this code:

```
int[] array = new int[] { 1, 2, 3, 4, 5 };
```

This creates a new integer array with five indexes, with the indexes containing the values 1, 2, 3, 4, and 5.

References versus Values

In the previous section, I showed you an array of integers, which are value types. That's pretty easy to understand. But what happens when you create an array of reference types, like a Spaceship?

```
Spaceship[] s = new Spaceship[5];
```

Does this create an array of five spaceships? No, it doesn't. It actually creates an array of five spaceship *references*. The following code produces the situation that Figure 4.5 depicts:

```
Spaceship s = new Spaceship[5];
s[0] = new Spaceship();
s[2] = new Spaceship();
```

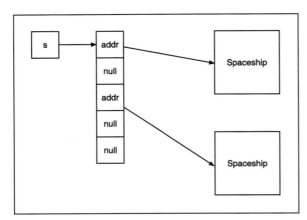

Figure 4.5 An array of references, where some are valid and others are null.

Indexes 0 and 2 are taken up by spaceships, but the rest are null pointers.

You can see that an array of reference types really just holds references, and not the actual types. You have to manually create each object in an array yourself if you need to use them. As you learned from Chapter 2 though, you can use for-loops to make this process very easy.

Inheritance and Arrays

One of the best things about arrays is that they fully support inheritance. Look at this code, for example:

```
Spaceship[] s = new Spaceship[4];
s[0] = new CombatShip();
s[1] = new CargoShip();
s[2] = new CargoShip();
s[3] = new CombatShip();
for( int i = 0; i < 4; i++ )
    s[i].LaserHit();    // hit each ship
```

This code creates an array of four spaceships, and then fills it in with two cargo ships and two combat ships. The last two lines show you a for loop that goes through the array and hits every ship with a laser beam. This works beautifully because the compiler knows that all Spaceships know how to get hit with a laser, and it doesn't care whether the spaceship is a combat ship or a cargo ship!

Multidimensional Arrays

So far, all I've shown you are one-dimensional arrays. If you know your geometry, you know that something in one dimension can only have a length defined; there's no width or height. In one dimension, you're pretty much limited to drawing straight lines. It's the same with arrays: a one-dimensional array can be viewed as a straight line.

If you take the geometry concept and expand it to two and three dimensions, you can imagine arrays looking like those in Figure 4.6.

A 2D array can be thought of as a square grid, like a chessboard. A 3D array can be thought of as a voluminous grid, much like a Rubik's cube.

You can have arrays of other dimensions too, such as 4D, 5D, or even up to 32D, but for most people, visualizing such arrays can be quite difficult, and they're really not seen much.

The Easy Way

C# differs from C/C++/Java in dealing with multidimensional arrays. If you're already familiar with those languages, then this may throw you off a little, but it's really not difficult.

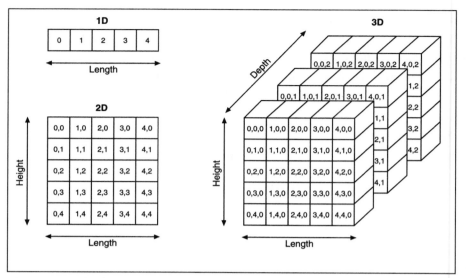

Figure 4.6 This figure shows you a visual layout of three different dimensional arrays.

Basically, to declare a 2D and a 3D array of ints, you would write this:

```
int[,] array2d;
int[,,] array3d;
```

And a 32D array:

```
int[,,,,,,,,,,,,,,,,,,,,,,,,,,,,,,] array32d;
```

You simply put *n-1* commas inside the parentheses to declare an *n*-dimensional array.

The next step is to actually create an array:

```
array2d = new int[5,5];   // 5x5 array, as seen in Figure 4.6
array3d = new int[5,5,3]; // 5x5x3 array, as seen in Figure 4.6
```

You can change the dimensions to whatever you need to fit your purposes. Accessing the elements in the array is easy, too:

```
array2d[0,0] = 100;   // top left square, see Figure 4.6 for reference
array2d[2,2] = 200;   // middle square
array2d[0,4] = 300;   // bottom left square
array3d[0,0,0] = 400;   // top left front cube
array3d[2,2,1] = 500;   // middle cube
array3d[4,0,2] = 600;   // top right back cube
```

The Hard Way

There is another way to create arrays, but it isn't as easy as the first method I showed you. This is the approach that languages like Java take, and it's really quite a pain in the butt sometimes. Basically, the idea is that a 2D array is just an array of 1D arrays. Sounds weird, doesn't it? But it makes sense. Look at Figure 4.7 for reference.

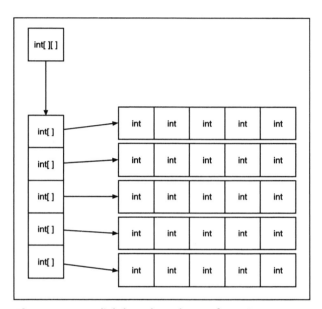

Figure 4.7 A slightly awkward way of creating a 2D array— by using a 1D array to store other 1D arrays.

An array can hold anything, so why not make it hold other arrays? Here's how you would declare a 2D and a 3D array in this fashion:

```
int[][] array2d;
int[][][] array3d;
```

Allocating the array, however, is a tricky task. You can't just say something like this:

```
int[][] array2d = new int[5][5];    // ERROR
int[][][] array3d = new int[5][5][3]; // ERROR
```

In the first example, you're trying to allocate six different arrays at one time (one array of arrays and five arrays of ints), and C# just doesn't allow you to do that. Instead, you need to do a little bit more work, first by allocating the array of arrays:

```
int[][] array2d = new int[5][];
```

then by creating each integer array individually:

```
for( int i = 0; i < 5; i++ )
{
    array2d[i] = new int[5];
}
```

Once you've done that, then you can start filling in the array:

```
array2d[0][0] = 100;
array2d[2][2] = 200;
array2d[0][4] = 300;
```

Of course, it gets even messier with a 3D array because you've got an array of arrays of arrays. (Say that three times fast.) So naturally, you've got a lot of work to do:

```
int[][][] array3d = new int[5][][];

// create the seconds dimension of arrays
for( int i = 0; i < 5; i++ )
{
    array3d[i] = new int[5][];
}

// now create the 3rd dimension of arrays:
for( int i = 0; i < 5; i++ )
{
    for( int j = 0; j < 5; j++ )
    {
        array3d[i][j] = new int[3];
    }
}
```

You can condense the loop if you want to, but I left the code uncondensed to clearly show you what is going on here.

The first thing I did in the previous example was to create an array. Then the next loop goes through and fills all five indexes with new arrays. At this point I have an array with five indexes, and each index has an array of five indexes.

Now I have something that, structurally, looks like that in Figure 4.7. The final loop goes through all 25 indexes in the 2D array on the right side of the figure and fills each one in with an array of three integers.

A huge mess, isn't it? This is why the first method I presented is preferred. The only benefit you enjoy with this method is the fact that you don't have to create rectangular arrays. Look at Figure 4.8, for example.

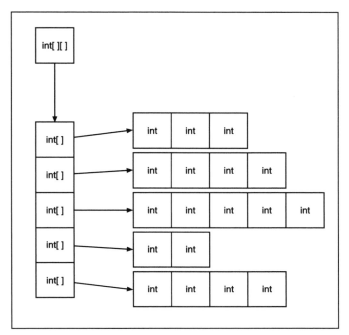

Figure 4.8 Using this method, you can create non-rectangular arrays.

Since you're storing arrays of arrays, the arrays in the last dimension don't have to be the same size. This can be pretty useful in some situations, but such situations don't come up too often.

Another Kind of Loop

Back in Chapter 2, I showed you how to perform various loops in C# using the for, while, and do while looping structures. There's actually one more loop in C# that I haven't talked about yet: the foreach loop.

The foreach loop is actually amazingly easy to use, but it can be used only on collections of data, such as arrays.

note

The foreach loop can be used on other collections that I haven't shown you yet. I'll get to those in Chapter 5.

Here's the basic syntax of the statement:

```
foreach( type variable in collection )
```

```
{
    // loop code here
}
```

The statement is going to treat every object inside `collection` as whatever type you specified for the type part, and you'll access the variable using `variable`. For example:

```
int[] array = new int[] { 1, 2, 3, 4, 5 };
int sum = 0;
foreach( int i in array )
{
    sum = sum + i;
}
```

This code goes through every index in `array` and sums them up.

Pretty much the only limitation on the `foreach` loop is that it's not allowed to physically alter the contents of the collection it's operating on. If you tried creating a statement like this instead of the previous one, you'd get a compiler error:

```
foreach( int i in array )
{
    i = 0;
}
```

That's because the compiler will treat the variable as read-only, so you can't change it. Unfortunately, this means you can only read values of value-type arrays, and you can't change the references in reference-type arrays. The good news, however, is that you *can* change the actual reference-types themselves, so if you have an array of classes, you can go ahead and change the classes as much as you want to—you just can't make the indexes in the array point to a different class.

Strings

Even in this day and age of fancy voice synthesis and interpretation, a whole heck of a lot of communication is still done via text. This is why almost every single language now has a very comprehensive string library. Not surprisingly, C# does, too.

Luckily, strings are very easy to use. If you're used to playing around with C's char*s (shudder), then you're going to love C#'s strings. They make using strings *fun*! Okay, I admit it: I have a strange string fixation.

Let me just jump right in and show you some examples:

```
string str = "Hello!";        // "Hello!"
str = str + " How are you?";  // "Hello! How are you?"
if( str == "Hello! How are you?" )
```

```
{
    str = "HI!";                 // "HI!"
}

if( str != "HI!" )
{
    // test fails so this code doesn't matter
}
```

Strings have the unique quality of being read-only. You can't change them, no matter how hard you try. If you want to change a string, you have to create a new one and overwrite it (like in line 2 in the previous example). This can be wasteful at times, but really, when was the last time you did a whole lot of processor-intensive text processing in a game? I thought so.

The string class, in addition to the basic stuff I just showed you, supports all sorts of useful functions:

```
string str = "Hello";
str a;
a = str.ToUpper();    // returns "HELLO"
a = str.ToLower();    // returns "hello"
a = str.Remove( 0, 2 );  // returns "llo"
a = str.Substring( 1, 3 ); // returns "ell"
```

And so on. There's a ton of functions; the most useful ones are listed in Table 4.1. Note that the variable str did not change in the previous example; each function returned a brand new string, rather than changing str.

note

If you need to do some heavy-duty string manipulation, then instead of using the string class, you should look into using System.Text.StringBuilder. Unfortunately, that goes beyond the scope of the book. I just wanted to let you know about StringBuilders, which are far more efficient for heavy duty text manipulation.

A string is essentially an array of characters, which is why I waited until you knew arrays before I exposed you to them. You can use a string almost exactly like an array when accessing individual characters:

```
string str = "hello!";
char c = str[0];  // 'h'
c = str[3];       // 'l'
```

Of course, as strings are read-only, you cannot change the characters like that—you must create a new string. It can be a pain in the butt, but that's just how it is.

Table 4.1 Useful String Functions

Function	Description
bool Endswith(string)	Determines if a string ends with string
string Insert(index, string)	Inserts string starting at index
string PadLeft(width, fillchar)	Increases string's width to width, inserting as many fillchars as needed to the left.
string PadRight(width, fillchar)	Same as PadLeft, but to the right.
string Remove(index, count)	Removes count characters starting at index
string[] Split()	Returns an array of all the words in the string
bool Startswith(string)	Determines if a string starts with string
string Substring(index, count)	Returns the sub-string starting at index which is count characters long
string ToUpper()	Converts lowercase characters to uppercase
string ToLower()	Converts uppercase characters to lowercase
string Trim()	Trims white space from front and back
string TrimEnd()	Trims white space from back
string TrimStart()	Trims white space from front

Summary

I hope this chapter has really expanded upon the knowledge you have of C#, especially in the area of polymorphism. Polymorphism is really an important concept in modern programming, so if you're still a little shaky on the subject, then it's really worth your time to go back and re-read this chapter and try to understand the material as best as you can. Don't worry too much about being a polymorphism expert, however: Throughout the rest of this book I'm going to be using polymorphism, so you'll understand it better as we go along.

You should also come away from this chapter knowing about how namespaces make your life easier (even if it doesn't seem like it!) and how to store data in basic arrays.

What You Learned

The main concepts that you should have picked up from this chapter are:

- How namespaces segment your programs.
- How to create namespaces.
- How to alias namespaces.
- How polymorphism makes your programs more flexible.

- How to use virtual functions and overriding.
- How to use abstraction.
- How to use `objects` to box and unbox value-types.
- How to use arrays.
- How to use multidimensional arrays.
- How to use the `foreach` loop on collections.
- How to use strings.

Review Questions

These review questions test your knowledge on the important concepts in this chapter. The answers can be found in Appendix A.

4.1. Are namespaces are a vital part of modern computer programming?

4.2. What can you do to make accessing namespaces like `Microsoft.DirectX.Direct3D` easier?

4.3. Polymorphism literally means what?

4.4. How does Polymorphism make your programs more flexible?

Questions 4.5 through 4.8 use the following code for reference:

```
abstract class Spaceship
{
    abstract public void MissileHit();
};

class CargoShip : Spaceship
{
    override public void MissileHit()
    {
        // some code here
    }
};

class CombatShip : Spaceship
{
    public void MissileHit()
    {
        // some code here
    }
};
```

4.5. Can you create instances of Spaceship?

4.6. Will the CombatShip class compile? If not, why?

4.7. Is the following code legal?

```
Spaceship s = new CargoShip();
```

4.8. Is the following code legal?

```
CargoShip s = new CombatShip();
```

4.9. How would you declare a 4-index integer array containing all 5s?

4.10. What's the easiest way to create a 5x5 2D array?

4.11. Why would you ever use the array-of-arrays method to create multidimensional arrays?

4.12. True or False: When you create an array designed to hold 10 Spaceships, all 10 ships are automatically created for you (assume Spaceship is a class, not a struct).

4.13. Is the following code legal? Why or why not?

```
int[] array = new int[5];
foreach( int i in array )
{
    i = 20;
}
```

4.14. Which lines in the following code are illegal?

```
1. string str = "HELLO";
2. char c = str[0];
3. str[1] = 'e';
4. str = str + " HOW ARE YOU?";
```

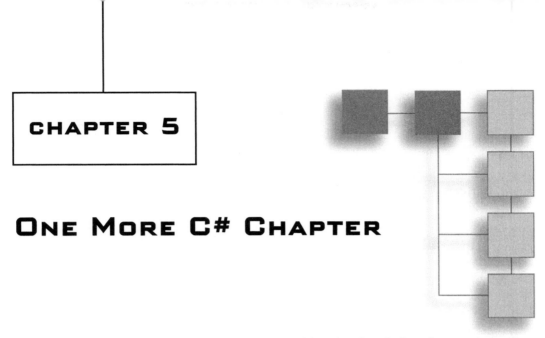

CHAPTER 5

ONE MORE C# CHAPTER

I'm sure all this stuff about C# is starting to get old; we're already five chapters in, and we have yet to get to some actual game-related programming! Argh!

Well, that just goes to show you how complex C# is—honestly, C# is one of the most complex computer languages ever written, and when combined with the .NET framework, it is one of the largest computer languages in existence, as well.

I have only a few more topics to cover before I move on to Windows programming and laying out the base framework of your computer game. In this chapter, I'll show you:

- How interfaces work.
- How interfaces differ from abstract classes.
- How to use interfaces to extend the capabilities of your classes.
- How to extend and combine interfaces.
- How exceptions make error handling easier and the rest of your code cleaner.
- How to create your own exceptions.
- How delegates make your programs more flexible.
- How to chain delegates.
- How to use array lists.
- How to use hash tables.
- How to use stacks and queues.
- How to read and write to text files.
- How to read and write to binary files.
- How to generate random numbers.

Interfaces

One more topic relating to inheritance that I haven't touched on yet is the topic of interfaces. I've used the term *interface* before, but C# actually has a keyword with the same name, which defines a construct slightly different from what you've seen before.

In Chapter 4, I showed you what an abstract class is, and how abstract functions define an interface. In computer science terms, that's correct, but C# actually has an interface keyword for defining real interfaces.

Look at this abstract class, for example:

```
abstract class Spaceship
{
    abstract public void LaserHit();
};
```

Anything that inherits from this class must define a LaserHit function, as all spaceships have that function.

On the other hand, you can redefine the spaceship and make an interface, rather than a class:

```
interface ISpaceship
{
    void LaserHit();
};
```

tip

It is common practice in C# to name interfaces with a capital I at the front. It helps code readability, but you're not required to do it.

Essentially, Spaceship and ISpaceship serve the same purpose: they define an interface that child classes must implement later on. Before I go into more detail about interfaces, let me show you how to inherit from these two different constructs.

For an easy point of reference, here's a combat ship definition that will inherit from the abstract Spaceship class (you've seen code like this before, in Chapter 4):

```
class CombatShip : Spaceship
{
    override public void LaserHit()
    {
        // some code
    }
};
```

There's nothing new in that code; I put it here only to illustrate the difference between inheriting an abstract class and an interface.

Here's how to inherit from an interface:

```
class CargoShip : ISpaceship
{
    public void LaserHit()
    {
        // some code
    }
};
```

That's it. The only difference is that when you inherit from an interface, you can't make the LaserHit function an override because there's nothing to override—interface functions aren't virtual unless you make them virtual in a child class like CargoShip.

Interfaces versus Abstract Classes

What is the difference between an interface and an abstract class? There are actually several differences that you probably wouldn't notice offhand. The next few subsections outline some of these differences.

Function Definitions and Data

The major difference between interfaces and abstract classes is that while abstract classes can act like interfaces, they are still essentially classes, and can hold things like data and function definitions. Interfaces cannot hold data or function definitions; they can only hold function *declarations* (the return type, name, and parameters of a function).

Virtual Functions

Abstract functions are assumed to be virtual. Any class that inherits from an abstract class is free to override any abstract function with its own implementation.

Interface functions, however, aren't virtual by default. Any function you define inside a class that uses an interface is a regular function by default; you need to explicitly make the function virtual in order to add the ability to override the function later on. Look at the following code:

```
class CombatShip : ISpaceship
{
    public void LaserHit()
    {
        // some code
    }
}
```

```
class AdvancedCombatShip : CombatShip
{
    new public void LaserHit()
    {
        // some code
    }
}
```

This code creates two classes using the ISpaceship interface, implementing the LaserHit function. This code doesn't use virtual functions; CombatShip.LaserHit is just a regular function.

Here's some example code that shows how the ISpaceship interface works:

```
ISpaceship s = new CombatShip();
s.LaserHit();      // calls CombatShip.LaserHit
s = new AdvancedCombatShip();
s.LaserHit();      // still calls CombatShip.LaserHit
```

The computer doesn't see AdvancedCombatShip.LaserHit when you're using the ISpaceship interface. In order to do that, you need to make it virtual:

```
class CombatShip : ISpaceship
{
    virtual public void LaserHit()
    {
        // some code
    }
}

class AdvancedCombatShip : CombatShip
{
    override public void LaserHit()
    {
        // some code
    }
}
```

Now the following code will work the way you expect it to when you use it with the new CombatShip and AdvancedCombatShip definititons:

```
ISpaceship s = new CombatShip();
s.LaserHit();     // calls CombatShip.LaserHit
s = new AdvancedCombatShip();
s.LaserHit();     // calls AdvancedCombatShip.LaserHit
```

Sometimes the default behavior of non-virtual functions in interfaces can work to your advantage; other times it may not. Just keep in mind that with interfaces you have more flexibility with your functions, but with abstract classes you're forced to use virtual functions.

Access

You can hide functions and data inside of abstract classes. Abstract functions don't have to be public; you can make them protected, if you wish.

Functions inside of interfaces on the other hand, are always public. The idea is that interfaces define functions that you want everyone to see.

Multiple Inheritance

Multiple inheritance is one of those ideas that seems sensible at first, but once you get to using it, it ends up annoying the heck out of you, which is why C# doesn't support it directly. However, C# does support a limited form of multiple inheritance, so I'm going to show you the theory behind it. Basically, the idea is that you can create a class that inherits from two different classes.

For example, you may want to create a flagship for your fleet of spaceships; the flagship will be a ship that combines both the weaponry of a combat ship and the cargo capacity of a cargo ship. Sounds great in theory, right? (See Figure 5.1.)

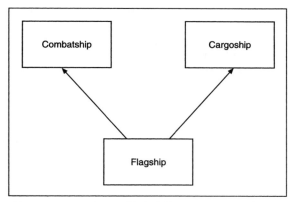

Figure 5.1 Using multiple inheritance to combine two classes into one.

Let me tell you right now: C# does not support multiple inheritance. It's just a huge mess. Let me give you an example showing you why multiple inheritance is a silly idea. Look at Figure 5.2; it shows *diamond inheritance*. In the figure, multiple inheritance doesn't seem like a major problem. We can all agree that a flagship is a spaceship, so what's the big deal?

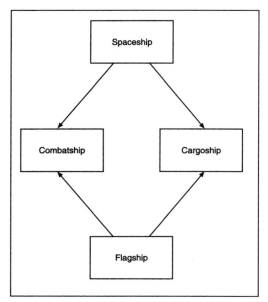

Figure 5.2 *Diamond inheritance,* in which two classes share a common base class.

Think about this: All spaceships can be hit by lasers. But combat ships get hit by lasers differently than cargo ships. So you have two different kinds of ships that can be hit, but they both react completely differently.

Now you make a flagship, which can also be hit by lasers. But how does it do it? Does it get hit by lasers like a combat ship or like a cargo ship? Who knows? There's really no easy way to concretely define exactly what should happen. The problem gets even worse when data is involved…but enough about that—multiple inheritance is just a pain in the neck.

C# has interfaces to solve the problem of multiple inheritance. In C#, a class can only inherit from one base. If you do the following, you'll get an error:

```
class FlagShip : CombatShip, CargoShip
```

But what if you defined an interface for the cargo ship instead?

```
interface ICargo()
{
    void LoadCargo();
    void DumpCargo();
};
```

Now try inheritance:

```
class FlagShip : CombatShip, ICargo
```

It works. Now a flagship is essentially a combat ship that can load and dump cargo. Unfortunately, you're going to have to recode the cargo functions on your own; that's just one of the limitations you'll have to deal with.

note

A better solution to the problem of combining capabilities would be to make all spaceships capable of handling cargo in the first place. For example, you could design combat ships to be able to carry a very small amount of cargo, such as the pilot's personal belongings, while a cargo ship can hold megatons of stuff. It's up to you.

Generally speaking, you really won't need multiple inheritance much; other solutions exist that work probably better.

Extending and Combining Interfaces

This concept is so simple that you've probably already figured it out: You can extend and combine interfaces. Say you've got a combat interface that can shoot lasers and missiles, but later on you want to make a special combat interface that can shoot nukes, too.

You could do this:

```
interface ICombat
{
    void ShootLaser();
    void ShootMissile();
}


interface INukeCombat : ICombat
{
    void Nuke();
}
```

Now you have an INukeCombat interface that has three functions: one for shooting lasers, one for shooting missiles, and one for nuking a planet from orbit (it's the only way to be sure).

Of course, you can combine interfaces as well:

```
interface IFlagShip : ICombat, ICargo
{
    // insert code here
}
```

Now you have a flagship interface that has functions to perform combat and cargo operations. Nothing special here.

Exceptions

I remember the bad old days of computer programming, before exceptions came along. I'm so glad those days are gone. I can remember writing code that looked like this:

```
error = Start Graphics Engine();
if( error )
    display error message

error = Set Resolution();
if( error )
    display error message


error = Start Sound Engine();
if( error )
    display error message
```

And so on. Maybe you still write code like that. If you do, you should stop; it's a pain in the butt. Exceptions are the solution to ugly code like that. Exceptions are special events that occur in *exceptional circumstances*. The idea is that you should write your code assuming that it's going to work, and have the error-handling portion somewhere else.

Let me explain. When you're running a program, many bad things can happen. You can run out of memory, for example, or a hardware device could fail. Or maybe a file that you need seems to have inexplicably disappeared. You'd better be prepared for when things go wrong.

Unfortunately, programmers are lazy. Admit it: you're lazy and you hate doing tons of work. Error-checking is just plain annoying and you don't want to deal with it.

The biggest kick in the butt, however, is realizing that 90 percent of everything you need to protect against almost never happens. Running out of disk space happens once in a blue moon. Some people think, "Well, as it almost never happens, I'm not going to protect against it." But that sort of thinking can come back to haunt you because sooner or later, it *will* happen. Nothing sucks more than having a program—especially a game—crash after it's been accumulating data for a long time. You need to protect your games, that's all there is to it.

Exception Basics

Exceptions are complex beasts, so I'll give you a simple overview of them first, and then I'll go on to the more advanced parts.

An Example of Exceptions

Take a look at this example:

```
try
{
    StartGraphicsEngine();
    SetResolution();
    StartSoundEngine();
}
catch
{
    // print an error message
}
```

The first thing you should notice is that this code is much cleaner than the example I showed you previously. You don't have annoying error-checking code mixed in all over the place. The main code is clean, and you can quickly see what it does. Start the graphic engine, set the resolution, start the sound engine. Badda-bing, badda-boom.

Obviously, if a problem occurs and one of those tasks can't be accomplished, then the game can't run. That's an exceptional circumstance.

What happens when an exceptional circumstance occurs is that each of those functions will *throw* an exception when something bad happens (I'll show you how to throw exceptions later). When an exception is thrown, the function immediately exits and execution keeps jumping out of each function until it finds a catch block. So, in the code I just showed you, if something goes wrong and you can't start the graphics engine inside of StartGraphicsEngine, then the function will throw an exception and execution will jump out of the function immediately, skip over SetResolution and StartSoundEngine without executing them, and start executing the code inside the catch block.

The try Block

The first part of the code example I showed you previously is the try block. A try block is a piece of code that tells the compiler, "I want to execute this code, but I know something bad may happen inside of it, so watch out for an exception." Every try block must be followed by a catch block, which I'll get to in the next section.

So what happens if you execute code that might throw an exception when it's not inside a catch block? Look at this code, for example (as usual, assume it's inside of a class):

```
public void Initialize()
{
    StartGraphicsEngine();
    SetResolution();
    StartSoundEngine();
}
```

Now, say someone calls Initialize. That calls StartGraphicsEngine, which tries to find a display device (note that this code is all just make-believe, serving only as an example). Assume that it can't find a display device. That's a pretty darn exceptional error, so the function says, "I give up, I can't start the graphics engine" and throws an exception. The code execution jumps out, back into the Initialize function. Rather than continuing, it sees that there is no try/catch block to handle the exception, and it jumps out again to whomever called Initialize.

Exceptions will keep jumping up until they find a try/catch block that can handle the exception. If they can't find one, then the entire program will eventually exit. The following is from Code Example 5.1, which can be found on the CD:

```
public class Class1
{
    static void Main( string[] args )
    {
        int[] array = new int[5];
        array[100] = 20;
        System.Console.WriteLine( "This should never be executed" );
    }
}
```

The example creates a new array with five indexes (0 through 4), and then tries assigning the value 20 to index 100.

The C# array class is smart; it realizes that you're doing something that just plain isn't right—the array isn't that big! Something really exceptional must have happened, so the array class throws an exception. The last line of code is skipped, and the program just exits out. You didn't catch the exception.

The catch Block

To catch exceptions and prevent your programs from spiraling out of control, use catch blocks. Here is Example 5.2 from the CD, which is a reworking of Example 5.1:

```
public class Class1
{
    static void Main(string[] args)
    {
        int[] array = new int[5];

        try
        {
            array[100] = 20;
            System.Console.WriteLine( "This should never be executed" );
```

```
        }
        catch
        {
            System.Console.WriteLine( "The exception was caught!" );
        }

        System.Console.WriteLine( "Execution continuing normally..." );
    }
}
```

Now the exception jumps right from the assignment line to the catch block. Once the catch block is done executing, execution continues on normally. The system has *handled* the exception, and knows that the problem doesn't exist anymore. At least it hopes so. It's really up to you to actually fix the problem inside the catch block.

The Finally Block

There are going to be times when you don't want code jumping around all over the place when an exception is thrown. For example, say you have a file that you've opened up, and in the process of working on that file, something bad happens and an exception is thrown. Instead of having execution immediately jump out, maybe you would like to make sure the file was properly closed first.

Well, then you'd do this:

```
try
{
    // open a file here
    ...
    // some exception may be thrown here
    ...
    // other code
}
catch
{
    // handle error here
}
finally
{
    // close the file here. This code will always execute
}
```

If you put the file-closing code inside the try block, then there's a chance it might not execute. If you put it in a catch block, then it will only execute when an exception is thrown.

You *could*, of course, put the same code in both a `try` block and a `catch` block, but that's code duplication, and code duplication is bad. Instead, put it in the `finally` block, thereby guaranteeing that the code will *always* be executed after the other blocks, no matter what happens.

note

> You should note that the scope for all three blocks is different. Anything you define inside a `try` block is *not* accessible outside of that block, so by the time you get to a `catch` block or `finally` block, everything declared inside the `try` block has gone out of scope and cannot be accessed. Therefore, in the previous example, you should declare (but not open) the file object *outside* of the `try` block.

Advanced Exception Topics

Exceptions are actually pretty advanced, and there's a lot to them. An exception is actually an object. Every time an exception is thrown, the system creates an exception object that contains information about what went wrong. All exceptions inherit from a common base class: `System.Exception`.

For example, in Examples 5.1 and 5.2, the exception that was thrown was of type `System.IndexOutOfRangeException`. That exception type tells you that you tried using an index that was out of range on a collection object.

Catching Specific Exceptions

Sometimes more than one error occurs in your code. Using a plain `catch` block catches all exceptions and assumes that you handled them; then it continues executing. But this is not always a good idea, and let me explain why. You are usually going to know what errors to expect in some code. When dealing with files, you know you're going to face the possibility that you're going to run out of space. But there's also the possibility that something completely unexpected will happen. A `catch` block is sort of like a contract. It says, "I'm going to handle this exception, and then the program is going to be able to keep running just fine after this." But if something completely unexpected happens, how can you be sure the problem is fixed? You can't!

So C# allows you to catch exceptions of specific types. Check it out:

```
try
{
    // try some code that may throw an index error
}
catch( System.IndexOutOfRangeException e )
{
```

```
    // print the error message:
    System.Console.WriteLine( e.Message );
}
```

Now you've just made your code able to catch index exceptions. All other exceptions will be ignored, and execution will keep jumping upward until it finds a catch block that can actually handle it.

You can also chain catch blocks, like this:

```
try
{
    // try some code that may throw an index error
}
catch( System.IndexOutOfRangeException e )
{
    // handle index error
}
catch( System.OutOfMemoryException e )
{
    // handle memory error
}
```

Each block will handle each error differently.

You may have noticed that in the previous examples I had a variable named e. That represents the actual exception object. Exceptions can store data specific to the error, in case you need to find out exact details of what happened.

Re-throwing Exceptions

There are going to be times when you want to catch an exception, but you won't be able to handle it. These situations usually arise when you only want to know that an exception has been thrown (and not actually fix the problem) so that you can log it somewhere or notify something. In that case, as you haven't handled the exception, you want to *re-throw* it. This is a very simple task:

```
catch
{
    // do some notification here
    throw;    // rethrow it
}
```

The exception has been re-thrown now, and will keep jumping up until another catch block catches it.

Creating Your Own Exceptions

You can create your own exception classes. It's really easy to do, and you should always inherit the classes from the base System.Exception object (or another built-in exception type, if your needs require it).

```
class FatalGameException : System.Exception
{
    // put some data about the game error in here
}
```

That's all there is to it!

Throwing your own exceptions is pretty darned easy, too:

```
throw new FatalGameException();
```

In a more complex program, you would make the constructor of the exception take some data about the game, but as this is just a simple example, I omitted that.

Delegates

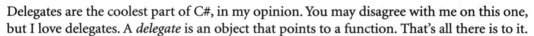

Delegates are the coolest part of C#, in my opinion. You may disagree with me on this one, but I love delegates. A *delegate* is an object that points to a function. That's all there is to it.

In C++, you had *function pointers*. The idea was that you had a variable that pointed to a function, and you could change the variable to point to other functions at run-time! Function pointers were useful, but ugly as all get-out and difficult to use. I'm not going to waste your time by showing you an example of them, but trust me—they were unbelievably ugly. C#, thankfully, has solved the ugliness-and-difficultness problem completely by creating delegates.

Creating a Delegate

In order to start using delegates, you first need to create a delegate-type definition, in order to tell the compiler what kind of function it's going to point to. Here's an example:

```
public delegate void MyDelegate();
```

This tells the compiler that you've created a delegate-type named MyDelegate, which points to functions that return nothing and have no parameters. Here's a sample Spaceship class that defines two functions, one static and the other non-static:

```
class Spaceship
{
    public static void InitializeShips()
    {
```

```
        // initialize all spaceships in the game here
    }

    public void LaserHit()
    {
        // get hit by a laser
    }
}
```

Later on, somewhere else, you can create a delegate pointing to those functions. Here's the code to make a delegate pointing to the static function:

```
MyDelegate d;                                   // declare delegate
d = new MyDelegate( Spaceship.InitializeShips ); // create delegate
d();                                // calls Spaceship.InitializeShips();
```

All you do is pass the name of the function (in this case Spaceship.InitializeShips) into the constructor of the delegate.

To create a delegate pointing to a non-static function, do this:

```
MyDelegate d;                      // declare delegate
Spaceship s = new Spaceship();     // create spaceship
d = new MyDelegate( s.LaserHit );  // create delegate
d();                               // calls s.LaserHit();
```

To create a delegate pointing to a non-static function requires a little bit more work; you need to actually have an instance of the Spaceship class. If you try saying new MyDelegate (Spaceship.LaserHit) your compiler is going to yell, "I don't know which spaceship to execute that on, stupid!"

All you need to do is call the delegate as if it were a function, and it will call whatever function you put into it.

Of course, you can create delegates that use different return values and parameters, as well:

```
class MyClass
{
    public static int MyFunction( int a, int b, float c )
    {
        // some code
    }
};

public delegate int MyDelegate( int a, int b, float c );
```

And then later on you could use the delegate like this:

```
MyDelegate d = new MyDelegate( MyClass.MyFunction );
int x = d( 1, 2, 3.141596 );
```

Or you could swap out MyClass.MyFunction with any function that returns an int and takes two ints and a float as parameters.

Chaining Delegates

C# took the idea of function pointers and went one step further, introducing *delegate multicasting*. That's a nice complex term, isn't it? I like to use the word *chaining*, instead, because it's more descriptive.

Delegate multicasting, or chaining, means that you're allowed to chain delegates together. Look at this code, for example (which uses the Spaceship class from the example I showed you previously):

```
MyDelegate d;                                    // declare delegate
Spaceship s = new Spaceship();                   // declare spaceship
d = new MyDelegate( Spaceship.InitializeShips ); // create delegate
d += new MyDelegate( s.LaserHit );               // chain a laserhit call
d();        // call InitializeShips and s.LaserHit!
```

If you execute a chained delegate, the code executes every function inside the delegate in the order that you added it. So the last line of the previous code example will call Spaceship.InitializeShips and then call s.LaserHit.

You can also remove delegates as well:

```
d -= new MyDelegate( Spaceship.InitializeShips );
d();        // only calls s.LaserHit now.
```

I really love this whole idea of chaining delegates. It adds so many possibilities to your programs.

note

If you chain delegates that return values, you may run into some problems. The way C# handles that situation is by returning the value of only the last function inside the delegate. All other return values are discarded. So don't return things that are absolutely vital to your program if you know the function is going inside a chained delegate.

Collections

Data collections are a huge topic in computer programming, and it deserves a whole book unto itself. I'm going to have to give you a limited rundown of C#'s collections here.

You've already seen one collection type in Chapter 4: the array. As I've already gone over arrays, in the subsections below I'll just show you the more advanced containers in C#.

The ArrayList

Arrays are great for storing information, but they have a large drawback: you can't resize them. If you want to resize an array, then you must create a new one, copy it over, and discard the old array. That's a lot of wasted effort.

Luckily, the .NET framework provides you with the System.Collections.ArrayList class, which is automatically resizable. It's fairly simple to use:

```
System.Collections.ArrayList list = new System.Collections.ArrayList();

// adding elements
list.Add( 20 );            // 20
list.Add( 30 );            // 20, 30
list.Add( 40 );            // 20, 30, 40
list.Insert( 1, 60 );      // 20, 60, 30, 40
list.Insert( 0, 90 );      // 90, 20, 60, 30, 40

// accessing elements
int x;
x = (int)list[0];          // 90
x = (int)list[2];          // 60

// finding elements
bool b;
b = list.Contains( 20 );   // true
b = list.Contains( 10 );   // false
x = list.IndexOf( 90 );    // 0
x = list.IndexOf( 30 );    // 3

// removing elements
list.Remove( 30 );         // 90, 20, 60, 40
list.RemoveAt( 0 );        // 20, 60, 40
list.Clear();              // empty!
```

That example should give you a pretty good idea of how array lists work. It's not really that difficult.

The only things you should be concerned about are removing and adding items into the middle of the list. Keep in mind that the .NET framework keeps the list stored in an array, so when you insert something in the middle, everything after that spot has to be moved up, and when you remove something in the middle, everything after that spot has to be moved down. It's not a huge deal, but you should be aware of it.

Another fact to remember is that array lists can store objects of any type. That means that you can perform operations like this, storing many different kinds of objects in the same list:

```
list.Add( 10 );
list.Add( "I am the very model of a modern major-general!" );
list.Add( new Spaceship() );
```

This also means that you need to cast objects when you take them out of the list again:

```
int x = (int)list[0];
string s = (string)list[1];
Spaceship sp = (Spaceship)list[2];
```

This can be a little tedious if you don't remember what you stored in your list.

The typeof Operator

If you are not sure of an object's type, you can perform a test on it like this:

```
if( list[0].GetType() == typeof(int) )
    // element is an int
if( list[1].GetType() == typeof(string) )
    // element is a string
if( list[2].GetType() == typeof(Spaceship) )
    // element is a spaceship
```

And that's how you can be sure.

The is Operator

Another operator you can use on types is the is operator, which is amazingly simple to use:

```
if( list[0] is int )
    // element is an int
if( list[1] is string )
    // element is a string
if( list[2] is Spaceship )
    // element is a spaceship
```

This method is a lot cleaner than the GetType method I showed you previously.

The as Operator

Another way to test the objects in your collection, if you know they are references and not value-types, is to use the as operator. Here's an example:

```
Spaceship s = list[2] as Spaceship;
```

If the element is a Spaceship, then s will hold a reference to the spaceship object inside the list. If it isn't a Spaceship, then s will hold null instead.

note

> You cannot use this operator with value-types, because it works by using references. When it fails, it returns a null reference, and value-types cannot be null.

Hash Tables

Hash tables are an extremely efficient collection type. They store key-value pairs, meaning they act sort of like an array, except you can use anything as the "index," not only numbers. Here's a simple example that uses strings as the key:

```
System.Collections.HashTable table = new System.Collections.HashTable();

// store some data in the table:
table["pi"] = 3.14159;
table["e"] = 2.71828;
table["fourty-two"] = 42.0;

// now retrieve it:
double d;
d = table["e"];          // 2.71828
d = table["fourty-two"]; // 42.0
d = table["pi"];         // 3.14159

// remove an entry:
bool b;
b = table.Contains( "pi" );  // true
table.Remove( "pi" );
b = table.Contains( "pi" );  // false
```

I don't really have the room to go over the internal details of a hash table, unfortunately. But let me give you a brief rundown of how they work. Whenever you insert a key/value pair into a table, the key values are *hashed* into a numerical value. C# does this by way of calling the GetHashCode function of the key object, which returns an int. All Objects have this function built in, so you can use anything as a key value. C# then treats this hash value as an index into the table, and quickly accesses the item for you.

note

I recommend that you create your own hash functions for your classes, as the built-in method isn't that good for custom data. Since it is unlikely that you'll need to use your own key types for a simple game, I'm going to leave this topic up to you to explore more on your own. I wrote an extensive chapter about hash tables in the book *Data Structures for Game Programmers*; though the book deals primarily with C++, the concepts remain the same no matter what language you use.

Stacks and Queues

The .NET framework also provides stacks and queues, which are simple linear containers that allow you to access data in a specific manner. Mainly, a queue is a first-in-first-out (FIFO) container (objects put in first will be removed first), and a stack is a last-in-first-out (LIFO) container (objects put in last will be removed first).

Here's an example of a queue:

```
System.Collections.Queue q = new System.Collections.Queue();
q.Enqueue( 10 );        // 10
q.Enqueue( 20 );        // 10, 20
q.Enqueue( 30 );        // 10, 20, 30
q.Enqueue( 40 );        // 10, 20, 30, 40
q.Enqueue( 50 );        // 10, 20, 30, 40, 50

// just look at the top
int x = (int)q.Peek();   // 10

// or look and remove the top
x = (int)q.Dequeue();    // 10,  q = 20, 30, 40, 50
x = (int)q.Dequeue();    // 20,  q = 30, 40, 50
x = (int)q.Dequeue();    // 30,  q = 40, 50
x = (int)q.Dequeue();    // 40,  q = 50
x = (int)q.Dequeue();    // 50,  q = {empty}
```

It's a pretty simple concept, and it's pretty handy.

Stacks are almost identical to queues, except in the way items are removed. Rather than take things off the front, stacks take things off the back:

```
System.Collections.Stack s = new System.Collections.Stack ();
s.Push( 10 );        // 10
s.Push( 20 );        // 10, 20
s.Push( 30 );        // 10, 20, 30
s.Push( 40 );        // 10, 20, 30, 40
s.Push( 50 );        // 10, 20, 30, 40, 50
```

```
// just look at the top
int x = (int)s.Peek();    // 50

// or look and remove the top
x = (int)s.Pop();    // 50,  s = 10, 20, 30, 40
x = (int)s.Pop();    // 40,  s = 10, 20, 30
x = (int)s.Pop();    // 30,  s = 10, 20
x = (int)s.Pop();    // 20,  s = 10
x = (int)s.Pop();    // 10,  s = {empty}
```

Other Collections

There are a bunch of other collections in C#, but the ones I've presented here are the collections you'll be using the most. I'll let you explore the other collection types on your own, as Microsoft has documented them really well in the MSDN (which can be found online at http://msdn.microsoft.com/). Just do a search for "System.Collections," and you should find more information than you'll need.

File Access

Games are complex creatures. The days when you could load up an arcade game and beat it in a few hours are gone; now games exist that literally take weeks of solid playing to complete.

Obviously, no one has enough stamina to play a game that long—that would be insane. So you need a way to store the game data so that a game player can come back and pick up where they left off.

Streams

In virtually any computer system, files are treated as abstract objects called *streams*. That's because you usually read or write a long "stream" of data at one time rather than skipping around all over the place.

Streams aren't just for files, though; they're used for all sorts of things, such as text input and output and network communication. In this section, however, you're only going to be concerned with file streams.

Reading and Writing

The base class for all streams in .NET is System.IO.Stream, which is an abstract class. Streams have all sorts of functions, but the functions you're going to be concerned with the most are Write, WriteByte, Read, and ReadByte.

The functions do exactly what they promise to do, and allow you to read or write arrays of bytes or just single bytes to a stream. For example (assume the stream s is already valid):

```
byte b;
b = s.ReadByte();    // read the first two bytes from
b = s.ReadByte();    // the stream

s.WriteByte( 10 );   // writes the value 10
s.WriteByte( 255 );  // writes the value 255

byte[] array = new byte[4];

// read into array starting at index 0, and read at most 4 bytes
s.Read( array, 0, 4 );
s.Write( array, 0, 4 );  // write everything back out again
```

This example is kind of silly because you won't often be combining read and write operations in the same general area of code. Most of the time, you're either performing one operation or the other, not both. This was just to show you how the functions worked.

Flushing and Closing

The two other major functions that streams support are Flush and Close.

Contrary to what you may think, when you write to a stream, what you write isn't actually written out immediately. The reason for this is that device access is slow. In terms of processing time required, it actually takes a long time to write one byte out to a file. There's a lot of overhead in such operations, so the amount of time it takes to write out one byte is only slightly smaller than the amount of time it takes to write out a bunch of bytes.

For this reason, streams use a *cache*. Whenever you write something to a stream, the computer holds on to it for a bit, and when the cache is full enough, the contents of the cache are finally written out to the actual device it's attached to. Unfortunately, this can be a pain in the butt because you have no idea when this is actually going to happen. Sometimes you need to make sure that something gets written out immediately. That's what the Flush method is for. Take a look:

```
s.WriteByte( 20 );   // cache a 20
s.Flush();           // make sure cache is manually written out immediately
```

note

Tests on my computer show that my file streams cache 1024 bytes before automatically writing them out to disk. Your results may vary.

And, of course, the `Close` function simply closes the stream so that no more reading or writing can be performed. Closing a stream also flushes it.

Readers and Writers

Reading and writing raw bytes to a stream gets tedious really quickly. You're going to want to read and write more important things, like ints and floats, or even text strings. Because of this, the .NET framework includes specialized classes, called *readers* and *writers*, that perform the reading and writing of datatypes automatically for you. These classes encapsulate a stream and allow you to read and write specialized data to a stream.

Text and Streams

The easiest pair of classes to use are the `System.IO.StreamReader` and `System.IO.StreamWriter` classes. They allow you to read and write strings to and from a file. Text files are usually called ASCII files, as they use the ASCII formatting standard—though that's not always the case. The .NET framework allows you to change the formatting, but you're not really going to be concerned with that unless you're doing international game development.

Reading

When reading from a text stream, there are only a few functions you should be concerned with: `Read`, `ReadLine`, and `ReadToEnd`.

`Read` reads a specified number of characters from a stream, stores them into a character array, and returns the total number of characters read. Here's an example (assume that `StreamReader` s is already set up with an underlying device; I'll show you how to do that in a little bit):

```
char[] buffer = new char[32];
int x;
x = s.Read( buffer, 0, 32 );   // read up to 32 characters and store them
                               // in buffer starting at index 0.
```

The x variable will now hold the number of characters actually read (if the stream doesn't have 32 characters to read, it will return as many as it can), and the buffer array will have everything that has been read.

An easier function to use is the `ReadLine` function:

```
string str;
str = s.ReadLine();   // reads the next line of text
```

That's all there is to it. The function returns a string, making things nice and easy for you.

The final option is to read the whole stream at once:

```
string str;
str = s.ReadToEnd();   // read EVERYTHING
```

That function also returns a string. You probably don't want to call this function on huge files, but I'm sure you've already figured that out.

Writing

There are primarily two functions that you should be concerned with when writing to StreamWriters: the Write function and the WriteLine function. I'm betting you can guess what they do.

```
int x = 10;
double y = 3.14159;
string s = "Hello there!";
s.Write( x );    // writes "10", as a string
s.Write( y );    // writes "3.14159" as a string
s.Write( s );    // writes "Hello there!"
// stream now contains "103.14159Hello there!"
```

The Write function has overloads to accept pretty much any of the built-in datatypes, making your job pretty easy—you don't have to manually convert everything to a string yourself.

WriteLine acts pretty much the same way, except that it writes a newline character after every write:

```
int x = 10;
double y = 3.14159;
string s = "Hello there!";
s.WriteLine( x );    // writes "10", as a string
s.WriteLine( y );    // writes "3.14159" as a string
s.WriteLine( s );    // writes "Hello there!"
// stream now contains:
// 10
// 3.14159
// Hello there!
```

Pretty easy, eh?

Binary Streams

Sometimes text files are too big. If you think about it, you're wasting space a lot of the time if you write out ASCII data. An integer is four bytes long inside a computer, but if you write out the individual characters of the number 1,000,000,000, you're taking up ten characters, over twice as big as four bytes the computer uses to store it.

Luckily, the .NET framework provides streams that allow you read and write binary values directly to a stream rather than converting them to and from strings. These classes are called the System.IO.BinaryReader and System.IO.BinaryWriter classes.

Reading

The BinaryReader class provides a lot of functions for reading binary data from a file. You need these, as pretty much every single native binary type is encoded differently. Here's a list of the reading functions:

- ReadBoolean
- ReadByte
- ReadBytes
- ReadChar
- ReadChars
- ReadDecimal
- ReadDouble
- ReadInt16
- ReadInt32
- ReadInt64
- ReadSByte
- ReadSingle
- ReadString
- ReadUInt16
- ReadUInt32
- ReadUInt64

Most of the functions are pretty self-descriptive, but a few of them need some explanation. For example, the function to read floats is called ReadSingle rather than ReadFloat. This is probably because the .NET datatype that represents floats is called System.Single.

The other functions that need explaining are the ReadChars, ReadBytes, and ReadString functions.

Reading characters and bytes is fairly straightforward; you tell the function how many you want to read and it returns an array of the characters that have been read:

```
char[] carray = s.ReadChars( 20 );  // read 20 chars if possible
byte[] barray = s.ReadBytes( 20 );  // read 20 bytes (signed) if possible
```

The size of the array may be less than the number of characters or bytes requested, depending on how many are left in the stream.

Reading a string is slightly more complicated. When reading strings in this method, the function assumes that the string has two parts: a descriptor describing how long the string actually is, and the actual string contents. The ReadString function assumes that the first byte (or more, depending on how long the string is, it varies) it reads from the stream is the size descriptor, and then it reads that many characters into a string and returns it. You'll need to use this method in conjunction with the System.IO.BinaryWriter.Write function.

```
string str = s.ReadString();
```

The other functions are fairly straightforward:

```
int x = s.ReadInt32();
uint y = s.ReadUInt32();
float z = s.ReadSingle();
```

And so on.

Writing

Writing binary data is incredibly simple because the BinaryWriter class automatically knows what kind of data you want to write just by looking at the type of the parameter you're passing in:

```
int x = 20;
float y = 12.32154;
char z = 'P';
s.Write( x );
s.Write( y );
s.Write( z );
```

And that's all there is to it.

File Streams

All the stream classes I showed you previously are basically interfaces for you. You use them to access actual streams. There are a bunch of streams, such as memory streams and network streams, in C#, but in this section you'll only be concerned with file streams.

With C#, file streams are pretty much a snap. You use the static System.IO.File class to open files for you, and it returns a System.IO.FileStream object that you can use with the readers and writers I showed you before.

There are a lot of functions in the File class that allow you to play around with files, but you're going to be primarily concerned with the functions that deal with opening files: OpenRead and OpenWrite. There's another one, Open, which allows you to configure exactly how a file is opened. I won't really get into that, though; the other functions give you enough functionality to work with at the moment.

Both OpenRead and OpenWrite return a FileStream object:

```
System.IO.FileStream file;

// write some stuff to file
file = System.IO.File.OpenWrite( "blah.txt" );
// <perform write operations on it here>
file.Close();

// now read the data back in:
file = System.IO.File.OpenRead( "blah.txt" )
// <perform read operations on it here>
file.Close();
```

The previous code segment allows you to read and write raw bytes using the ReadByte and WriteByte functions, but you're not going to be very interested in performing those operations because reading and writing raw bytes is tedious. Instead, you're probably going to want to encapsulate the file stream into a reader or writer.

Here's an example showing how to write using a StreamWriter object:

```
System.IO.FileStream file;
System.IO.StreamWriter writer;

// open the file
file = System.IO.File.OpenWrite( "blah.txt" );

// create a writer with that file
writer = new System.IO.StreamWriter( file );

writer.WriteLine( "Hello all you happy people!" );
writer.WriteLine( 542 );
writer.Close();
```

And you've now written two lines of text to a file named "blah.txt". Here's how you would read it all back in:

```
System.IO.FileStream file;
System.IO.StreamReader reader;

// open the file
file = System.IO.File.OpenRead( "blah.txt" );

// create a reader with that file
reader = new System.IO.StreamReader( file );
```

```
string str;
str = reader.ReadLine();  // "Hello all you happy people!"
str = reader.ReadLine();  // "542"
int i = Int32.Parse( str );  // convert value to integer
reader.Close();
```

If you prefer using binary files, then you should use the binary readers and writers (`BinaryReader` and `BinaryWriter`) like I showed you before.

Random Numbers

Random numbers are used quite often in game programming, as they're used to simulate different chaotic circumstances that can be found in the real world. The .NET framework provides a really neat system for generating random numbers.

In order to begin using random numbers, the first thing you need to do is to create a number generator, like this:

```
System.Random r = new System.Random( 0 );
```

The integer passed into the constructor is called a *seed value*. Random number generators aren't truly random; instead, they use algorithms to generate *pseudo-random numbers*, or numbers that seem random to you and me, but which aren't mathematically random (meaning they aren't completely chaotic). For games, pseudo-random numbers do just fine.

Seeds

The seed value determines where to start generating numbers. If you give a seed to a random number generator and pull off five numbers from it, and then give a totally different generator the same starting seed, its first five numbers will be identical. For example:

```
System.Random r = new System.Random( 0 );
int x = r.Next();     // should hold 1559595546
System.Random s = new System.Random( 0 );
int y = s.Next();     // should also hold 1559595546
```

Whenever you want a generator to generate the same sequence of numbers, give it a common seed.

You're not required to have a seed, however. In fact, most of the time you probably don't want to set a hard-coded seed because that will make your game seem less random, as it will be generating the same sequence of random numbers every time someone plays.

Instead, you can create a generator like this:

```
System.Random r = new System.Random();
```

When you don't provide a seed, the system uses a seed based on the current time for you automatically, so you don't have to worry about it.

Generating Numbers

As you can guess, the Next function returns the next random number in the sequence.

note

All of the following generation examples assume that they are run one after another. If run this same code you should get the same results, as you're using the same seed.

Here's an example:

```
System.Random r = new System.Random( 0 );
int x;
x = r.Next();    // 1559595546
x = r.Next();    // 1755192844
x = r.Next();    // 1649316166
x = r.Next();    // 1198642031
x = r.Next();    // 442452829
x = r.Next();    // 1200195957
```

Now those are absolutely huge numbers, and they're probably not going to be too useful to you. Luckily, the .NET framework provides a few other ways to generate numbers that have a bit more meaning to them. For example, you can generate numbers from 0 to a specified amount:

```
x = r.Next( 100 );    // 90
x = r.Next( 100 );    // 44
x = r.Next( 100 );    // 97
x = r.Next( 100 );    // 27
```

That call generates numbers between 0 and 100. There's another version of the function as well, which allows you to specify a lower bound:

```
x = r.Next( 50, 100 );    // 64
x = r.Next( 50, 100 );    // 73
x = r.Next( 50, 100 );    // 81
x = r.Next( 50, 100 );    // 73
```

This time, you're generating numbers from 50 to 100.

Other Generation Techniques

There are two other ways you can generate random numbers using the Random class: you can generate double-precision numbers, and you can generate arrays of random bytes.

Both are pretty straightforward:

```
double d;
d = r.NextDouble();   // 0.98215125314060192
d = r.NextDouble();   // 0.030366990729406004
d = r.NextDouble();   // 0.86237015382497118
d = r.NextDouble();   // 0.99534708121574811
```

Doubles are generated between the values 0.0 and 1.0.

And finally, you can fill an array with random bytes:

```
byte[] b = new byte[10];
r.NextBytes( b );   // 173, 80, 209, 217, 253, 8, 179, 134, 239, 176
```

That's pretty much everything you'd be interested in with the System.Random class.

Above and Beyond

I've mentioned a few times before that C#, combined with the .NET class library, is one of the largest and most complex programming languages in existence. Obviously, a book this size cannot possibly hope to cover it all. I showed you the major parts of the language—the stuff you'll use most often, and stuff that's important to game programming.

Unfortunately, there is still a ton of things that I haven't covered. In the following subsections I'll go over some topics I think are worth looking into on your own free time.

The Preprocessor

In the olden days of computer programming, some programming languages (most notably C) had a *preprocessor*, a special phase of the compiling process that would go through your code and perform simple text-replacement operations. I don't want to get into a large discussion about why this was needed, suffice to say that it was.

Unfortunately, it's an ugly beast, and I'm quite glad to see it thrown by the wayside in most modern languages. C# has decided to include a very limited preprocessor that allows you to selectively compile different pieces of code depending on the value of preprocessor values. You probably won't need to use it for anything, but if you're interested, you might want to look into it.

Operator Overloading

C# has inherited a rather neat feature from C++: *operator overloading*. This is the feature that allows you to define new operators for classes, so that you can do things like this:

```
Spaceship s = new Spaceship();
Spaceship t = new Spaceship();
s = s + t;
```

Operator overloading allows you to use the standard operators (such as +, -, *, /, and so on) on your own custom classes.

Of course, what exactly does adding a spaceship to another spaceship accomplish? Who knows? That's pretty much why I haven't gone over it; there's really little real-world use for operator overloading outside of mathematical classes. If you want to look into it, go ahead.

Variable Parameter Lists

C# allows you to create functions that can take a variable number of parameters. Personally, I've never really needed something like this, but I suppose it can come in handy in some situations. Look up the `params` keyword if you're interested.

Unsafe Code

C# allows you to create blocks of so-called *unsafe code*. This is primarily to allow you access to old C APIs, and it allows you to have direct memory access without any garbage-collection protection. I really wouldn't recommend using unsafe code unless you know exactly what you're doing.

C# 2.0 Features

C# 2.0 is a brand-new release that adds a few features to the language, such as *generics* (similar to C++'s templates, but not quite as powerful) and *iterators*, which are structures used to examine contents of data structures. None of these features are essential to game programming, and as the current .NET framework release still does not support those features, you wouldn't be able to use them, anyway.

Summary

This was the last chapter on the C# language itself. You learned a lot of advanced material here; the worst of it is over now, and you can finally move on to creating your very own games in C#! Throughout the next few chapters, I'm going to be taking you through how to use Managed DirectX 9 in combination with C# to make a simple arcade-style shooter game.

What You Learned

The main concepts that you should have picked up from this chapter are:

- How interfaces work
- How exceptions make error-handling easier and the rest of your code cleaner
- How delegates make your programs more flexible

- How to use more advanced data structure collections
- How to read and write to files
- How to generate random numbers

Review Questions

These review questions test your knowledge on the important concepts exposed to you in this chapter. The answers can be found in Appendix A.

5.1. Can an interface hold function declarations?

5.2. Can an interface hold function definitions?

5.3. Can an interface hold variables?

5.4. Are interface functions virtual by default?

5.5. Fill in the blank: Interfaces are C#'s way of supporting a limited form of _____ inheritance.

5.6. How does using exceptions make your code cleaner?

5.7. Which lines of the following code will *not* be executed?

```
1:   public void Foo()
2:   {
3:       try
4:       {
5:           int[] array = new int[3];
6:           array[3] = 10;
7:           array[2] = 5;
8:       }
9:       catch
10:      {
11:          System.Console.WriteLine( "EXCEPTION!" );
12:      }
13:      finally
14:      {
15:          System.Console.WriteLine( "Process Completed" );
16:      }
17: }
```

5.8. Using the code from Question 5.7, which lines of code will *always* be executed?

5.9. How do you re-throw an exception without modifying it?

5.10. True or False: A delegate can point to *any* public function, static or non-static, as long as the signatures are the same.

Use the following code for Questions 5.11 and 5.12:

```
class Foo
{
    static public int DoubleMe( int p )
    {
        return p * 2;
    }

    static public int TripleMe( int p )
    {
        return p * 3;
    }

    public delegate int MyDelegate( int );
}
```

5.11. Assume that the following code is run. What is the value of i?

```
Foo.MyDelegate d = new Foo.MyDelegate( Foo.DoubleMe );
int i = d();
```

5.12. Assume that the following code is run. What is the value of i?

```
Foo.MyDelegate d = new Foo.MyDelegate( Foo.DoubleMe );
d += new Foo.MyDelegate( Foo.TripleMe );
int i = d();
```

5.13. What is the primary difference between an Array and an ArrayList?

5.14. Why is it considered an expensive operation to insert or remove items in the middle of an ArrayList?

5.15. Fill in the blanks: Hash tables store _____/_____ pairs.

5.16. Text files are good for storing data that you want people to read easily. Name one reason why you would prefer a binary file instead.

5.17. If you give two generators the same seed and then get a number from each of them, will they be the same?

5.18. Name one reason why the capability of setting your own random seed is a good thing.

On Your Own

On your own, you should look into some of the topics I listed that this book does not cover. It's not necessary to do so in order to successfully finish reading this book, but a little extra knowledge has never hurt anybody.

PART II

GAME PROGRAMMING IN C#

CHAPTER 6
Setting Up a Framework 123

CHAPTER 7
Direct3D 145

CHAPTER 8
DirectInput 197

CHAPTER 9
DirectSound 219

CHAPTER 10
Programming the Keyboard, Mouse, and Joystick 227

CONCLUSION 283

You've just completed five chapters that showed you most of what you should need to know about C# in order to get on your way into game programming, but you're not all the way there yet! You've only learned about the C# language itself—you've yet to learn many general game programming concepts or which important multimedia components you'll need to create your own games. This part of the book aims to remedy that problem by teaching you how to build a framework in C#, as well as how to use the graphics, input, and sound libraries of DirectX. Finally, in this part of the book, I'll show you how to assemble a game on your own.

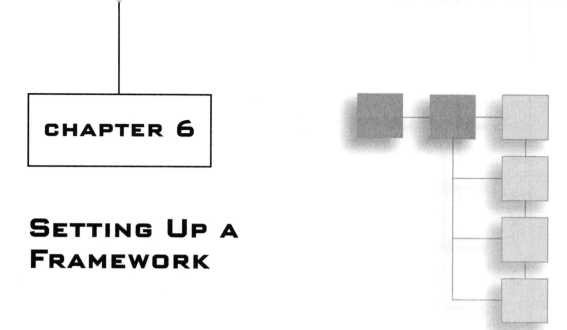

CHAPTER 6

SETTING UP A FRAMEWORK

So far all you've been doing is simple console-mode stuff. That's great, but it really doesn't help you make a game with all the graphical goodness that DirectX provides. I'm going to cut right to the chase and leave out all the stupid GDI and GUI control stuff because, as a game programmer, you probably aren't going to need to know it anyway. Learning about the GUI components may come in handy later on, when you make complicated game resource editors, but unfortunately, there's just not enough room to include that information in this book.

This chapter will teach you:

- How to create a new project in SharpDevelop.
- How to create a new project in Visual C#.
- How to use project wizards to create a framework.
- How to use the basic features of a form.
- How to use form event handlers.
- How to use the DirectX high precision timer.
- How to use the Advanced Framework's timer.
- How the Advanced Framework works.
- How to play nicely with the operating system.
- How to handle losing window focus.

Creating a Project

The absolute neatest thing about today's modern Integrated Development Environments (IDEs) is that they contain wizards.

A *wizard* is simply a simple program that performs a complex task for you, handling all the messy little details so that you don't have to waste your time handling them yourself.

In the bad old days of game programming, people would spend hours piecing together a little *framework* to use. A framework, in a programming sense, is something that would not contain code that was specific to any single game, and so could be used over and over with a variety of different games. Frameworks would typically have code to handle interfacing with the operating system and so on.

Today, both of the major C# IDEs (VC# and SharpDevelop) have wizards that will generate frameworks for you automatically.

SharpDevelop

In SharpDevelop, creating a Direct3D project is pretty easy. All you have to do is go to the File menu, click on New, and then select Combine. The project wizard will pop up, displaying a screen something like that in Figure 6.1.

n o t e

In some older versions of the SharpDevelop IDE, you'll select New Project rather than New Combine, so don't be discouraged if the New Combine option doesn't appear. A project is a collection of source files, and a combine is a collection of projects. As with all software, versions may vary, so be sure to read the documentation of the version you're using to figure out how to create a combine.

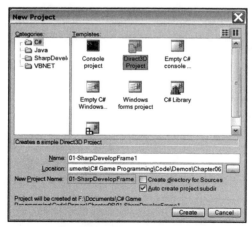

Figure 6.1 The SharpDevelop project wizard.

The wizard is pretty robust and gives you a lot of options. The option you're interested in is shown in Figure 6.1: Direct3D Project. The wizard asks you for a name for your project and a place to put it in, and that's about all. Once you've entered in this information, the wizard will automatically generate source code files and project files for you, and you'll be ready to go! Figure 6.2 shows the final product.

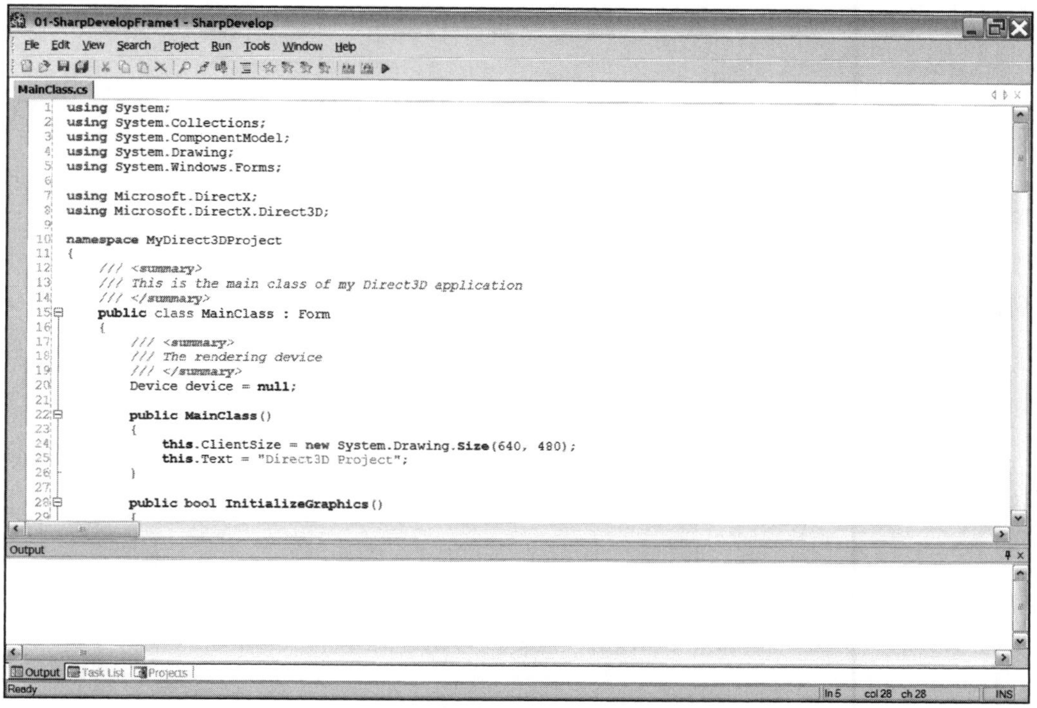

Figure 6.2 The final result of the SharpDevelop project wizard

You now have a simple framework that will allow you to create your very own Direct3D projects.

Files

On my version of SharpDevelop (0.99), the wizard created four files, which you can find on the CD as Demo 6.1. They are

- 01-SharpDevelopFrame1.cmbx
- 01-SharpDevelopFrame1.prjx
- AssemblyInfo.cs
- MainClass.cs

The first two files are the combine file and the project file, respectively. They simply store information about your project files. The next file, AssemblyInfo.cs, is a C# source file that contains information that tells .NET how your project is assembled—you're more than likely not going to need to touch this file at all. The final file is what you saw in Figure 6.2. This source file contains all the code you need in order to start making your own Direct3D application.

Explanation of the Code

The code is fairly straightforward, but you haven't seen a lot of the things in it before, so I'm going to go over it piece by piece in the next subsections.

The Libraries

The first part of the framework is the libraries used:

```
using System;
using System.Collections;
using System.ComponentModel;
using System.Drawing;
using System.Windows.Forms;

using Microsoft.DirectX;
using Microsoft.DirectX.Direct3D;
```

You've used the first two libraries before, but you haven't used the next five.

- System.ComponentModel holds various classes needed for basic control behavior in a windowed program.
- System.Drawing holds classes that are used for (obviously) drawing functions.
- System.Windows.Forms holds classes that are used for displaying forms.
- Microsoft.DirectX holds DirectX information.
- Microsoft.DirectX.Direct3D holds information about Direct3D.

The Class Outline

The main class, with all the code chopped out, looks like this:

```
public class MainClass : Form
{

    Device device = null;

    public MainClass()
    public bool InitializeGraphics()
```

```
virtual void InvalidateDeviceObjects(object sender, EventArgs e)
virtual void RestoreDeviceObjects(object sender, EventArgs e)
virtual void DeleteDeviceObjects(object sender, EventArgs e)
virtual void EnvironmentResizing(object sender, CancelEventArgs e)

virtual void FrameMove()
virtual void Render()
public void Run()

override void OnPaint(PaintEventArgs e)
override void OnKeyPress(KeyPressEventArgs e)

static void Main()
}
```

note

I removed the `protected` tags from a lot of the functions because it made them too long to fit on the page. Anything that doesn't have an access modifier on it in the previous code listing is supposed to be protected.

The first thing you should notice about this class is that it inherits from `System.Windows.Forms.Form`, which is a class that you need to use whenever you make a windowed application. Whenever you open up a new Windows program, the window you see is called a *form*, and the `Form` class provides all of the functionality needed to operate a form. So whenever you create a new windowed program, you must derive from the `Form` base class.

The `Mainclass` contains a Direct3D device, named `device`. I'll get into Direct3D devices in a later chapter.

The Constructor

The constructor of your class sets up the form:

```
public MainClass()
{
    this.ClientSize = new System.Drawing.Size(640, 480);
    this.Text = "Direct3D Project";
}
```

The constructor sets the size of the window to 640×480, and then sets the window title to Direct3D Project. Obviously, you're going to want to change these values to whatever you would like them to be later on.

Initializing the Graphics

The next function initializes the graphics engine. I'm just going to do a brief rundown of the code here, and then give you a far more in-depth tutorial on graphics in Chapter 7, "Direct3D."

```
public bool InitializeGraphics()
{
    try {
    PresentParameters presentParams = new PresentParameters();
    presentParams.Windowed   = true;
    presentParams.SwapEffect = SwapEffect.Discard;

    device = new Device(0, DeviceType.Hardware, this,
            CreateFlags.SoftwareVertexProcessing, presentParams);
```

The previous code creates a new graphics device. It's not going to make a whole lot of sense to you right now, but don't worry that much about it. Just know that it works, and that I'll get to it in much more detail in Chapter 7.

The next part of the code sets up the event handlers (which are delegates):

```
device.DeviceLost      += new EventHandler(this.InvalidateDeviceObjects);
device.DeviceReset     += new EventHandler(this.RestoreDeviceObjects);
device.Disposing       += new EventHandler(this.DeleteDeviceObjects);
device.DeviceResizing  += new CancelEventHandler(this.EnvironmentResizing);
```

The first three events handle whenever a device is lost (say, if the user switches to another window), the device is reset for any reason, or the device is disposed of. These first three events are solid events; when they happen, you have to handle them. No ifs, ands, or buts about it—the operating system is telling you something happened and your event handler has to take care of the situation.

The final event handles when the graphics device is resized, which is a special kind of event because it can be cancelled. A cancelable event is an event that your program can decide to reject. For example, if the user says he's going to resize your game window, your program will get the event, but you can tell the operating system, "Nope, it's not gonna happen!" and the event won't complete. This behavior is used mostly to prevent forms from closing before the user saves his data in windows applications.

The final part of the code returns true for a successful initialization, or catches any DirectXExceptions that may have been thrown and returns false:

```
    return true;
    } catch (DirectXException) {
        return false;
    }
}
```

The Event Handlers

There are four event handlers to handle the four events you saw earlier:

```
virtual void InvalidateDeviceObjects(object sender, EventArgs e)
virtual void RestoreDeviceObjects(object sender, EventArgs e)
virtual void DeleteDeviceObjects(object sender, EventArgs e)
virtual void EnvironmentResizing(object sender, CancelEventArgs e)
```

All four of these functions are protected, and none of them has any code in them. The code is something you're supposed to put in them yourself, depending on how you want the program to respond. The first parameter for each function is the sender, the object that is sending the event to the handler. In this case, the sender would be the Direct3D device variable sending the messages, but it's never a good idea to assume so.

The second parameter for each is the event arguments (EventArgs), which describes information about the event for you. I'll go into much more detail about these in Chapter 7.

Game Processing

Most game frameworks are very similar; they have separate functions to perform game logic, and then draw the current scene to the user. This framework is no exception, and provides these two functions for you:

```
protected virtual void FrameMove()
{
    // TODO : Frame movement
}
```

The FrameMove function is completely bare; you have to fill it in yourself. That function is where you would put all of your actual game logic calculations, AI processing, physics modeling, network communication, and so on.

```
protected virtual void Render()
{
    if (device != null) {
        device.Clear(ClearFlags.Target, Color.Blue, 1.0f, 0);
        device.BeginScene();

        // TODO : Scene rendering

        device.EndScene();
        device.Present();
    }
}
```

The next function renders the scene. It makes sure that there actually is a Direct3D device created, and if so, it clears the screen to blue and tells the device that it's going to start drawing a scene. (As I've said previously, I'll get into the graphics stuff in detail in Chapter 7.) Then the function ends the scene drawing and tells the device to present the scene to the viewer; this is just fancy-talk for saying it's going to show what was actually rendered onto the monitor (or whatever device the user is using to view the game).

Next is the Run function, which is called when someone wants the game to run:

```
public void Run()
{
    while (Created) {
        FrameMove();
        Render();
        Application.DoEvents();
    }
}
```

This is just a simple loop that keeps looping while the form is "created." Created is a Boolean property of the form that stays true when the form is valid, and turns false when the form is closed. For each loop, the function performs the game logic, renders the scene, and tells your application to handle all the events.

note

The Application class is a static class that represents your application and provides useful functions, such as telling the program to handle events or to immediately shut down.

Windows Event Handlers

Every form has built-in event handlers for handling basic windows events, such as key presses and repainting the scene. Incidentally, the framework has functions to handle these events, also.

You should note that you don't need to add these basic events to any event delegates anywhere—Windows automatically knows to call these events when actions occur.

note

The Form class has the event-handling functions built-in already, but they usually do nothing by default, which is why you must create your own and specify them as overrides. On occasion, however, they *will* perform extra functions, so you must remember to call the base versions on your own if you want to use the extra functionality. Look at the OnKeyPress example a bit further on to see what I'm talking about.

```
protected override void OnPaint(PaintEventArgs e)
{
    this.Render();
}
```

The OnPaint event occurs whenever the program needs to be repainted, such as when a window is on top of your form and is then moved off, and so on. The framework simply tells the renderer to re-render the scene.

Next you have the key press event:

```
protected override void OnKeyPress(KeyPressEventArgs e)
{
    base.OnKeyPress(e);
    if ((int)e.KeyChar == (int)System.Windows.Forms.Keys.Escape) {
        this.Close();
    }
}
```

The first thing this function does is call the base keypress function, Form.OnKeyPress. This is because the Form.OnKeyPress function actually does some useful processing for you. For example, if you have any GUI components on the screen, then pressing Tab should cause the window focus to go to the next GUI component. The Form.OnKeyPress function handles that for you, and I doubt you want to re-implement that functionality on your own.

Then Form.OnKeyPress checks to see if you pressed Escape, and if so, the form is told to close.

note

This is going to change later on. It's a bad idea to have a game close automatically when you press Escape inside of it.

The Entry Point

The final part of the framework is the entry point:

```
static void Main()
{
    using (MainClass mainClass = new MainClass()) {
        if (!mainClass.InitializeGraphics()) {
            MessageBox.Show("Error while initializing Direct3D");
            return;
        }
        mainClass.Show();
        mainClass.Run();
    }
}
```

This simply creates a new MainClass object (your window) and tries to initialize it. If it can't be initialized, then an error message appears onscreen and the application exits.

note

This example uses the using keyword in a way that you haven't seen before. The code creates a *using-block*, in which the variable mainClass is valid. As soon as the block ends, C# immediately destructs the mainClass variable instead of waiting for the garbage collector to get around to it later on.

If the window was created successfully, then the Main function tells the window to show itself, and then calls the Run function. When you load this project up and run it, you should get what you see in Figure 6.3.

Figure 6.3 The framework window in action; it's blank because nothing is being rendered yet!

Pressing Escape will cause the program to exit.

If you're using SharpDevelop, load Demo 6.1 and hit F5. If you're using Visual C#, then you need to do a bit more work to use this framework; I'll go over it in the next section.

Visual C#

Visual C# is a very popular C# IDE made by Microsoft; it can be found in the Visual Studio package or as a product on its own. It's a lot more complex than SharpDevelop, but that's to be expected, as SharpDevelop is free, and VC# costs lots of money.

The framework from Demo 6.1 works perfectly well in Visual C#. You don't even need to make any code changes. That's the great thing about .NET and C#—they're all completely standardized, so the code will work across any compiler. With C++, you don't really have that luxury because it's implemented in 500 different ways across 500 different compilers. C# really makes your life so much easier.

To create a new project in Visual C#, open the File menu and select New Project. VC#'s project wizard should pop up and give you a bunch of options. You want to create an empty C# project, like Figure 6.4 shows.

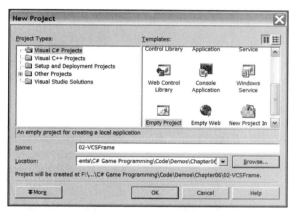

Figure 6.4 The Visual C# project wizard

Next copy over the two .cs files from Demo 6.1 into the Demo 6.2 directory, and add them into the project manually.

You're not done yet, unfortunately. C# projects can't compile unless they know about all of the references needed for the project. In this case, you're going to need to import the System and DirectX DLLs into your project. To do this, click on Project, Add Reference. A dialog box will appear, allowing you to make your project reference certain DLLs that you need. For this particular framework, you're going to need to import the System.dll, System.Drawing.dll, System.Windows.Forms.dll, Microsoft.DirectX, and Microsoft.DirectX.Direct3D modules. (See Figure 6.5.) Appendix A goes over this process in more detail.

Once you've done that, your program knows what modules it needs to compile correctly, and you can hit F7 to compile and F5 to run the program. You'll get the same output that you saw in Figure 6.3

Visual C#'s D3D Framework

You can use Visual C#'s application wizard to create a different D3D framework, but I'm not going to actually do so for this book. If you've ever used it, you'll know why. The framework produced by Visual C# is incredibly complex and would take several chapters just to explain; I'm going to keep things nice and simple.

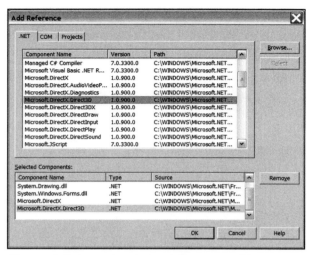

Figure 6.5 Importing the modules you need into your project.

---

note

The VC# D3D framework creator created a full 180 kilobytes of code for me. That's a lot of code.

---

note

You should also note that the very latest version of the DirectX SDK (the Summer 2004 release, as of this writing—which this book *doesn't* use) removes the D3D Framework Wizard from Visual C#. Instead, you can find a brand new framework already coded for you in one of the demo directories.

The good thing is that the framework that SharpDevelop works perfectly, whether you're using VC# or SharpDevelop.

The Advanced Framework

The framework SharpDevelop provides is okay for a generic framework, but it doesn't really meet your needs as a game programmer. On the other hand, the VC# framework is overkill. I've created another framework built on top of the SharpDevelop framework that will be just right. All of the code for this framework can be found in the Demo 6.3 directory on the CD.

Have You Got the Time?

Almost all games are time-based. Rare is the game that doesn't require some use of a timer device. Unfortunately for game programmers, .NET wasn't really designed with us in mind. The .NET framework was designed with application programmers in mind, so all it includes is a timer system that isn't very accurate. When is the last time you saw a regular word-processing application require a millisecond-accuracy timer, anyway?

Luckily for you and me, the DirectX team at Microsoft decided to fix this problem and gave us a handy, high-precision timer, with time accuracy that no sane game programmer would ever need. We're talking about microsecond accuracy here. I'm happy with just milliseconds, though.

note

All Intel-compatible CPUs since the original Pentium have had a *performance counter* in them, which is what Windows uses to obtain this ultra-high-precision timing.

Microsoft provided a file called DXUtil.cs that contains this timer, but it's kind of hidden away in the SDK. You can find it if you go into the Samples\C#\Common directory inside wherever you installed the DirectX 9 SDK.

Here's an example of how to use the timer:

```
float time = DXUtil.Timer( DirectXTimer.GetAbsoluteTime );
```

The DXUtil class is static, and the Timer function returns a given time, depending on what values pass into it. The values are all part of an enumeration called DirectXTimer. The valid values are listed in Table 6.1.

Table 6.1 Timer Function Options

Value	Result
Reset	Resets the application time value of the timer to 0
Start	Starts the timer if it has been stopped. Affects only application time.
Stop	Stops the application time of the timer from advancing
Advance	Moves the application time of the timer forward by 0.1 seconds
GetAbsoluteTime	Gets the absolute system time (usually how long the computer has been running, but not guaranteed)
GetApplicationTime	Gets the application time value
GetElapsedTime	Gets the amount of time passed since the last retrieval of the elapsed time

So there's a fair amount of available options. You'll notice that the time is represented as a float; that's actually pretty handy. The unit of the float is the *second*, meaning that 1.0 represents one full second, and 0.001 represents one millisecond, and so on. The reason this is handy is that most of the time, you represent speeds and other assorted time-based values in games as "units per second." For example, a rocket may move 10 feet per second, so to get the amount of feet it moved for any given timer result, you just multiply the timer result by 10.

The DirectX timer keeps track of two different times, the absolute time and the application time. The absolute time usually represents how long the Windows operating system has been running since the last reboot (but this isn't guaranteed), and the application time is modifiable by you.

Let me show you how to play around with the timer a bit:

```
// get the absolute time:
float t;
t = DXUtil.Timer( DirectXTimer.GetAbsoluteTime );
t = DXUtil.Timer( DirectXTimer.GetApplicationTime );
```

After those two calls, t was around 68,000 seconds for both calls, differing only by a few milliseconds. That's around 19 hours, which is, coincidentally, the last time I rebooted.

When you first start your program, the application timer has the same value as the absolute timer, so it's not really useful. To make it useful, you need to reset it:

```
DXUtil.Timer( DirectXTimer.Reset );
t = DXUtil.Timer( DirectXTimer.GetApplicationTime );
```

Now t will hold the number of seconds that have elapsed since the application timer was reset (probably much fewer than zero; on my system I got 0.000000838095332 as the result, meaning that 0.84 microseconds elapsed between those two calls).

You can also stop the timer:

```
DXUtil.Timer( DirectXTimer.Reset );
DXUtil.Timer( DirectXTimer.Stop );
f = DXUtil.Timer( DirectXTimer.GetApplicationTime );
f = DXUtil.Timer( DirectXTimer.GetApplicationTime );
DXUtil.Timer( DirectXTimer.Start );
f = DXUtil.Timer( DirectXTimer.GetApplicationTime );
```

The first time f was retrieved on my machine the result was 0.00000139482561 seconds. The very next line performs the call again, and the result is the same: 0.00000139482561 seconds. That means that 1.39 microseconds elapsed from the time the timer was reset to the time the timer was stopped, and, obviously, the timer doesn't advance when it's stopped.

After the timer was started again on my machine, f was filled in with 0.00000391111143, or 3.9 microseconds. This goes to show you that the time between resetting and stopping the timer added to the time between starting it up again and retrieving its value is a total of 3.9 microseconds. The amount of time spent retrieving the value while the timer was stopped isn't counted at all.

Finally, the timer makes it easy to retrieve the elapsed time between calls:

```
DXUtil.Timer( DirectXTimer.GetElapsedTime );
f = DXUtil.Timer( DirectXTimer.GetElapsedTime );
```

The first call is to simply reset the elapsed time counter, so I don't bother getting the value. The next call gives me how much time has elapsed since the last time I got the elapsed time value. In my case, it is simply 0.000000838095332 seconds, or 0.84 microseconds.

Problems with the Timer

I don't like the DirectX application timer for one reason: it's static, meaning that there's only one timer. It isn't very useful to have only one high-resolution timer in your entire program, because there are probably a lot of things that need timing, not just one thing. So I went ahead and did the reasonable thing: I created my very own expandable timer class, which you can find along with the Advanced Framework inside the Demo 6.3 directory in the file Timer.cs. This timer class is built on top of the existing DirectX timer, but it allows you to create many different timers, all running on different clocks. Most of the code is pretty straightforward and is built on top of the existing DirectX timer code, so I'm just going to show you the AdvancedFramework.Timer class outline and how to use it, instead of wasting precious time documenting silly timer code.

Here's the class outline:

```
public class Timer
{
    public static float Now()
    public Timer()

    public void Reset()
    public void Reset( float p_time )

    public float Time()
    public float Elapsed()

    public void Pause()
    public void Unpause()
}
```

The Now function is simply a wrapper around the absolute time function inside the DirectX timer. It's a static function, so you don't need any actual timers to call it:

```
float f = AdvancedFramework.Timer.Now();
```

There are two Reset functions, allowing you to reset the timer to 0 or to whatever time you want:

```
AdvancedFramework.Timer t = new AdvancedFramework.Timer();
t.Reset();          // to 0
t.Reset( 60.0f );   // to 60 seconds
```

Then you can use the timer to get the amount of time passed since it was last reset:

```
f = t.Time();       // amount of time since last reset
```

or to get the amount of time elapsed since the last call to Elapsed:

```
t.Elapsed();        // reset elapsed timer
f = t.Elapsed();    // time since last call
```

And, of course, you can pause and unpause the timer:

```
t.Pause();          // pause timer
// time does not advance for this timer anymore
t.Unpause();        // unpause timer
```

This timer is a heck of a lot easier to use than the DirectX timer.

Changes to the Framework

As I said earlier, the Advanced framework is built on top of the SharpDevelop framework, with lots of minor changes that make it easier to use, cleaner to look at, and more game-related.

Namespaces

Here is an example of how the new framework makes things cleaner: the Microsoft.
DirectX.Direct3D namespace is no longer implicitly used via the using command. That can make things somewhat confusing. All major DirectX components have classes they call Devices, such as a DirectSound.Device and a DirectInput.Device. Therefore, it's a bad idea to have code like this:

```
using Microsoft.DirectX.Direct3D;
using Microsoft.DirectX.DirectSound;
// later:
Device d = null;    // ERROR: what kind of device? Direct3D or DirectSound?
```

So the Advanced Framework uses namespace aliasing to create three new namespaces:

```
using Direct3D = Microsoft.DirectX.Direct3D;
using DirectSound = Microsoft.DirectX.DirectSound;
using DirectInput = Microsoft.DirectX.DirectInput;
```

Now you can just say `Direct3D.Device` or `DirectSound.Device`, and your program will be much more readable.

The Game Class

The Advanced Framework calls its main class `Game`. This isn't really an important change (the old framework called it `MainClass`), as you're probably going to end up changing it anyway, but I felt that `MainClass` sounded silly.

Along with the name change, I've added a bunch of static variables near the top of the framework so that you can change them easily if you need to:

```
static string gametitle = "Advanced Framework";
static int screenwidth  = 640;
static int screenheight = 480;
```

If you recall, these values were kind of hidden away inside the `MainClass` constructor in the first framework, so you had to hunt that function down if you wanted to change them.

Also added are some other statics:

```
static Timer gametimer  = null;
static bool paused       = false;

Direct3D.Device graphics     = null;
DirectSound.Device sound     = null;
DirectInput.Device keyboard  = null;
DirectInput.Device mouse     = null;
DirectInput.Device gameinput = null;
```

A game timer is defined that will keep track of the current game time for you, and a `paused` variable is defined that determines whether the game is paused or not. Lastly, there are five devices defined: the graphics device; the sound device; and three input devices representing a keyboard, a mouse, and any other game input device (usually a joystick or a gamepad) that may be used.

Function Changes

The old framework just initialized the Direct3D system using an `InitializeGraphics` function. This new framework takes it one step further and adds two functions: `InitializeSound` and `InitializeInput`. You get a free cookie if you can guess what those do. I'm not going to post their code here, as you wouldn't understand it now, anyway—I'm going to postpone that until Chapters 8 and 9.

The old `FrameMove` function has changed its name; it is now called `ProcessFrame`. I think that sounds better and more descriptive of what it actually does.

```
protected virtual void ProcessFrame()
{
    if( !paused )
    {
        // do processing here
    }
    else
        System.Threading.Thread.Sleep( 1 );
}
```

The ProcessFrame function has a little addition this time: It checks to see if the game is paused or not. If the game is not paused, then you should go ahead and perform your game calculations. If the game is paused, then the function tells the system thread to sleep for one millisecond.

---

tip
___

Here is something that most game programmers tend to forget: You are not the sole owner of a computer system. On today's modern computers, it's not uncommon for someone to be running hundreds of processes at the same time, and therefore you need to share nicely with all of the other processes. When you tell the current thread to sleep, you're telling the operating system, "I don't really have any processing to do right now, so go ahead and work on something else that might need it." If you don't have this line in your program, then your game will eat up as much of your processor's resources as it can grab, even while it's paused. This is a very bad thing.

___

The Render and Run functions haven't changed significantly, so I'm leaving those out of the description here.

Events

One thing you have to watch out for in a windowed game is losing focus. In a multi-tasking operating system like Windows, it's very easy for the user to decide to stop playing your game and check another window for something on a whim. Naturally, your game shouldn't be selfish; it should say, "Okay user, go ahead and use another program. I'll just sit here *sniff* and wait for you to return." Whenever your program loses focus (meaning the user has switched to a different program), the OnLoseFocus event gets executed:

```
protected override void OnLostFocus( EventArgs e )
{
    base.OnLostFocus( e );
    Paused = true;
}
```

You tell the base `Form` class that the program has lost focus, and then set the `Paused` property to `true`, telling the game that it has been paused. I'll get to this property in the next subsection.

note

It might seem like a good idea to unpause the game when the program regains focus (with the `OnGotFocus` event), but it's really not. The reasoning is thus: What if the user paused the game manually, then exited, and then re-entered? Should the game automatically unpause? Probably not. Therefore, it's just safer to leave the game paused and make the user manually unpause it.

The Paused Property

The Advanced Framework has a property in it named `Paused`, which wraps around the `paused` Boolean variable:

```
public bool Paused
{
    get { return paused; }
    set
    {
        // pause the game
        if( value == true && paused == false )
        {
            gametimer.Pause();
            paused = true;
        }

        // unpause the game
        if( value == false && paused == true )
        {
            gametimer.Unpause();
            paused = false;
        }
    }
}
```

The code is fairly straightforward. The `get` action simply returns the value of the `paused` variable. The `set` action is a bit more complex; it performs the actual pausing and unpausing of the game. If you set `Paused` to `true`, then the game checks to see if the game isn't already paused (if it is, the function does nothing). If not, then the function pauses the game timer and sets the `paused` variable to `true`. Unpausing does the opposite; it unpauses the timer and sets `paused` to `false`.

The Entry Point

The entry point for the framework has been changed a bit in the Advanced Framework, as well:

```
static void Main()
{
    try
    {
        Game game = new Game();
        game.InitializeGraphics();
        game.InitializeSound();
        game.InitializeInput();

        game.Show();
        game.Run();
    }
    catch( Exception e )
    {
        MessageBox.Show( "Error: " + e.Message );
    }
}
```

The game is created, and the three main media components are initialized, the game form is shown, and then it is run. Finally, there's a catch-block that catches any exceptions and prints out the error message to the user. This is a little different from the old framework; it used Boolean return values in the initialization functions to determine if there was an error. Here, I simply converted it entirely to an exception-based system.

Summary

You now have a robust framework with which you can begin to design your games. Unfortunately, as you don't really know how to use DirectX yet, you're going to have to continue reading! Oh darn!

The good news is that the next three chapters are going to explain all of that confusing DirectX mumbo-jumbo that you saw within the frameworks. I wouldn't worry too much, however. Managed DirectX 9 is a huge improvement over the older versions, and it is incredibly easy to use compared to what it used to be.

What You Learned

The main concepts that you should have picked up from this chapter are:

- How to create a new project in SharpDevelop.
- How to create a new project in Visual C#.
- How to use project wizards to create a framework.
- How to use the basic features of a form.
- How to use Form event handlers.
- How to use the DirectX high-precision timer.
- How to use the Advanced Framework's timer.
- How the Advanced Framework works.
- How to play nicely with the operating system.
- How to handle losing window focus.

Review Questions

These review questions test your knowledge on the important concepts exposed to you in this chapter. The answers can be found in Appendix A.

6.1. Why is it a good idea to use a project wizard to start your projects?

6.2. True or False: All windowed programs must have a class that inherits from System.Window.

6.3. True or False: Default Form event handlers do nothing, so you don't ever have to call the base version of the functions.

6.4. Why is it a better idea to use the AdvancedFramework.Timer class instead of the DXUtil.Timer function?

6.5. What does System.Threading.Thread.Sleep() do?

On Your Own

This chapter introduced you to a lot of concepts that I'm not really going to expand on. For example, the System.Windows.Forms.Form class is incredibly complex and has literally dozens of functions and properties in it, but I showed you only a handful. Generally speaking you're probably not going to be concerned with them, but it helps to be knowledgeable about these kinds of things; this knowledge will come in mighty handily if you ever decide to make a GUI-based resource editor for your game. So you should look into forms programming on your own if you're interested in learning all about it.

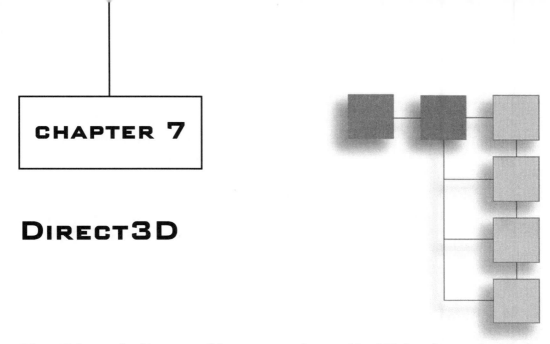

CHAPTER 7

DIRECT3D

Direct3D has evolved into one of the most complex graphics APIs in existence. Luckily for you and me, it's also amazingly flexible. Direct3D has come a very long way since the days of yore, and even though each release becomes more complex, Microsoft has also managed to make each release simpler to use. I can't tell you how many times I heard people complaining about the number of lines of code required to simply set up a rendering device back when DirectX 5 was king. You don't have to deal with that because DirectX 9 has come to save the day.

In this chapter, you will learn:

- How to create a Direct3D Device.
- What a back buffer is.
- How to make sure a device is available for you to use.
- What display formats (pixel formats) are.
- How the updated framework looks.
- How to handle multitasking in fullscreen mode.
- How to draw a triangle.
- How to use colors and alpha blending.
- How textures and texture coordinates work.
- How to use D3DX to load a texture quickly.
- How to use triangle strips and fans to optimize your geometry.
- How to use D3DX to handle sprites for you easily.
- How to load fonts and draw text.

DirectX Versions

During writing of this book, Microsoft rudely introduced a new version of the DirectX SDK. The newest version, as of this writing, is DirectX 9.0c, whereas this book uses DirectX 9.0b. I've included the 9.0b SDK on the CD for you, in the /extras directory, so you can use that version if you don't have it installed.

Unfortunately, if you have the newest version installed, then some of the code examples will not compile for you, as the Direct3D D3DX libraries have changed in a few key places. I didn't have the time update the code examples to get them into this book by printing time, but I will try my best to release a 9.0c version of all the code examples on my Web site (http://ronpenton.net) later on.

One Device to Rule Them All

The core component of Direct3D is the `Direct3D.Device`. A Direct3D device simply represents whatever device you're using to render with, which is almost always your video card.

note

DirectX uses vague terms like "device" because in the future, there may be no such thing as a video card, and you may be using something entirely different.

In Demos 6.1, 6.2, and 6.3, you were presented with Direct3D initialization code. It probably didn't make much sense to you at the time, but here's where I explain it all to you.

It's All about Presentation

Direct3D devices are amazingly configurable. Because of this, Microsoft has created a special class that allows you to describe exactly how you want to configure your graphics device. This class is called `Direct3D.PresentParameters`. It has a whole load of properties, a lot of which I won't have room to cover here. Table 7.1 lists the properties you will be concerned with in this book.

note

If you're interested in learning about all those advanced properties that I don't use in this book, you should check out a book on Direct3D, such as *Beginning DirectX 9*, by Wendy Jones.

Buffers and Buffer Swapping

If you don't know anything about graphics drawing, then this section is for you. In the old days of game programming, graphics hardware was very primitive, and you only had enough graphics memory to hold what was actually on the screen. The old systems would

Table 7.1 `Direct3D.PresentParameters` Properties

Property	Description
Windowed	Determines if the program is windowed or not
SwapEffect	Tells Direct3D how to swap back buffers
BackBufferCount	Tells Direct3D how many back buffers there should be
BackBufferFormat	Tells Direct3D what format back buffer you want to use
BackBufferHeight	Tells Direct3D what window height you want to use
BackBufferWidth	Tells Direct3D what window width you want to use

draw a scene, clear the screen, and then draw the next scene. This resulted in a bad flickering effect because the screen would literally change to black for a few milliseconds before it was updated with the new data. Figure 7.1 shows this effect. Not very many games were made like this because they would give users headaches.

note

A method called *dirty rectangles* was invented to take care of the problem at first. Whenever something moved on the screen, the computer would keep track of a rectangle around the area where something changed, and then redraw the rectangle that changed, without blanking anything. Thankfully, we don't have to do this anymore.

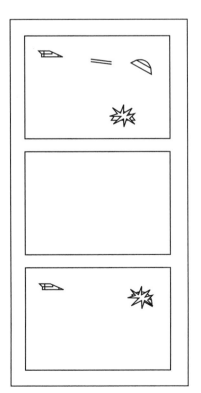

Figure 7.1 The flickering effect

As graphics hardware became more advanced, a new method called *buffer swapping* or *back-buffering* was introduced. The idea is to keep two buffers, a front buffer and a back buffer, open at all times. You draw to the back buffer, and when you want the data to be presented to the screen, the back buffer is swapped with the front buffer, and the old front buffer becomes the back buffer. This method is shown in Figure 7.2.

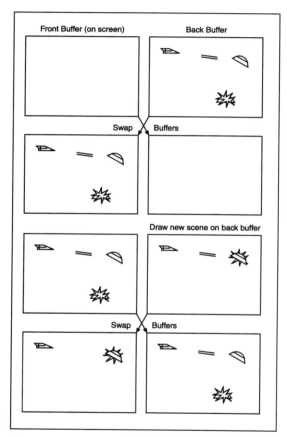

Figure 7.2 Back buffer can prevent flickering.

At one point, it was determined that buffer swapping took a very long time and the games were actually sitting there waiting for the buffers to swap before they could start writing to the back buffer again. This was especially true in the days when memory busses were incredibly slow. To fix the problem, game programming pioneers decided to add another buffer into the mix—to create *triple-buffering*. While the back buffer was being swapped onto the front buffer, the game would actually begin writing to a third buffer rather than waiting for the buffer swap to finish. Of course, memory bus speeds started catching up to the resolutions that games used, and you don't often see triple-buffering anymore.

note

DirectX supports up to three back buffers, giving you the option of using *quadruple-buffering* if you'd like. I personally don't see much need for that much buffering, but you can try it out just for kicks.

The following subsections will describe the three different ways to perform buffer swapping in DirectX 9.

Copying

The first swap effect is `Direct3D.SwapEffect.Copy`. This format requires that your program have exactly one back buffer. Every time you present the current scene, DirectX copies everything from the back buffer onto the front buffer. Naturally, this can take quite a long time. Think about it: If you have a game running at a reasonable resolution, say 1280×960, using 32-bit color, your screen is going to take up 4.68 megabytes of space. A 1600×1200 screen takes up 7.32 megabytes. So when you perform copying, you're trying to copy 4–8 megs of information over onto the primary buffer somewhere around 30–60 times per second. That's a transfer rate of anywhere from 120 to 480 megs per second.

Flipping

The second swap effect is `Direct3D.SwapEffect.Flip`. Flipping works on multiple back buffers by flipping whichever buffer is currently displayed on the screen. If your application is full-screen, then there usually won't be any actual memory copying going on. If your application is windowed, however, there will be memory copying, as your program only controls part of the screen.

Discarding

The final swap effect—the one you're probably going to end up using almost exclusively—is `Direct3D.SwapEffect.Discard`.

Recently, video cards started getting *really* complex; video card makers have figured out all sorts of ways to make presenting graphics even faster than the traditional methods. Some of them have created some really neat algorithms that only update parts of the screen that have actually changed, and they don't really tell us how they do it. The end result is that the video card hardware does a lot less work than it used to, and it does everthing automatically. In this case, you would use the discarding method to swap your buffers.

Creating a Device

The constructor for the `Direct3D.Device` class is a behemoth, unfortunately. There are five parameters to the constructor; these are listed in Table 7.2.

Table 7.2 `Direct3D.Device` **Parameters**

Parameter	Description
`int adapter`	The ID of the adapter you want to use
`DeviceType deviceType`	The kind of device you want to create
`Control renderWindow`	A reference to the window you will render to
`CreateFlags behaviorFlags`	Flags representing the device behavior
`PresentParameters presentation Parameters`	The presentation parameters

The Adapter

Every graphics adapter on your computer is assigned an ID number. Most computer systems only have one graphics adapter, your main video card. The main graphics adapter is always given an ID of 0, so that's almost always what you're going to pass into the constructor of your graphics device.

The Device Type

You have the option of creating several different kinds of graphics devices. Generally you're only going to be concerned with two values: `Direct3D.DeviceType.Software` and `Direct3D.DeviceType.Hardware`. There's a third value, `Direct3D.DeviceType.Reference`, but it's used only for debugging purposes and should never be used for any actual releases.

Software devices generally support most features, but your CPU must perform all of the processing, like lighting and transforming things, itself.

Hardware devices, on the other hand, offload heavy graphics processing onto your video card, which acts sort of like a parallel processor, therefore freeing up your CPU for other important things, such as AI and physics calculations.

Hardware devices used to be pretty rare, but you can pretty much assume that most computers support basic hardware acceleration nowadays, and you're probably going to want to create a hardware device.

Behavior Flags

There are several flags that determine how a graphics device will behave, and they pertain mostly to vertex processing. Table 7.3 lists the values that are most relevant to you and me.

Other options exist, but you would only be concerned with them if you were creating a really complex program. You probably don't need to bother with them (I never have).

Table 7.3 Useful `Direct3D.CreateFlags` values

Value	Meaning
HardwareVertexProcessing	Your graphics hardware will take care of vertex transformations
SoftwareVertexProcessing	Your CPU will take care of vertex transformations
MixedVertexProcessing	Your graphics card and CPU will share vertex transformation processing

Hardware vertex processing is one of the major revolutions in modern graphics hardware; it allows you to offload the very heavy graphics processing onto your video card, allowing your CPU to focus on things like physics and AI processing instead. The original NVIDIA GeForce card was the first to support hardware vertex processing, and it's gotten to a point where you can almost assume that everyone supports it now. I say *almost* because there are still slackers out there who haven't updated their video cards yet.

The Manager

You can go ahead and create any kind of device you want—the compiler's not going to stop you. You can say, "Hey computer, give me a hardware renderer with full vertex processing and a huge resolution!" and your compiler will say, "Okay!" Maybe that code will even run on your pimped-out development rig that you piled your life savings into. Then you distribute your game to your less-fortunate friends, telling them how awesome it is...and they tell you that you suck because it doesn't work on their computers. Why?

Well, you can't assume that everyone will have the hottest hardware. That's just life. A computer can have literally trillions of combinations of hardware, and it's almost impossible to make something work on every single computer out there, unless you revert to 100 percent software processing mode.

You need to check whether devices are available before you go around creating them. The good folks at Microsoft have provided the handy-dandy `Direct3D.Manager` class to give us this functionality. As with all things DirectX, the class is big and has a bunch of functions that you'll use once in a blue moon, so I'll show you only the parts that are important to you and me.

Checking Device Availability

The first thing you're going to want to do in your game is check whether a certain kind of device is available to you. This is accomplished using the `Direct3D.Manager.CheckDeviceType` function:

```
public static bool CheckDeviceType(
    int adapter,
    DeviceType checkType,
    Format displayFormat,
    Format backBufferFormat,
    bool windowed
);
```

The adapter is the adapter ID I told you about previously, which means you're probably just going to use 0. The checkType represents the kind of device that you are checking whether the adaptor supports. The displayFormat and backBufferFormat arguments determine what kind of back buffer and display mode you'll want to use; I'll get to that in just a moment. Finally, the last parameter determines whether you want to use windowed mode or not.

Display Formats

Display formats are a tricky thing to get into, because there are so many different formats on so many different video cards. So Direct3D provides this nice Direct3D.Format enumeration that lists every possible display format known to man. Okay, maybe not *every* format, but it lists a ton of them. I counted 46 just looking at the documentation. Wow.

note

In the old days, we had standardized formats like EGA and VGA, but hey—who needs standards anymore? Ugh. That is one of the things I miss about the old days, but never mind that.

So what is a display format? Basically, a display format tells you how each pixel on a screen is represented. The very first display formats were *monochrome*, meaning each pixel could be either blank or one color (usually white, depending on the monitor), and each pixel could be represented by a single bit. Later, computers got a lot more complex and could use 2-bits (four colors) or 4-bits (16 colors) to store a color information, usually preset color values. The next major revolution was *palletized color*, in which you had an 8-bit pixel format (256 colors) wherein each color value pointed to a color within a palette. None of this is really important anymore because the world has moved on to (fanfare, please) true color!

True color presented game programmers with the ability to show lush worlds full of vibrant colors. For the first time, we had display formats able to display 16 thousand or 24 million different colors all at the same time.

A true color pixel is represented by 16 or 32 bits of data, and is stored in a format that looks like R5G6B5 (16 bits), X8R8G8B8 (32 bits), or something similar. For the first

R5G6B5, that means that the pixel stores five bits of red information (32 values), six bits of green information (64 values), and five bits of blue information (32 values). The actual color of the pixel is determined by the color created when those three components are combined. For example, if you had a 16-bit pixel that has (31, 63, 31), you'll get a white pixel, as all the colors are at their full intensity, and when you combine all of those colors, you get white. Likewise, if you had (0, 0, 0), you'd have black, and if you had (31, 31, 0), you'd have orange (full red, half green, no blue).

There are also 16-bit formats, such as X1R5G5B5, that use five bits for each color and the last bit isn't used.

32-bit formats tend to be a bit more formalized. There are chiefly two variants: X8R8G8B8 and A8R8G8B8. In the first format, the X means that eight bits are ignored and not used at all. In the second format, the A stands for *alpha*, which is an extra eight bits of data that can be stored per pixel and usually represents transparency effects. A pixel with 0 alpha is completely clear, 255 alpha is fully colored, and 127 alpha means that it is blended with 50 percent translucency with the pixel below it. I'll get more into alpha later on.

You're probably going to want to use a 32-bit color format. A few years ago, there was a huge performance difference between 16- and 32-bit colors, but it's not really a problem anymore. The only time you should really be concerned about using 16-bit colors is when you know you're using an older graphics card and every bit of speed counts. The major downside of using 16-bit color is that you sometimes get bad banding effects; you can see this effect in Figure 7.3.

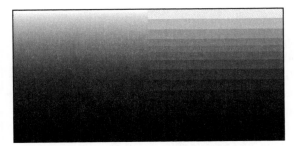

Figure 7.3 The left shows a 32-bit rendering of a color gradient, and the right shows a banded 15-bit rendering of a color gradient.

note

I intentionally exaggerated the banding in Figure 7.3 because it's hard to get the idea without seeing it on a computer screen. But generally, that's what banding looks like—you can see "lines" in between the colors of a gradient because there's not enough colors to represent a smooth transition.

Performing a Device Check

Now you can perform a device check:

```
bool b;
b = Direct3D.Manager.CheckDeviceType(
    0,                                    // default adapter
    Direct3D.DeviceType.Hardware,    // we want hardware rendering!
    Direct3D.Format.X8R8G8B8,        // 32 bit color
    Direct3D.Format.X8R8G8B8,        // backbuffer the same
    true );                          // in windowed mode
```

If b is true, then you know you have a hardware device that can support the format you want. If b is false…well, sorry. Try a different format.

Using the Current Format

If you're lazy (and what self-respecting game programmer isn't?), then the easiest way to pick a display format is to just go ahead and use the one the user is already using for Windows. You can do this by using the Manager class to obtain the current display format:

```
Direct3D.Format current;
current = Direct3D.Manager.Adapters[0].CurrentDisplayMode.Format;
```

Now current will have the current display mode. And that mode is guaranteed to work, unless the user is doing something silly, like using Windows in a graphics mode that their video card doesn't support.

Checking Device Capabilities

Occasionally, you may want to check a device to see if it supports the capabilities you want. I must warn you, however, that if you look at the Direct3D.Caps structure, you may become frightened. It has a full 63 properties, many of which are structures that have *even more* properties of their own! Direct3D has a *ton* of options. The good thing is that almost everything I use in this book is pretty much standard on computers nowadays, so you don't have to go fumbling around the device capabilities. But here's how to retrieve a Caps structure for a particular device, in case you've ever wondered:

```
Direct3D.Caps caps =
    Direct3D.Manager.GetDeviceCaps( 0, Direct3D.DeviceType.Hardware );
```

And now the caps structure will hold every thing you ever wanted to know (or didn't want to know) about the device.

Updating the Framework

Now that you know how to create devices, you can update the framework from Chapter 6 to add the ability to make fullscreen games. Sounds easy enough, right? Well, it's not.

A common theme you'll see in programming is that you're supposed to *play nice* with the operating system. The days where a game could take control of the entire operating system are long gone, and we'll never see them again (unless you're working on a console game system such as the Xbox or the Gamecube or whatever they make next).

The operating system is running dozens of programs, and at any minute, the user might decide to switch out of your program for a minute to check his e-mail or something. If you don't allow the user to do so, he may become angry with you. In windowed mode, your program is a window and plays nicely with the graphics system. In fullscreen mode, however, it's a mess.

When you create a fullscreen application, you're being greedy. You're telling the operating system that you want the entire screen for yourself. That's not an unreasonable request— we all know that playing games in fullscreen is the best way to go. But when a user switches out, your program is still running, but Windows destroys your graphics device (how dare they!) and leaves it up to you to fix it when the user goes back to your program.

Pain in the butt. When I talk to new Direct3D users, one of the most common questions they ask is, "How do I disable Alt+Tab?" not "How do I properly handle multi-tasking?" They would rather just lock the user into the program and be done with it. How I wish life were that easy.

The new, updated framework, which fixes these problems, can be found on the CD as Demo 7.1.

Setting Up a Device

The new framework can support windowed or fullscreen mode. In order to facilitate this, a new Boolean has been added to the framework:

```
static bool windowed     = false;
```

When false, the framework will create a fullscreen application, and when true, a windowed mode will be made.

The next change from the old framework occurs within the InitializeGraphics function, which now creates a device based on whether you want it windowed or not. The windowed part is easy:

```
public void InitializeGraphics()
{
    // set up a device
    Direct3D.PresentParameters p = new Direct3D.PresentParameters();
    p.SwapEffect = Direct3D.SwapEffect.Discard;

    if( windowed == true )
```

```
    {
        p.Windowed = true;
    }
```

All you need to do is set the Windowed property of the parameters to true; everything else can be left to the defaults.

Setting up a fullscreen device is a little different:

```
    else
    {
        Direct3D.Format current =
            Direct3D.Manager.Adapters[0].CurrentDisplayMode.Format;

        p.Windowed = false;              // fullscreen
        p.BackBufferCount = 1;           // one back buffer
        p.BackBufferFormat = current;    // use current format
        p.BackBufferWidth = screenwidth;
        p.BackBufferHeight = screenheight;
    }
```

Rather than search for a valid pixel format, I used the system's current format (I showed you how to do this earlier), set Windowed to false, and gave the device one back buffer. For a fullscreen app, you must set the size of the back buffer as well, so it is set to whatever screenwidth and screenheight are set to.

tip

Now you can see why I made screenwidth and screenheight static variables of the Game class: they're used in at least two different places, and if you change their values in one place, you might forget to change them in the other.

Now that your parameters are set up, you can create the device as usual:

```
    graphics = new Direct3D.Device(
        0, Direct3D.DeviceType.Hardware, this,
        Direct3D.CreateFlags.SoftwareVertexProcessing, p );

    // Setup the event handlers for the device
    graphics.DeviceLost
        += new EventHandler( this.InvalidateDeviceObjects );
    graphics.DeviceReset
        += new EventHandler( this.RestoreDeviceObjects );
    graphics.Disposing
        += new EventHandler( this.DeleteDeviceObjects );
```

```
graphics.DeviceResizing
    += new CancelEventHandler( this.EnvironmentResizing );
}
```

The last section of code shouldn't be anything new to you; it's the same stuff you've seen since Demo 6.1.

Note that this code assumes I'll be using a hardware device with software vertex processing. I'm not going to be doing anything in this book that requires the speed of hardware vertex processing, but I would like to use the color shading that a hardware device offers.

This code should work on probably 99 percent of all computers out there. Seriously—any computer that can't run this code has a video card older than the 3DFX Voodoo 1 video card, which was released in 1996.

Handling MultiTasking

The ability to handle proper multitasking requires a lot of code updates because it's a fairly complex process. Whenever someone switches out of your fullscreen application, windows invalidates your display device, so you'd better not try drawing anything on it unless you want your program to blow up.

The first change from the old framework is the addition of another Boolean:

```
static bool graphicslost = false;
```

This will be turned true whenever the graphics device is lost, so that you know not to draw anything, and you know that you should try reacquiring the graphics device when you can.

The next change is to make it so your window cannot be resized:

```
protected virtual void EnvironmentResizing( object sender, CancelEventArgs e )
{
    e.Cancel = true;
}
```

I explained this in Chapter 6. Setting the Cancel property to true tells the operating system that you're canceling the resize event because you don't want anything to resize your window. If you allow resizing, then Windows tries, for some odd reason, to mess up your window size whenever you multitask.

The final change takes place inside of the Render function.

note

All of the following code occurs within the block that starts with if(graphics != null). I removed that part because the margins of this book aren't wide enough to show the entire thing.

Now that you have the basics set up, it's time to look at the code inside of the Render function:

```
if( graphicslost )
{
    try
    {
        graphics.TestCooperativeLevel();
    }
```

If the graphics device has been lost, then I call the TestCooperativeLevel function, which tests to make sure that the device is valid and cooperating with the operating system. Obviously, as graphicslost is true, you know the device is not cooperating, but there's one bit of information that you don't know: Can the device be required or not? Calling this function allows you to find out.

When the device is lost and you call this function, it will throw an exception of type DeviceLostException or DeviceNotResetException. The first exception means that the device is lost, and it still cannot be reacquired. In that case, just return and don't do any rendering:

```
catch( Direct3D.DeviceLostException )
{
    // device cannot be reacquired yet, just return
    return;
}
```

On the other hand, if DeviceNotResetException is thrown, then you know that the device is still lost, but it's now safe to reset the device, so that's exactly what you're going to do:

```
catch( Direct3D.DeviceNotResetException )
{
    // device has not been reset, but it can be reacquired now
    graphics.Reset( graphics.PresentationParameters );
}
graphicslost = false;
}
```

Isn't that nice? The Direct3D.Device class provides a handy-dandy Reset function. All you need to do is pass in some presentation parameters and you're set. Also luckily for you, your device still remembers the presentation parameters you were using last, so that's what you reset the device to. Then set the graphicslost Boolean to false, as the device is no longer lost.

The final piece of code is a change to the actual rendering code (the changes in the code have been bolded):

```
try
{

    graphics.Clear( Direct3D.ClearFlags.Target, Color.Blue, 1.0f, 0 );
    graphics.BeginScene();

    // TODO : Scene rendering

    graphics.EndScene();
    graphics.Present();
}

// device has been lost, and it cannot be re-initialized yet
catch( Direct3D.DeviceLostException )
{
    graphicslost = true;
}
```

A try-block has been added around the rendering loop, and a catch-block has been added to the end, to catch if the device happens to get lost. If it does get lost, then the graphicslost Boolean is set to true, and the rendering function will try to reacquire it the next time a loop occurs.

Now the framework handles multitasking in fullscreen mode properly.

Actually Drawing Stuff

Direct3D is much easier to set up than it used to be. Setting up Direct3D used to be a monumental effort, and doing so caused many a programmer to run off into the abyss, screaming his head off. The fact that I've taken around 15 pages to show you how to set up Direct3D should be a testament to how complex it used to be, and should make you thankful that it's so much easier now. But I'm sure you're sick of learning how to set up a device, and you just want to get to drawing stuff. Can't say I blame you.

Direct3D is a triangle-rastering system. That's really all it does: draw triangles. The reason is that a triangle is the simplest geometric shape that you can make that has an area to it. You can draw almost *any* three-dimensional object onto a 3D screen by just turning it into hundreds, thousands, or even millions of triangles.

note

Okay. Technically, you can't draw *any* 3D object using triangles. There are many objects, like spheres and other curvy things, that just can't be defined precisely by using triangles. However, if you use enough triangles, it *looks* like a curvy object. It's our little secret; you don't have to tell your users that your spheres are actually massive collections of tiny triangles.

note

Unfortunately, I don't have room to get into complex 3D topics like 3D transformations, pixel shaders, and so on. This means that I'm going to stick to some fairly simple graphics options for the remainder of the book. If you're looking for a more comprehensive look into graphics programming, I suggest *Beginning Direct3D Game Programming, Second Edition*, by Wolfgang Engel.

Vertexes

Now you're going to draw some triangles! The first thing you're going to do is create something in which to store your geometry. Since Direct3D draws triangles, you obviously need some way to store triangle data. Triangle data is stored in objects called *vertexes*. A *vertex* at its simplest is a point defined in 3D space. Direct3D supports all kinds of vertex formats, however, many of which contain additional data.

Direct3D provides you with the Direct3D.CustomVertex class, which defines a lot of different vertex structures. These are listed in Table 7.4.

Table 7.4 Custom Vertex Formats

Vertex	Transformed	Color	Texture	Normal
PositionOnly	no	no	no	no
PositionColored	no	yes	no	no
PositionTextured	no	no	yes	no
PositionNormal	no	no	no	yes
PositionColoredTextured	no	yes	yes	no
PositionNormalColored	no	yes	no	yes
PositionNormalTextured	no	no	yes	yes
Transformed	yes	no	no	no
TransformedColored	yes	yes	no	no
TransformedTextured	yes	no	yes	no
TransformedColoredTextured	yes	yes	yes	no

The first thing you'll notice is that there are two major types of vertexes: *position* vertexes and *transformed* vertexes. Position vertexes are untransformed, meaning that their position is defined somewhere in your world and they need to go through the Direct3D transformation pipeline in order to be converted into *screen coordinates*. Transformed vertexes are in screen coordinates already, so if you put the x and y values of a transformed vertex to (100, 200), then that vertex is going to be drawn 100 pixels from the left side of the screen and 200 pixels down from the top of the screen.

Color data is fairly obvious; it defines what color the vertex is. Texture coordinates are a somewhat complex idea that I will go into later on in this chapter. *Normals* are a complex topic that I don't have room to get to, however.

note

> You may not have heard of normal data before. A *normal* is simply a 3D vector that is perpendicular to the face of the triangle; this data helps Direct3D figure out how light affects the face of a triangle. You should note that the only vertexes that have normal data are untransformed vertexes. This is because the D3D transformation pipeline takes care of lighting calculations as well. It assumes that transformed vertexes have already had lighting calculations performed on them; therefore, a normal vector is not needed on transformed vertexes.

Defining Some Vertexes

For a simple demonstration (this is Demo 7.2 on the CD), I'm going to show you how to draw a simple triangle. The first thing you need to do is create a structure in which to hold your vertexes. For this demo, I'm just going to use transformed colored vertexes:

```
Direct3D.CustomVertex.TransformedColored[] vertexes = null;
```

I simply declared an empty array of transformed and colored vertexes.

The next step is to create three vertexes and initialize them:

```
public void InitializeGeometry()
{
    vertexes = new Direct3D.CustomVertex.TransformedColored[3];

    // top vertex:
    vertexes[0].X = screenwidth / 2.0f;  // halfway across the screen
    vertexes[0].Y = screenheight / 3.0f;  // 1/3 down screen
    vertexes[0].Z = 0.0f;
    vertexes[0].Color = Color.White.ToArgb();
```

The array is created with enough room to store three vertexes (three vertexes make a triangle, after all), and then the X, Y, Z, and Color information for each vertex is filled in.

note

> I'm sure you understand the x and y information, but the z might throw you off, so let me go off on a tangent and explain it for you. In a 3D program, when you transform pixels into 2D screen-space, you retain *depth* information, so that you know which pixels are closer to the viewer. If you have a *depth buffer* created (which I won't show you in this book), then D3D does depth-checking. When you draw a pixel, D3D checks the depth buffer to see if another pixel has been drawn there already. If the previous pixel is closer to the viewer, then the new pixel isn't drawn, as it won't be seen anyway. I don't need the depth buffer, and I always set the Z to 0.

The next two vertexes are defined:

```
// right vertex:
vertexes[1].X = (screenwidth / 3.0f) * 2.0f;  // 2/3 across the screen
vertexes[1].Y = (screenheight / 3.0f) * 2.0f;  // 2/3 down screen
vertexes[1].Z = 0.0f;
vertexes[1].Color = Color.White.ToArgb();

// left vertex:
vertexes[2].X = screenwidth / 3.0f;  // 1/3 across the screen
vertexes[2].Y = (screenheight / 3.0f) * 2.0f;  // 2/3 down screen
vertexes[2].Z = 0.0f;
vertexes[2].Color = Color.White.ToArgb();
}
```

And you're done defining your triangle.

Note that the triangle has its vertexes defined in clockwise order. This is done because Direct3D, by default, doesn't draw triangles where the vertexes are counter-clockwise. This is called *backface culling*, and I'll explain it a bit more in the next section.

Final Touches

There are a few more steps that need to be taken in order to complete the demo. The first step is to turn off backface culling. *Backface culling* is a feature that is very useful in 3D applications because most triangles can only be seen from one side. Imagine a cube: You cannot see the inside of a solid cube, so the faces on the inside of the cube should never be shown. Direct3D knows this, and doesn't waste its time drawing something that cannot be seen anyway. For this reason, you should design all your 3D models with their triangles defined in clockwise order when you're looking at the side that's supposed to be visible. When you look at the triangle from the other side, the vertexes will be counter-clockwise, and Direct3D will know not to draw them.

Unfortunately, if you're only doing 2D work in Direct3D, this gets to be a problem. I don't want to have to remember to make my triangles clockwise all the time—what a pain in the butt! So I turn that option off inside the InitializeGraphics function:

```
graphics.RenderState.CullMode = Direct3D.Cull.None;
```

The final thing you need to do is actually draw the triangle, which is inside the Render function:

```
graphics.Clear( Direct3D.ClearFlags.Target, Color.Black, 1.0f, 0 );
graphics.BeginScene();

graphics.VertexFormat =
```

```
    Direct3D.CustomVertex.TransformedColored.Format;
graphics.DrawUserPrimitives(
    Direct3D.PrimitiveType.TriangleList,
    1, vertexes );

graphics.EndScene();
graphics.Present();
```

The first and last two lines of this code should be familiar to you, as you've seen them before, back in Chapter 6. The graphics device is cleared to black (I changed it from blue because blue got annoying), and the device is told that you're going to start rendering a scene.

The bold part of the code is all the new stuff I added. I tell the graphics device what kind of vertexes it's going to be rendering (transformed colored vertexes), and then I call the DrawUserPrimitives function to draw a list of triangles (my list only contains one triangle, but it's still a list). The last parameter is the array of vertexes.

The final piece of code tells the device that I'm done drawing and that it should present the scene to the user.

Figure 7.4 shows what the program looks like when you run it.

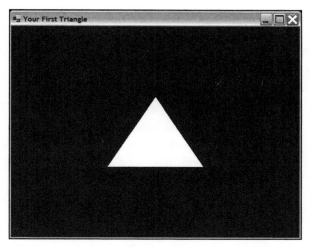

Figure 7.4 Your very first triangle. Your parents will be so proud.

Colors and Alpha

Okay, you can draw triangles now. I'm sure you're happy that you've accomplished something, but if you try showing this to someone else, they'll probably look at you like you're crazy and say. "What? It's just a triangle." Non-programmers just don't understand.

Let's go on to some more advanced stuff, like colors and alpha.

Playing with Colors

One of the neatest features of Direct3D is that it has automatic triangle shading built in. Don't like a solid white triangle? Make the vertexes different colors! Go into Demo 7.2 and go crazy! Personally, I prefer a lovely combination of aquamarine, cornflower blue, and lemon chiffon:

```
vertexes[0].Color = Color.Aquamarine.ToArgb();
vertexes[1].Color = Color.CornflowerBlue.ToArgb();
vertexes[2].Color = Color.LemonChiffon.ToArgb();
```

I feel like I'm picking out wallpaper.

Of course, you don't have to use the preset windows colors (especially as the color names seem like they came right out of *Martha Stewart Living*). You can create your very own numeric color combinations, instead:

```
vertexes[0].Color = Color.FromArgb( 0, 127, 0, 255 ).ToArgb();
```

This code uses the `System.Drawing.Color` class to create a color and retrieve the integer value. This color is a kind of indigo-purple color, having half-intensity red, no green, and full-intensity blue (127, 0, 255).

Playing with Alpha

You have seen the term *alpha* a few times before in this book, but you've never actually had a chance to see what it is. Simply put, alpha information is just extra information that can be tacked onto a color, and it's up to you to figure out what you want to do with it.

The most common use for the alpha channel is for translucency, via a process called *alpha blending*. With alpha blending, the computer calculates a new color based on what you want to draw and what is already there. You need to set up the Direct3D device with an algorithm that will perform these blends. Check out Figure 7.5.

When you have blending enabled and you try drawing a pixel, the computer will read the pixel that's already on the screen, and blend it with the pixel you're trying to draw using any operation that you tell it to.

The basic algorithm that blending follows is this:

```
newcolor = [sourcecolor * sourcefactor] operation [destcolor * destfactor]
```

The source color is the color that you're drawing, and the destination color is the color that is already on the screen. Let's say you have the source factor set to 1.0, the destination factor set to 0.0, and the operation set to "add." The equation becomes:

```
newcolor = [sourcecolor * 1.0] + [destcolor * 0.0]
```

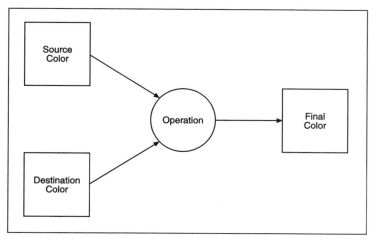

Figure 7.5 A blend operation

or, simplified, it becomes:

```
newcolor = sourcecolor
```

which means that you're not really blending anything; you're simply drawing the new color on the screen.

An Example of Translucency Blending

Now that you see how alpha blending works in a very basic manner, let me show you a more advanced method that actually performs translucency calculations. If you set the source blend factor to the source alpha value, and you set the destination blend factor to the inverse of the source alpha value (one minus the alpha value), you now have translucency blending enabled.

Let's say you have two pixels, one blue and one red. The blue is the destination color—it's already on the screen. For this example, the red has an alpha value of 191 (or about 0.75, if you look at it as a fraction out of 255), meaning that you want it to be 75 percent solid, or 25 percent translucent. The operation will stay at "add:"

```
newcolor = [red * 0.75] + [blue * (1.0 - 0.75)]
```

And simplified:

```
newcolor = [red * 0.75] + [blue * 0.25]
```

So what color does that end up being, exactly? Let's perform the actual calculations and find out:

```
newcolor = [(255,0,0) * 0.75] + [(0,0,255) * 0.25]
newcolor = (191,0,0) + (0,0,63)
newcolor = (191,0,63)
```

So the new color is (191, 0, 63), which is a bluish-red; it looks like a dark-pink carnation color to me. If you set the alpha value of the red pixel to 255, then the operation would look something like this:

```
newcolor = [(255,0,0) * 1.0] + [(0,0,255) * (1.0 - 1.0)]
newcolor = (255,0,0) + (0,0,0)
newcolor = (255,0,0)
```

Meaning that the red is fully solid, and none of the original color shows through it. Likewise, an alpha value of 0 means that the new pixel is completely transparent, and an alpha value of 127 (0.5) means that it's 50 percent translucent, giving you (127,0,127), a dark purple.

Setting Up Alpha Blending

Alpha blending isn't enabled by default in Direct3D. You need to do it yourself:

```
graphics.RenderState.AlphaBlendEnable = true;
```

But your job doesn't end there. After that, you need to set up the blending operation:

```
graphics.RenderState.AlphaBlendOperation = Direct3D.BlendOperation.Add;
```

Technically, you don't have to write this option out because the default blend operation is Add, but it's always safe to make your code more readable.

Table 7.5 lists the different blend operations available to you.

You can achieve a variety of different effects by playing around with the operation.

The next step is to set the blend factors. In this case, I'm going to be setting them up to perform translucency blending:

```
graphics.RenderState.DestinationBlend = Direct3D.Blend.InvSourceAlpha;
graphics.RenderState.SourceBlend = Direct3D.Blend.SourceAlpha;
```

You can use different blend factors to achieve different effects if you don't want translucency blending. The available blend factors are listed in Table 7.6.

Table 7.6 doesn't list all of the available blends, but it does list the most useful ones. The four blend options not shown in the table are either obsolete or useful only in special circumstances. I've never used them before, and you probably shouldn't worry about them.

Table 7.5 `Direct3D.BlendOperation` **Values**

Value	Effect
Add	Adds the two colors together
Subtract	Result is the source minus the destination color
RevSubtract	Result is the destination minus the source color
Min	Uses whatever color is darker
Max	Uses whatever color is lighter

Table 7.6 Useful `Direct3D.Blend` **Values**

Value	Factor
Zero	$(0, 0, 0, 0)$
One	$(1, 1, 1, 1)$
SourceColor	(A_s, R_s, G_s, B_s)
InvSourceColor	$(1 - A_s, 1 - R_s, 1 - G_s, 1 - B_s)$
DestinationColor	(A_d, R_d, G_d, B_d)
InvDestinationColor	$(1 - A_d, 1 - R_d, 1 - G_d, 1 - B_d)$
SourceAlpha	(A_s, A_s, A_s, A_s)
InvSourceAlpha	$(1 - A_s, 1 - A_s, 1 - A_s, 1 - A_s)$
DestinationAlpha	(A_d, A_d, A_d, A_d)
InvDestinationAlpha	$(1 - A_d, 1 - A_d, 1 - A_d, 1 - A_d)$
SourceAlphaSat	$(1, \min(A_s, 1 - A_d), \min(A_s, 1 - A_d), \min(A_s, 1 - A_d))$

*The subscript $_s$ refers to the source component, and the subscript $_d$ refers to the destination component.

Another Demo

Now that you know how to color vertexes and perform alpha calculations on them, you can play around with those features. To demonstrate this, I've created Demo 7.3, which demonstrates the creation of *two* triangles! This demo is pretty much the same as Demo 7.2, with a few things changed. I'll only be showing you what has changed.

Here's the triangle setup:

```
public void InitializeGeometry()
{
    vertexes = new Direct3D.CustomVertex.TransformedColored[6];
```

```
// triangle 1:

// top vertex:
vertexes[0].X = screenwidth / 2.0f;  // halfway across the screen
vertexes[0].Y = screenheight / 3.0f;  // 1/3 down screen
vertexes[0].Z = 0.0f;
vertexes[0].Color = Color.FromArgb( 255, 255, 0, 0 ).ToArgb();

// right vertex:
vertexes[1].X = (screenwidth / 3.0f) * 2.0f;  // 2/3 across the screen
vertexes[1].Y = (screenheight / 3.0f) * 2.0f;  // 2/3 down screen
vertexes[1].Z = 0.0f;
vertexes[1].Color = Color.FromArgb( 255, 0, 255, 0 ).ToArgb();

// left vertex:
vertexes[2].X = screenwidth / 3.0f;  // 1/3 across the screen
vertexes[2].Y = (screenheight / 3.0f) * 2.0f;  // 2/3 down screen
vertexes[2].Z = 0.0f;
vertexes[2].Color = Color.FromArgb( 255, 0, 0, 255 ).ToArgb();


// triangle 2:

// bottom vertex:
vertexes[3].X = screenwidth / 2.0f;  // halfway across the screen
vertexes[3].Y = (screenheight / 3.0f) * 2.0f;  // 2/3 down screen
vertexes[3].Z = 0.0f;
vertexes[3].Color = Color.FromArgb( 127, 255, 0, 0 ).ToArgb();

// right vertex:
vertexes[4].X = (screenwidth / 3.0f) * 2.0f;  // 2/3 across the screen
vertexes[4].Y = screenheight / 3.0f;  // 1/3 down screen
vertexes[4].Z = 0.0f;
vertexes[4].Color = Color.FromArgb( 127, 0, 255, 0 ).ToArgb();

// left vertex:
vertexes[5].X = screenwidth / 3.0f;  // 1/3 across the screen
vertexes[5].Y = screenheight / 3.0f;  // 1/3 down screen
vertexes[5].Z = 0.0f;
vertexes[5].Color = Color.FromArgb( 127, 0, 0, 255 ).ToArgb();
}
```

The first triangle stays in the same position, but I've changed the colors. The vertexes are red, green, and blue, now, and each vertex has a full 255 for its alpha value, meaning that it's perfectly solid.

The second triangle is flipped upside-down; it has the same colors, but the alpha value for each vertex is set to 127, which means that I want to draw it at 50 percent translucency.

The only other change needed from Demo 7.2 is the change to make the renderer draw two triangles now, instead of just one:

```
graphics.DrawUserPrimitives(
    Direct3D.PrimitiveType.TriangleList, 2, vertexes );
```

Now you can load up Demo 7.3 and run it; you should obtain the results shown in Figure 7.6.

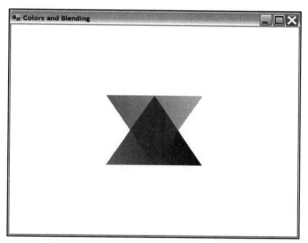

Figure 7.6 Demo 7.3, with coloring and alpha blending in action

You can see that the regular triangle is visible through the upside-down triangle because the upside-down triangle is 50 percent translucent.

Texturing and Other Shapes

The ability to show pretty, colored triangles is cool, but if that were all you could do, your games would end up looking more like a 1980s-era Kraftwerk music video than a high-tech computer game.

Because of this, a technology called *texturing* was invented to make your triangles look more detailed. In addition to texturing, I'll also be showing you how to optimize your geometry by using advanced primitive collections, such as triangle-strips and triangle-fans.

Texturing

To make your objects look better, you need to add detail to them. You can do so using textures, which are images that are stretched onto your triangles. You can make a polygonal mountain in your game, but it will look pretty silly if it's made only of solid-colored triangles. To make the mountain look better, you're going to want to find some sort of image that looks like rock, and then put that rock texture on every triangle in the model.

I'm not going to do anything so bold. In fact, I'm merely going to show you how to load one texture from a file. Direct3D makes this incredibly easy to do with the TextureLoader class.

Here's how you define a texture:

```
Direct3D.Texture texture = null;
```

I think that was a no-brainer.

Loading a Texture

And now, to load a texture:

```
texture = Direct3D.TextureLoader.FromFile(
    graphics, "texture.jpg", 0, 0, 0, 0, Direct3D.Format.Unknown,
    Direct3D.Pool.Managed, Direct3D.Filter.Linear,
    Direct3D.Filter.Linear, 0 );
```

Well, that's a heck of a lot of options. Luckily for you, you're probably just going to want to use the default options for a texture. Let me explain what those options are and what they do anyway. Here is the full definition of the TextureLoader.FromFile function, so you can see all the options first:

```
public static Texture FromFile(
    Device device,
    string srcFile,
    int width, int height,
    int mipLevels,
    Usage usage,
    Format format,
    Pool pool,
    Filter filter,
    Filter mipFilter,
    int colorKey
);
```

The first parameter is, obviously, the graphics device, and the second parameter is the name of the file you want to load. This function can load tons of different graphics file formats: .BMP, .JPG, .PNG, .TGA, .DDS, .DIB, .HDR, .PFM, and .PPM. So you're pretty much set on that front.

Next up are the width and height. You can set these manually, but why bother? If you leave them as 0, then the program uses the size of the image from the file you loaded automatically.

The next variable determines how many mip-levels are defined for this texture. This is used for mip-mapping. *Mip-mapping* essentially takes your texture and generates a chain of smaller images (if your texture is 64×64, a complete mip-chain will hold 32×32, 16×16, 8×8, 4×4, 2×2, and 1×1 versions of the texture, as well), which D3D displays when your texture is shrunken. Mip-mapping produces really good-looking results, and your video card won't have to hold huge versions of your textures when you're looking at stuff that's far away. For what I'm doing in this book, you don't really have to worry about mip-mapping, so just leave this parameter at 0, and D3D will automatically generate a full chain for you.

The usage parameter lets D3D know if you're going to be using this texture for any special purposes, such as rendering stuff onto the texture dynamically, allowing you to create animated textures in your game (this can be useful for water/plasma/fire effects). I won't be using this feature either, so I leave it at 0.

The format parameter is the color format of the texture; you can set it to anything you like. If you pass in Direct3D.Format.Unknown, then D3D uses the same color format of the file.

The pool parameter determines where the texture will be placed in memory. If you use Direct3D.Pool.Managed, it tells Direct3D to manage the texture for you automatically. This is what you should probably always use, unless you're going to be doing some special work on the texture and you require it to be in a particular place in memory.

note

Whenever you lose your Direct3D device, *all* of your textures are lost as well. If you use the managed memory pool, however, Direct3D takes care of reloading all of your textures automatically. Managed memory pools are your friend.

The next two parameters are filters; they determine how the texture is filtered when it's expanded or shrunken. If you don't have a filter, then D3D performs a straight pixel resize, and that can end up looking bad. The linear filter is usually the best one to use in both cases; it doesn't produce perfect-looking results, but it's faster than most of the other filters and most of the time you can't really tell what kind of improvements the other slower filters provide.

The final parameter is the *color key*. This means that whenever D3D sees a pixel that matches the color of the color key, it will not draw that pixel. Bitmaps and textures are always 2D rectangles, but images don't always have to be rectangle-shaped. For example, a person is not shaped like a rectangle—there's going to be pixels in the image of the person that you don't want to show. These pixels are usually drawn in one particular color, so if you set that color as the color key, then those pixels will never be drawn. To disable color keying, just use the value 0.

Texture Coordinates

There's a fundamental difference between textures and triangles: textures are rectangular; triangles aren't. Therefore, it's kind of hard to just say, "Draw this texture on this triangle" because the computer doesn't know what part of the texture to draw. This is what texture coordinates are used for.

Texture coordinates are simply a way of telling the computer what part of a texture to draw on a triangle.

Texture coordinates are very similar to the standard 2D (x, y) scale, except that textures use two different letters, (u, v). Figure 7.7 shows the coordinate system used for textures.

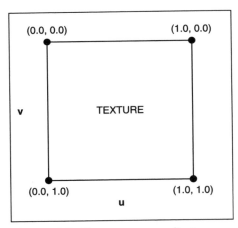

Figure 7.7 How texture coordinates are arranged

As you can see in Figure 7.7, the top-left of a texture is referred to as (0.0, 0.0), the top right is (1.0, 0.0), and so on. All coordinates range from 0.0 to 1.0. Figure 7.8 shows an example of mapping a texture onto a triangle.

So, to set up a triangle like the second one shown in Figure 7.8, you would do something like this:

```
Direct3D.CustomVertex.TransformedTextured[] vertexes =
    new Direct3D.CustomVertex.TransformedTextured[4];


// top-left vertex:
vertexes[0].Tu = 0.5f;
vertexes[0].Tv = 0.0f;
```

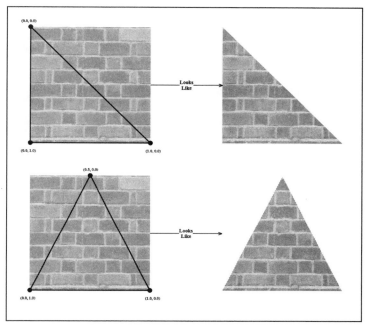

Figure 7.8 This shows how textures are mapped onto triangles using texture coordinates.

```
// bottom-left vertex:
vertexes[1].Tu = 0.0f;
vertexes[1].Tv = 1.0f;

// bottom-right vertex:
vertexes[2].Tu = 1.0f;
vertexes[2].Tv = 0.0f;
```

The actual screen coordinates of those vertexes don't matter at this point; no matter how you move them around, the texture will stretch to fit the entire triangle.

Other Forms of Geometry

Let's say you want to make a square, which requires four vertexes. But Direct3D can only draw triangles, so you make a square by combining two triangles. But there's a problem with this method: two triangles have six vertexes, not four. Two of the vertexes are shared between the triangles.

It's a waste of memory to have those extra vertexes, and if you're using Direct3D to transform your vertexes, then you're wasting valuable processing time, too. If only there were a way to create two triangles using only four vertexes…

Ah, but there is! The DirectX team thought about this problem long before you did, and they included different types of primitives for you to use. The primitives you used in Demos 7.1 and 7.2 are called *triangle lists*, which are simply a list of triangles wherein every three vertexes defines a single triangle.

Another kind of primitive is the *triangle strip*, which is a strip of triangles. Figure 7.9 shows this primitive.

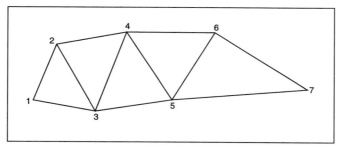

Figure 7.9 A triangle strip that defines five triangles using seven vertexes.

So, using a triangle strip, you can define many triangles connected to each other, all sharing common vertexes. This is a very efficient way of defining 3D objects.

Still another primitive is the *triangle fan*. A triangle fan is a collection of triangles that are all connected to the same vertex, the first one in the array. You can see a triangle fan in Figure 7.10.

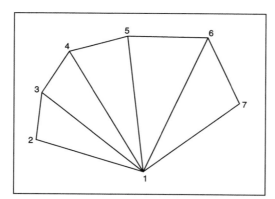

Figure 7.10 A triangle fan that defines five triangles using seven vertexes.

Using these other types of primitives is pretty simple, as all you have to do is change a parameter in the DrawUserPrimitive call. You'll see this done in Demo 7.4.

Demo 7.4

Demo 7.4 builds upon Demo 7.3; it puts a textured square on the screen instead of colored triangles.

The demo first has to declare the vertexes and the texture:

```
Direct3D.CustomVertex.TransformedTextured[] vertexes = null;
Direct3D.Texture texture = null;
```

Then I create the four vertexes and load the texture:

```
public void InitializeGeometry()
{
    vertexes = new Direct3D.CustomVertex.TransformedTextured[4];

    // top-left vertex:
    vertexes[0].X = screenwidth / 4.0f;
    vertexes[0].Y = screenheight / 4.0f;
    vertexes[0].Z = 0.0f;
    vertexes[0].Tu = 0.0f;
    vertexes[0].Tv = 0.0f;


    // top-right vertex:
    vertexes[1].X = (screenwidth / 4.0f) * 3.0f;
    vertexes[1].Y = screenheight / 4.0f;
    vertexes[1].Z = 0.0f;
    vertexes[1].Tu = 1.0f;
    vertexes[1].Tv = 0.0f;

    // bottom-left vertex:
    vertexes[2].X = screenwidth / 4.0f;
    vertexes[2].Y = (screenheight / 4.0f) * 3.0f;
    vertexes[2].Z = 0.0f;
    vertexes[2].Tu = 0.0f;
    vertexes[2].Tv = 1.0f;

    // bottom-right vertex:
    vertexes[3].X = (screenwidth / 4.0f) * 3.0f;
    vertexes[3].Y = (screenheight / 4.0f) * 3.0f;
    vertexes[3].Z = 0.0f;
    vertexes[3].Tu = 1.0f;
    vertexes[3].Tv = 1.0f;
```

```
texture = Direct3D.TextureLoader.FromFile(
    graphics, "texture.jpg", 0, 0, 0, 0, Direct3D.Format.Unknown,
    Direct3D.Pool.Managed, Direct3D.Filter.Linear,
    Direct3D.Filter.Linear, 0 );

}
```

And finally, I render the square:

```
graphics.Clear( Direct3D.ClearFlags.Target, Color.White , 1.0f, 0 );
graphics.BeginScene();

graphics.SetTexture( 0, texture );
graphics.VertexFormat = Direct3D.CustomVertex.TransformedTextured.Format;
graphics.DrawUserPrimitives(
    Direct3D.PrimitiveType.TriangleStrip, 2, vertexes );

graphics.EndScene();
graphics.Present();
```

The most important step here is the first bold line. Whenever you draw something that's textured, you need to tell the graphics device what texture you're going to be using. Then you tell the device what kind of vertexes you're drawing, and finally you draw a strip of two triangles. You should get a window that looks like that in Figure 7.11.

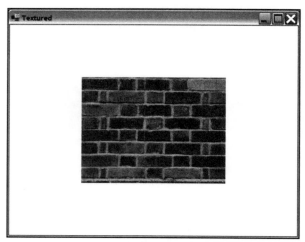

Figure 7.11 The result of Demo 7.4; a textured triangle strip

Sprites

Using Direct3D is sort of overkill when you want to draw simple 2D sprites, but it provides a lot of nice features that DirectDraw (the old 2D drawing API of DirectX) never did.

Setting up a 2D sprite system is a fair amount of work, so Microsoft went ahead and gave us a nice handy `Direct3D.Sprite` class to handle the messy details. No messing around with vertexes or anything else—just a nice, comprehensive sprite class.

caution

The `Sprite` class, along with other helper classes used in this book—such as `Direct3D.Texture-Loader` class and the `Direct3D.Font` class—belong to the D3DX library, which is not part of the core of Direct3D. D3DX is a library designed to make your life easier, and it really does help.

Unfortunately, D3DX has undergone many changes, and is still changing to this day. The D3DX functions that you see in this book are part of the DirectX 9.0b SDK, which was released in the summer of 2003. Since then, there has been another DirectX SDK update, DirectX 9.0c, which has changed a *lot* of the functions and makes them incompatible with the old versions. The reason I chose to use DirectX 9.0b is that it works with more compilers. DX9.0b works with Visual Studio 2002, SharpDevelop, and Visual Studio 2003. DirectX 9.0c, however, only works with Visual Studio 2003.

The Sprite Class

The `Sprite` class is actually confusingly named, as it doesn't actually represent a sprite. It's just a helper class that accepts drawing information that you pass in and creates the sprites for you. Let me show you an example.

First, you need to create the variable:

```
Direct3D.Sprite sprite = null;
```

And then you must initialize it using the graphics device:

```
sprite = new Direct3D.Sprite( graphics );
```

Now that you have the class created, you can draw sprites with it:

```
graphics.Clear( Direct3D.ClearFlags.Target, Color.White , 1.0f, 0 );
graphics.BeginScene();

sprite.Begin();
sprite.Draw( texture,
    new Rectangle( 0, 0, 512, 512 ),
    new Vector2( 1.0f, 1.0f ),
    new Vector2( 256.0f, 256.0f ),
    0.0f,
```

```
    new Vector2( 0.0f, 0.0f ),
    Color.White );
sprite.End();

graphics.EndScene();
graphics.Present();
```

Whoa! That's a lot of code inside the Draw function! It just goes to show you how powerful the function is.

Now let me explain exactly what is going on. The first thing you need to do, when drawing sprites, is tell the Sprite class that you're going to start sending it sprite information, by calling Begin. Once you've done that, you can use the Draw function to give it sprite information.

The Draw function takes a whole load of parameters, as you can plainly see. Here's the full function declaration:

```
public void Draw(
    Microsoft.DirectX.Direct3D.Texture srcTexture,
    System.Drawing.Rectangle srcRectangle,
    Microsoft.DirectX.Vector2 scaling,
    Microsoft.DirectX.Vector2 rotationCenter,
    System.Single rotation,
    Microsoft.DirectX.Vector2 translation,
    System.Drawing.Color color )
```

The first parameter is, of course, the texture that you want to use for the sprite. The second parameter might not be so obvious to you, however.

The second parameter is a rectangle object, which defines which part of the texture you want to draw. This is necessary because you might only want to draw part of a texture as your sprite, and not the entire thing. In the example I gave above, I defined a new rectangle that encompassed an area of 512×512 pixels because that's how large the texture I was using is. You can use smaller area if you want to.

The next parameter is a 2D vector that determines how the object is scaled. If you pass in (1.0, 1.0), then it's not scaled at all. Likewise, (0.5, 0.5) would shrink it by half, and (2.0, 2.0) would double the size.

The parameter after that is also a 2D vector, this time describing the rotation center of the sprite. Imagine taking a nail and pushing it through a piece of paper, and then spinning the paper around the nail. This is exactly what a rotation center is. I put it at (256, 256), which is the center of a (512, 512) texture. You don't have to rotate your sprites around the center if you don't want to, however. It's up to you.

note

The rotation center of the sprite is actually kind of confusing, and it took me a while to figure out exactly what the value means because the Managed DirectX documentation is pretty bare. The rotation center of the sprite is *unscaled*, meaning that if you scale the sprite, the rotation center of the sprite will not move along with it. If your sprite is 128×128 in size, and you set the rotation center to (64,64), then it will rotate around the center of the sprite—but *only* if you use a scaling vector of (1.0, 1.0). If you scale the sprite to 64×64 by using a (0.5, 0.5) scaling vector, then the rotation center is still at (64,64), and your sprite will end up rotating around the lower-right corner of itself, rather than the center.

After that is a floating point number representing the rotation angle of the sprite, which is given in radians.

note

A radian is simply a measurement of an angle that ranges from 0 to 2π (approximately 6.28). You can think of 360 degrees being equal to 6.28 radians, and 180 degrees equal to 3.14 radians. The equation for getting radians from degrees is *radians = degrees / (180/π)*.

The next parameter is a vector that describes the translation of the sprite on the screen. If you use (0,0), then the sprite will be drawn at the upper-left of the screen, and if you use (100,0), it will be drawn 100 pixels from the left of the screen, and so on.

The final parameter is simply the color of the sprite, if you want to shade it or use alpha blending. In my example, I used Color.White, giving you an unshaded sprite. You can just as easily use any other color combination.

Making the Code Better

The drawing code I showed you previously is a mess. There is no way you should ever use code that looks like that. It's large and inefficient, and somewhat difficult to manage, as well. To make things better, I decided to make my own Sprite class, one that will manage stuff like position, rotation angle, and scaling on its own.

A Better Sprite Class

You can find this Sprite class inside of Demo 7.5, in the file Sprite.cs. Here's a listing of the data members:

```
public class Sprite
{
    Direct3D.Texture texture;
    Drawing.Rectangle rect;
    DirectX.Vector2 scaling;
```

```
DirectX.Vector2 offset;
DirectX.Vector2 anchor;
float angle;
Drawing.Color color;
}
```

The class will keep track of a texture, the source rectangle, a scaling vector, an offset vector, an anchor point, a rotation angle, and the color of the sprite.

Everything there, except the anchor point, correlates directly to the parameters you pass into the `Direct3D.Sprite.Draw` function. An anchor point is similar to the rotation center of a sprite, but not exactly.

I told you previously that the rotation center doesn't scale along with the size of your sprite, and that that can be a pain in the butt. Furthermore, if you change the scaling factor of the sprite, then the left-hand corner stays where it was and all the other sides increase in size. Take a look at Figure 7.12 for reference.

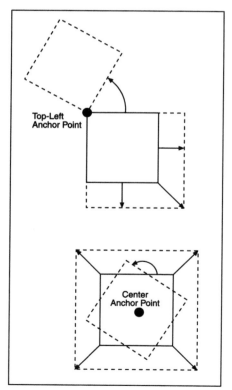

Figure 7.12 How an anchor point should
affect scaling and rotation of a sprite

When the anchor point is at the top-left corner, the entire sprite rotates around that point and scales around that point, so it never grows upwards or to the left—it simply scales down and to the right.

If you have the anchor point in the center, however, the entire thing scales evenly around that point.

To make things simple, my Sprite class will use texture coordinates to define the anchor point, meaning that it will be defined on a 0.0 to 1.0 scale. Therefore, (0.5, 0.5) is the exact center of the sprite, (0.0, 1.0) is the bottom-left corner, and so on.

Properties

The new Sprite class is based almost entirely on properties for retrieving and setting the values. Most of the properties are pretty boring, so I'm only going to show you the code for the important ones. Here's a listing of all the properties in the class:

```
public Direct3D.Texture Texture
public int Width          // can only get
public int Height         // can only get
public float XScale
public float YScale
public float Scale        // can only set
public float X
public float Y
public float XAnchor
public float YAnchor
public float Angle
public Drawing.Color Color
```

Most of these, such as Texture, XScale, YScale, X, Y, XAnchor, YAnchor, Angle, and Color, should be obvious to you.

Width and Height are read-only; you can't set their values because they are read directly from the texture you give it. These two values tell you the width and height of the texture.

Scale is only settable; it's a shortcut used to set both the X and the Y scale of the sprite at the same time.

Some of the properties take care of extra housekeeping work. The Texture property, in particular, does this—whenever you set a new texture, it resets the internal rect structure for you so that you don't have to manually set a new rectangle every time you change textures.

Drawing

The most complex part of the new class is the Draw function. Here's the declaration:

```
public void Draw( Direct3D.Sprite renderer, Camera camera )
```

The function takes a Direct3D.Sprite as its first parameter and a 2D vector representing the camera.

A *camera* is a really simple concept to understand; it's basically the coordinates of a camera in *world space*. Imagine your game world as one large 2D grid; you can give it any dimensions you want—let's say, -1000 to 1000 in both the vertical and horizontal directions, giving you a universe size of 2000×2000 units. Your screen obviously can't display the whole thing at once—the camera can only be pointing at one small section of the universe at any given time. Figure 7.13 shows a diagram of this setup.

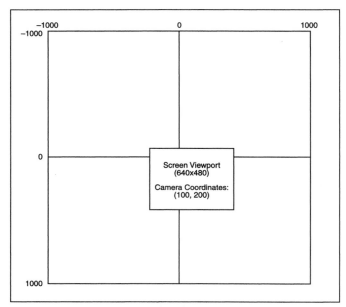

Figure 7.13 A screen viewport applied to a universe

For example, if your screen is 640×480, then you can only display that many pixels. So, in a simple 2D world, a camera usually has two coordinates, denoting which part of the universe to show. I prefer that these coordinates be defined at the center of the screen, so that if you tell your camera to point to universal coordinates (100, 200), then those coordinates will be displayed at the exact center of the screen.

Begin Note

I'll show you how to use the Camera class that I defined as part of the framework (which can be found in the Sprite.cs file in Demo 7.5) in the next section.

Without further ado, here's the drawing function:

```
public void Draw( Direct3D.Sprite renderer, Camera camera )
{

    // calculate the actual width and height:
    float w = XScale * Width;
    float h = YScale * Height;
```

The first step I take is to calculate the actual width and height of the sprite, which is the width and height multiplied by the scaling factors.

Here's the next step:

```
    // calculate the actual anchor point in sprite coordinates:
    DirectX.Vector2 scaledanchor = anchor;
    scaledanchor.X *= w;
    scaledanchor.Y *= h;
```

This step creates a new vector that will store the actual anchor point of the sprite. For example, if you have a 512×512 sprite scaled by 0.25, then w and h will both be 128. Now, if you have the anchor point set to (0.5, 0.5)—which is the center of the texture—this step will multiply 128 * 0.5, giving you 64 for both the X and Y values of the scaled anchor. This makes sense, as the center of a 128×128 sprite is (64, 64).

Next, I offset the sprite by the scaled anchor point:

```
    DirectX.Vector2 newoffset = offset;
    newoffset.X -= scaledanchor.X;
    newoffset.Y -= scaledanchor.Y;
```

The anchor point determines where the sprite should be drawn. If a sprite is at coordinates (100, 100), and the anchor point is in the center of the sprite, then whenever you draw that sprite, you will want the center of the sprite to be drawn at (100, 100). Unfortunately, Direct3D.Sprite draws sprites at the upper-left corner of the sprite, so if you tell it to draw a sprite at (100, 100), then the upper-left corner of the sprite will be at (100, 100). To fix this, I modify the offset of the sprite by the values of the scaled anchor. So, using the data that I showed you previously, the anchor point would be moved left 64 pixels and up 64 pixels, giving you a new offset of (36, 36) and ensuring that the center of the sprite will be drawn at (100, 100) like you wanted.

Finally, the sprite is sent to the Direct3D.Sprite device:

```
    renderer.Draw(
        texture,
        rect,
        scaling,
```

```
        scaledanchor,
        angle,
        newoffset - camera.Offset,
        color );
}
```

The only line that should concern you is the line that contains newoffset - camera.Offset. This simply moves the sprite by whatever offset the camera has. If a sprite is supposed to be drawn at (0,0), and the camera is at (0,0), then nothing happens. If the camera is looking at (100, 0), however, then the sprite is moved left by 100 pixels to give the appearance that the camera has moved to the right. Pretty clever, isn't it?

The Camera Class

The Camera class I made is somewhat simple. I had to add a fair amount of code to make it handle some housekeeping work automatically, but in the end, it came out incredibly easy to use.

Basically, a camera knows how big the screen is and where it's pointing to on the screen, and it has a few vectors to hold this information:

```
public class Camera
{
    DirectX.Vector2 position;
    DirectX.Vector2 screensize;
    DirectX.Vector2 finaloffset;
}
```

If the camera is pointing at (0, 0), then that's what's stored in position. If the screen is 640×480, then (640, 480) is stored in screensize.

You need to do little bit more work, which is why there's a third vector, finaloffset. Basically, this vector stores a calculated offset based on the vector's position and screen size. For an example, say you want to draw something at (0, 0), and you want the camera pointed at (0, 0) as well. Direct3D.Sprite will draw everything at (0, 0) at the upper-left hand corner of the screen, but that's not what you want. As you want (0, 0) to be drawn at the center of the screen, you need to move the screen halfway to the left and halfway down. So, if the screen is 640×480, then you need to subtract 320 pixels from the X component, and 240 from the Y component. These values are calculated with the two calculation functions:

```
void CalculateXOffset()
{
    finaloffset.X = position.X - (screensize.X / 2);
}
```

```
void CalculateYOffset()
{
    finaloffset.Y = position.Y - (screensize.Y / 2);
}
```

The position data and the screen width data are accessed via properties like this:

```
public float X
{
    get { return position.X; }
    set { position.X = value; CalculateXOffset(); }
}
```

Note that whenever you set a new value, the offsets are recalculated so that later on you can just call the `Offset` property (which is read-only) to get the final offset vector. You've seen this used previously in my `AdvancedFramework.Sprite.Draw` function.

Cameras also have mandatory constructors to set screen size and position:

```
AdvancedFramework.Camera c;
c = new AdvancedFramework.Camera( 640, 480, 100, 100 );
c = new AdvancedFramework.Camera( 640, 480 );
```

The first camera points to (100, 100), and the second one is at (0, 0).

Demo 7.5

Now that you have a functional sprite and camera class, you can build a program to show-case these capabilities. I've created Demo 7.5 to do this.

The Data

This demo will need to store some data, specifically the sprites, a camera, the Direct3D variables, and some other auxiliary variables:

```
Direct3D.Texture texture = null;        // the texture
Direct3D.Sprite spriterenderer = null;  // the sprite renderer
Sprite[] sprites = null;                // array of sprites
int numsprites = 4;                     // number of sprites
Camera camera = null;                   // the camera
float movingx = 0.0f;                   // how fast is camera moving in x?
float movingy = 0.0f;                   // how fast is camera moving in y?
```

This demo will be animated and more interactive than any of the previous demos, so I've included two floats to describe how fast the camera is moving in the x and the y directions.

Setting Up the Data

As with previous demos, all of the data is set up within the InitializeResources function.

First, the texture:

```
public void InitializeResources()
{
    texture = Direct3D.TextureLoader.FromFile(
        graphics, "texture.bmp", 0, 0, 0, 0, Direct3D.Format.Unknown,
        Direct3D.Pool.Managed, Direct3D.Filter.Linear,
        Direct3D.Filter.Linear, Color.FromArgb( 0, 0, 255 ).ToArgb() );
```

This is very similar to what you've seen before, with one change: I've added a color key of pure blue. The texture for this demo is a brick bitmap with a large blue circle in the middle, and I want the blue circle to be completely transparent, so I set the color key to blue; when the texture is loaded, the blue is ignored.

note

In order to use color keys, you need to use a lossless graphics format like BMPs or TGAs. You cannot use lossy formats like JPGs for color keying because they don't store the data in a pure manner. If you made a JPG with a pure blue circle in the middle, the JPG compression process would change the color slightly.

note

There are two different kinds of image formats out there: lossy and lossless. A lossless image format stores image data precisely; every pixel in the image is preserved exactly as how it should be. Lossy image formats, however, "lose" information. JPGs in particular are notorious for this. In order to get a better compression ratio, the lossy image formats *approximate* what colors exist in the image, and you get an image that looks good to the human eye—the exact pixel information is not stored, as with lossless formats. Whenever you use color keying, you *must* use lossless formats.

Next, the sprite renderer and the sprite array are created:

```
    spriterenderer = new Direct3D.Sprite( graphics );
    sprites = new Sprite[numsprites];
```

Then the sprites are initialized:

```
    for( int i = 0; i < numsprites; i++ )
    {
        sprites[i] = new Sprite();
        sprites[i].Texture = texture;
        sprites[i].Scale = (i+1) * 0.2f;
        sprites[i].X = i * 75.0f;
```

```
        sprites[i].Y = i * 75.0f;
        sprites[i].Angle = i;
        sprites[i].XAnchor = 0.5f;
        sprites[i].YAnchor = 0.5f;
    }
```

Each sprite will use the same texture, and each sprite will be scaled differently. For example, the first sprite will be scaled at 0.2, the next at 0.4, the next at 0.6, and so on.

The same goes for position; the first is at (0,0), the next is at (75,75), the next at (150,150), and so on.

Each sprite starts out with a different angle as well: 0 radians, 1 radian, 2 radians, and so on.

Finally, every sprite is anchored at its center point.

I decided to have some fun and play around with colorizing some of the sprites as well:

```
        sprites[0].Color = Color.FromArgb( 127, 127, 255, 0 );
        sprites[1].Color = Color.FromArgb( 127, 255, 0, 127 );
        sprites[2].Color = Color.FromArgb( 127, 0, 127, 255 );
```

The first one is a reddish-green, the next is a bluish-red, and the final one is a greenish-blue. The fourth sprite (index 3) isn't colored at all. Note that the first three sprites are also at 50 percent translucency, which should produce some pretty effects.

Finally, the camera is created:

```
        camera = new Camera( screenwidth, screenheight );
}
```

Animating the Data

This is the first demo to use animation. The animation information is going to be stored within the ProcessFrame function:

```
if( !paused )
{
    float t = gametimer.Elapsed();

    camera.X += (movingx * t);
    camera.Y += (movingy * t);

    for( int i = 0; i < numsprites; i++ )
    {
        sprites[i].Angle += 1.0f * t;
    }
}
```

The first thing the function does is get the amount of time elapsed since the last frame and store it in t.

Next, the camera is moved using the movingx and movingy variables. For example, if movingx holds 100.0f, then that means the camera is going to be moving by 100 pixels per second to the right.

The final step is to loop through all four sprites and rotate them. They'll be rotating at a rate of 1 radian per second—which is approximately 57 degrees per second—counter-clockwise.

Rendering

Rendering the sprites is a simple process; you merely need to go through the array and draw each one:

```
graphics.Clear( Direct3D.ClearFlags.Target, Color.White , 1.0f, 0 );
graphics.BeginScene();

spriterenderer.Begin();

for( int i = numsprites - 1; i >= 0; i- )
{
    sprites[i].Draw( spriterenderer, camera );
}

spriterenderer.End();

graphics.EndScene();
graphics.Present();
```

Instead of rendering the sprites from first to last (which would put the smallest one on the bottom), I go the other way around and draw the last sprite first. This is so that you can see the pretty blending effects the sprites give you.

Each sprite has its Draw function called, using the sprite renderer and the camera, making the code pretty darned easy to use.

Interaction

The last change made to the demo is to make it interactive. Since you don't have DirectInput up and running yet, I've just implemented a very rudimentary input system using Windows OnKeyDown and OnKeyUp events, which you've seen used in the frameworks given previously.

I'm adding the following lines to `OnKeyDown`:

```
if( e.KeyCode == System.Windows.Forms.Keys.W ) { movingy = -100.0f; }
if( e.KeyCode == System.Windows.Forms.Keys.S ) { movingy = 100.0f; }
if( e.KeyCode == System.Windows.Forms.Keys.A ) { movingx = -100.0f; }
if( e.KeyCode == System.Windows.Forms.Keys.D ) { movingx = 100.0f; }
```

When the user presses the W key on the keyboard, the camera will start moving upwards at 100 pixels per second. Likewise, S will move the camera down at 100 pixels per second, A will move it left by 100 pixels per second, and D will move it right by 100 pixels per second.

When the user stops holding down those keys, the camera movement should stop; so add the following lines to `OnKeyUp`:

```
if( e.KeyCode == System.Windows.Forms.Keys.W ) { movingy = 0.0f; }
if( e.KeyCode == System.Windows.Forms.Keys.S ) { movingy = 0.0f; }
if( e.KeyCode == System.Windows.Forms.Keys.A ) { movingx = 0.0f; }
if( e.KeyCode == System.Windows.Forms.Keys.D ) { movingx = 0.0f; }
```

Whenever the keys are released, the movement is halted.

Run the Demo and Watch the Prettiness

Finally, you can compile and run the demo, and you'll get something that looks like that Figure 7.14.

You can move the demo around using the W, A, S, and D keys on your keyboard, and you can pause and unpause it using P. You should note that the animation will stop when you multitask out of the window (because of the auto-pausing in the framework). Other than that, just sit back and enjoy the pretty animated sprites.

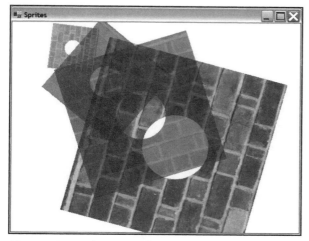

Figure 7.14 The output for Demo 7.5

Fonts

The D3DX library also provides a handy Font class for you to use. In the past, you would have to make your own font textures or go around messing with GDI to draw fonts. Well, no more!

Creating a System Font

The .NET framework has fonts built into it using the System.Drawing.Font class. This class can be used to represent any kind of system font, which are usually true-type files (.ttf). In order to draw fonts in your game, you need to first access a system font. Luckily for you, this is incredibly easy:

```
System.Drawing.Font sysfont;
sysfont = new System.Drawing.Font(
    "Arial", 16,
    System.Drawing.FontStyle.Bold |
    System.Drawing.FontStyle.Italic );
```

This code creates a new object that represents the Arial font, with a size of 16 points, using a bold and italic style. You combine flags using the binary or operator, as seen in the code. Table 7.7 lists the available styles.

Table 7.7 Font Styles

Style	Description
Bold	Text is in bold, thick letters
Italic	Text is slanted
Regular	No effect
Strikeout	Text has a line through the center
Underline	Text has a line underneath

Creating a Direct3D Font

Now that you have a system font, you can go ahead and make a Direct3D font:

```
Direct3D.Font font;
font = new Direct3D.Font( graphics, font );
```

All you need to do is pass in a reference to the graphics device and a reference to the windows font object, and you're all set to go!

Drawing Text

Now that you have your font classes all set up, you can just cut to the chase and start drawing text. Marvelous!

Draw text using the `DrawText` function of `Direct3D.Font`. Here's a sample:

```
Rectangle rect = new Rectangle( 0, 0, 640, 100 );
dxfont.DrawText(
    "Hello there!",
    rect,
    Direct3D.DrawTextFormat.NoClip,
    Color.CornflowerBlue );
```

This code creates a rectangle that represents a box at the top of your rendering window, 640 pixels wide and 100 pixels tall. This is the rendering area that the font will be drawn into.

The next step is to draw the text "Hello there!" inside of that rectangle, using the `NoClip` text formatting option and the color cornflower blue.

You really only have to be concerned with the formatting options, which allow you to tell the renderer exactly how you want the text drawn. Table 7.8 lists the most useful options.

Table 7.8 Useful `DrawTextFormat` Values

Value	Purpose
WordBreak	If the text is longer than the box you give it, this option will break the text up onto the next line or however many lines it needs to fit the entire text.
VerticalCenter	Centers the text vertically
Top	Forces the text to be drawn at the top of the rectangle (default)
Bottom	Forces the text to be drawn at the bottom of the rectangle
SingleLine	Forces text to be drawn on a single line, ignoring newline characters.
NoClip	By default, the Font class clips the text into the rectangle you provide, so nothing is drawn outside the box. This disables that feature and makes drawing faster.
Center	Centers the text horizontally
Right	Forces the text to be drawn at the right margin
Left	Forces the text to be drawn at the left margin (default)

Demo 7.6

Demo 7.6 demonstrates the various font options that you can use. Overall, this is a remarkably simple demo.

The first step is to declare the font resources:

```
Font windowsfont = null;
Direct3D.Font dxfont = null;
```

And then initialize the resources when the program is loaded:

```
public void InitializeResources()
{
    windowsfont = new System.Drawing.Font(
        "Arial", 16, System.Drawing.FontStyle.Bold );
    dxfont = new Direct3D.Font( graphics, windowsfont );
}
```

Finally, all I do is just draw a bunch of text strings on the screen inside of the Render function:

```
graphics.Clear( Direct3D.ClearFlags.Target, Color.White , 1.0f, 0 );
graphics.BeginScene();

Rectangle rect = new Rectangle( 0, 0, 640, 100 );
dxfont.DrawText(
    "Welcome to Demo 7.6",
    rect,
    Direct3D.DrawTextFormat.NoClip,
    Color.CornflowerBlue );

rect = new Rectangle( 0, 50, 640, 100 );
dxfont.DrawText(
    "Here's some more text! Centered!",
    rect,
    Direct3D.DrawTextFormat.Center |
    Direct3D.DrawTextFormat.NoClip,
    Color.PaleVioletRed );


rect = new Rectangle( 0, 100, 300, 300 );
dxfont.DrawText(
    "This is a paragraph of wrapped text in a 300x300 box!",
    rect,
    Direct3D.DrawTextFormat.WordBreak |
    Direct3D.DrawTextFormat.NoClip,
    Color.MediumOrchid );

rect = new Rectangle( 0, 150, 640, 300 );
dxfont.DrawText(
```

```
    "Isn't text exciting?",
    rect,
    Direct3D.DrawTextFormat.Right |
    Direct3D.DrawTextFormat.NoClip,
    Color.LawnGreen );

graphics.EndScene();
graphics.Present();
```

This demonstration produces the output seen in Figure 7.15.

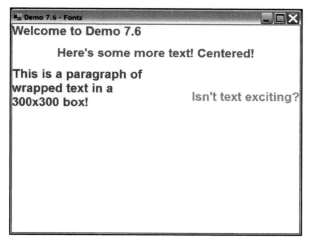

Figure 7.15 The output from Demo 7.15

Summary

This has been the biggest chapter in the book so far, and I've got some bad news for you: You've barely just scratched the surface of Direct3D. I really wasn't kidding when I said that Direct3D is one of the largest and most complex APIs in the world. There is just an incredible amount of things inside the API that allow you to make some really unbelievable games.

There's a ton of things that I just didn't have room to cover, such as vertex buffers, index buffers, lighting, 3D transformation calculations, meshes, vertex shaders, pixel shaders, volume textures, fog, depth buffers, keyframe animation, point sprites, particles.... But don't be discouraged! You've already got a good head start and you can start making your own 2D games right now if you wanted to. The next subject this book is going to go over is input and sound programming, which are smaller (but still very important) parts of game programming.

What You Learned

The main concepts that you should have picked up from this chapter are:

- How to create a Direct3D Device.
- What a back buffer is.
- How to make sure a device is available for you to use.
- What display formats (pixel formats) are.
- How the updated framework looks.
- How to handle multitasking in fullscreen mode.
- How to draw a triangle.
- How to use colors and alpha blending.
- How textures and texture coordinates work.
- How to use D3DX to load a texture quickly.
- How to use triangle strips and fans to optimize your geometry.
- How to use D3DX to handle sprites for you easily.
- How to load fonts and draw text.

Review Questions

These review questions test your knowledge on the important concepts exposed to you in this chapter. The answers can be found in Appendix A.

7.1. What's the difference between a hardware device and a software device?

7.2. Why would you prefer to use a hardware device over a software device?

7.3. Why are back buffers used?

7.4. Why is 32-bit color preferred to 16-bit color?

7.5. What is alpha information?

7.6. Why bother handling multitasking?

7.7. Why does Direct3D draw primarily triangles?

7.8. What purpose do textures serve?

7.9. How can you optimize your geometry so that you don't waste time and space working on duplicate vertexes?

7.10. Why use the D3DX library?

On Your Own

There is so much you can do on your own from what you've learned in this chapter. With the way the AdvancedFramework's sprite system is set up, you can move a camera around in world-space to make the sprites move around on the screen, but the framework isn't as complex as it could be. Look into using matrixes and the Direct3D.Sprite.SetWorldViewLH function to make the sprite engine able to rotate and zoom the camera as well. You should take note that this function has been removed from the D3DX library in DirectX 9.0c, so if that's what version you're using, look into using the Direct3D.Sprite.Draw2D functions with matrixes instead. You can accomplish some really neat effects that way.

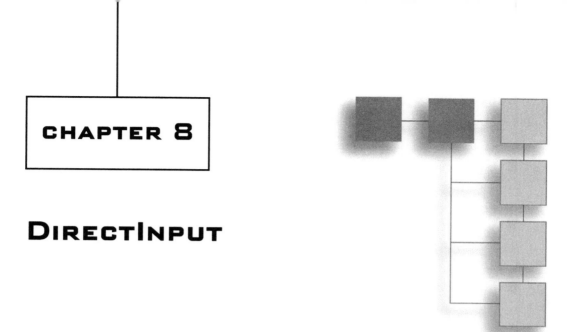

CHAPTER 8

DIRECTINPUT

You've seen some rudimentary input programming already, in Chapters 6 and 7. Those chapters used Windows events to determine when a key was pressed on the keyboard. While handling input like that is great for things like Windows applications, it's not really suitable for a game environment. Games typically require quick handling of input and more control over the actual devices—control that standard Windows events just don't give you. That's why there's DirectInput, the DirectX API that gives you as much control as possible over an input device.

In this chapter, you will learn:

- How to get information from keyboards.
- How to get information from mice.
- How to get information from game devices like joysticks and steering wheels.
- How to use force feedback to send data back to a game device.

Keyboards

The keyboard was one of the very first computer input devices available. It's difficult to find a PC without a keyboard nowadays, and you can probably assume that anyone playing a PC game has a keyboard.

The Advanced Framework from Demo 7.1 includes code that creates a keyboard, but I didn't go over what it all meant.

Just as in Direct3D, the DirectInput API has a Device class that represents actual input devices:

```
DirectInput.Device keyboard = null;
```

Creating a Device

Once you've created a variable to store your device, you need to create the device:

```
keyboard = new DirectInput.Device( DirectInput.SystemGuid.Keyboard );
```

The constructor for a Device takes a *globally unique identifier* (GUID) as its parameter. A GUID is simply a 128-bit number that has been assigned to each device on your system. As a keyboard and a mouse are assumed to exist on a PC system, DirectInput has a class that returns the GUID of the keyboard and mouse devices for you; the class is named DirectInput.SystemGuid. The Keyboard member returns the GUID of the system keyboard and the Mouse member returns the GUID of the system mouse.

The next step is to set the cooperation level of the device:

```
keyboard.SetCooperativeLevel(
    this,
    DirectInput.CooperativeLevelFlags.Background |
    DirectInput.CooperativeLevelFlags.NonExclusive );
```

A common theme you should see in game programming is that *you do not own the machine you're running on.* That keyboard belongs to the user, not your program. This means you have to tell DirectInput how you want to access the device. Table 8.1 lists all the flags you can use.

It's a good idea to create devices like the keyboard and the mouse with the NonExclusive flag because they are used by everything. If you don't want your program grabbing input while your window is minimized, then you should use Foreground mode. Unfortunately, if you do that, your devices become unacquired whenever someone switches out of the program, and your program will have to reacquire them manually. I prefer to use Background mode and just not gather input while the application is minimized.

The next step after setting a cooperation level is to acquire the device:

```
keyboard.Acquire();
```

And now you can use the keyboard with DirectInput instead of Windows event messages.

Table 8.1 Input Device Cooperation Flags

Flag	Meaning
NoWindowsKey	The windows key is disabled (keyboards only)
Background	The device can be accessed even when your app is in the background
Foreground	Device can only be used when your application is the active one
Exclusive	Program requests to use device exclusively
NonExclusive	Device can be shared among other programs

Gathering Input by Polling

There are two ways to gather input from a keyboard. The first method is by polling the keyboard and asking it, "Which keys are pressed right now?" Another method is to use an event notifier; this is very similar to what you've seen already with the windows OnKeyDown events. (I won't be going over the second method because it involves *multithreading*, which is a topic this book doesn't have room to cover.)

Here's how to poll the keyboard:

```
DirectInput.Key[] keys = keyboard.GetPressedKeys();
```

The GetPressedKeys function only works with keyboards, and it returns an array of DirectInput.Keys, which is just an enumeration representing the various keys on a keyboard. Here are a few examples of DirectInput.Key values: DirectInput.Key.Return, DirectInput.Key.Q, DirectInput.Key.Numpad6, and so on. There's a ton of them.

Demo 8.1 shows you interactively how getting keyboard data works by printing out a string containing all the keys pressed. Figure 8.1 shows the demo in action. As the code really is amazingly simple, I'm not going to bother showing it here; you already know all the basics about getting keyboard data this way, anyway (it only takes one line!).

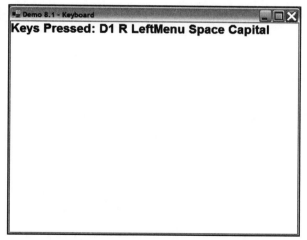

Figure 8.1 This demo uses polling to get keyboard data.

The screenshot shows that the keys 1, R, Left+Alt, Space, and Caps Lock are pressed down. DirectInput uses odd names for the keys sometimes; for example, Left+Alt is called DirectInput.Key.LeftMenu, for some odd reason. Look at your SDK docs for a complete listing of key names.

You should note that most keyboards can only store the data required to show that about five keys are being pressed at any given time. It all depends on the keyboard. For example, if I hold down S, D, and F, nothing else will register when I press those keys down. That's just how the hardware works.

Mice

Mice are amazingly useful devices, and like keyboards, you can't really find a computer without one. Mice are just a little harder to use than keyboards.

Mice are different from keyboards in that they store how much distance they have moved in a 2D grid, so that every time you poll a mouse, you get information on what buttons are pressed and also how much the mouse has moved since the last time you polled it.

Creating a Mouse

Creating a mouse is also amazingly simple, and the process is almost identical to what you used to create a keyboard device. The following code assumes that mouse is a DirectInput.Device:

```
mouse = new DirectInput.Device( DirectInput.SystemGuid.Mouse );
mouse.SetCooperativeLevel(
    this,
    DirectInput.CooperativeLevelFlags.Background |
    DirectInput.CooperativeLevelFlags.NonExclusive );
mouse.SetDataFormat( DirectInput.DeviceDataFormat.Mouse );
mouse.Acquire();
```

The only line that differs significantly from the keyboard code is the line in bold. That line tells the device that it is going to be accepting data for a mouse object.

Polling a Mouse

A mouse object can be polled by retrieving the CurrentMouseState property of your Device, which returns a DirectInput.MouseState object:

```
DirectInput.MouseState state = mouse.CurrentMouseState;
```

The state structure will have some variables that you're interested in looking at:

```
int deltax = state.X;    // how many units mouse has moved horizontally
int deltay = state.Y;    // how many units mouse has moved vertically
int deltaz = state.Z;    // how many units mouse-wheel has moved

byte[] buttons = state.GetMouseButtons();
if( buttons[0] == 128 )
```

```
       // button 0 is down
if( buttons[1] == 128 )
       // button 1 is down
// and so on...
```

For the X, Y, and Z variables, the value returned is an integer that can be positive or negative. The actual meaning of this value depends on the system, so it varies; this is why it's usually a good idea to let your player have the ability to adjust the mouse sensitivity (by multiplying the delta values with some constant).

To get button state information, you simply call the GetMouseButtons function of the state structure, which returns an array of bytes. Each byte represents a button, and the button can be in one of two states: 0 or 128. 0 means the button is not pressed, and 128 means it is pressed. That's all there is to it.

Demo 8.2 demonstrates these abilities within the ProcessInput function. Again, you've already seen how the functions work, so there's no need to show you the demo code. Figure 8.2 shows the output of Demo 8.2.

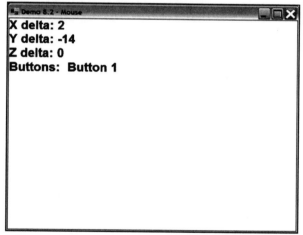

Figure 8.2 Demo 8.2 on the CD-ROM

Game Devices

The other major type of input device is the generically named game device. A *game device* is simply any device designed for games that isn't a mouse or a keyboard. It could be a joystick, a steering wheel, a game pad, foot pedals, or anything else you can think of.

Game devices are similar to mice—they have one or more axes, and they have a variety of buttons. But they can also be very complex, and can include a variety of controls that a mouse just can't have, including sliders, a rotation axis, three standard axes, buttons, and even a point-of-view hat. Throughout this section, I will use the term *joystick* to mean any type of game device.

Finding a Game Device

As not all computers have game devices, you can't just assume that you're going to have a game device available. And since the advent of USB ports, you can't assume that the system will only have one game device either; you could have a variety of devices on one machine.

You need some way of retrieving a device GUID from the computer. Luckily for you, DirectInput provides a handy Manager class that will gather a list of available devices for you. Here's an example:

```
foreach( DirectInput.DeviceInstance i in
    DirectInput.Manager.GetDevices(
    DirectInput.DeviceClass.GameControl,
    DirectInput.EnumDevicesFlags.AttachedOnly ) )
{
    // do something with "i" here
}
```

The Manager.GetDevices function returns a list of DeviceInstances; which ones it gets depend on what parameters you pass in. The first parameter determines what class of device you want to find; this can be a Pointer (a mouse device), a Keyboard, a GameControl (joystick-type device), Other (drawing pads and other oddball stuff), or All.

The next parameter determines which flags the devices must have. For the example, I used the AttachedOnly flag, which only finds attached devices. If you don't use that flag, then the function could return a pointer to a joystick that the user unplugged but forgot to uninstall —you don't want to be using devices that aren't actually attached to the system.

The other two important flags are AllDevices and ForceFeedback. The ForceFeedback flag will only return devices that have force feedback effects; I'll cover feedback effects later in this chapter.

Creating a Game Device

Once you have found a device that you want to use, you can create it just as you would create a mouse or a keyboard:

```
gameinput = new DirectInput.Device( i.InstanceGuid );
gameinput.SetCooperativeLevel(
    this,
    DirectInput.CooperativeLevelFlags.Background |
    DirectInput.CooperativeLevelFlags.NonExclusive );
```

```
gameinput.SetDataFormat( DirectInput.DeviceDataFormat.Joystick );
gameinput.Acquire();
```

The previous code segment is meant to be placed inside the `foreach` block from the code segment that finds devices, so `i` is a `DirectInput.DeviceInstance` object representing an attached game controller. Other than that, there's nothing new about this code.

Getting Joystick Axis Data

As so many different variations of joysticks exist, you don't really know what axes, sliders, buttons, and hats any particular device is going to have. The `JoystickState` structure has variables to hold everything you could possibly imagine. Table 8.2 lists some of the properties of a joystick state structure.

Table 8.2 `DirectInput.JoystickState` Properties

Property	Description
X	X axis absolute location
Rx	X axis rotation angle
ARx	X axis angular acceleration
AX	X axis acceleration
FRx	X axis torque
FX	X axis force
VRx	X axis angular velocity
VX	X axis velocity

* You can replace X with Y or Z for each of these variables in order to access the same information for the Y and Z axes.

That's a heck of a lot of information! Chances are, you're not even going to need most of it. Most of the time, the only information you're going to need here is the X, Y and Z variables, and possibly the Rx, Ry, and Rz variables. It all depends on how your joystick works.

On my joystick (Logitech Wingman Force 3D), for example, the X and Y variables represent the left-right and up-down locations of the stick, respectively. Rz represents the left-right rotation of the stick, and Z isn't used. But another joystick I own, which is the same brand, uses the Z variable to represent the throttle slider. Everything depends on the particular joystick.

tip

It is a very good idea to let your players configure their own joysticks within your program.

DirectInput handles devices with up to five axes of data, but you can only get the first three axes with the properties you know about so far. In order to get the additional two axes (typically called the *u* and *v* axes), you need to use some other functions. The function you'll be mainly concerned with is the GetSlider function, which returns an array of two integers. The first integer represents the absolute position of the *u* axis, and the second represents the absolute position of the *v* axis.

Three other functions, which you probably won't need to use, are GetASlider, GetFSlider, and GetVSlider, which return arrays of two ints representing the Acceleration, Force, and Velocity of the two sliders.

note

It seems strange that the way you access the XYZ axes is completely different from the way you access the UV axes, and no one is really sure why that is. Most likely it is the result of an oversight of some sort on the part of the DirectX team. They are aware of this inconsistency, and it will most likely be fixed in a future version of the API.

Modifying Axis Attributes

DirectInput allows you to modify attributes of axes, and this becomes useful in many situations, so you can fine-tune how your devices are used.

Modifying the Range

If you start up a program and begin receiving axis data from a joystick, you're probably going to get data in the range of 0 to 65,535, but that isn't guaranteed. Furthermore, most of the time the data doesn't entirely make sense in that range because the zero-position of the axes is going to show up as 32,768, which isn't really useful. The zero-position of an axis usually means that you're not moving at all, so you'd think that value would be 0, right? Well, it's not. But you can change the values that an axis returns to you.

Every joystick element actually has a DirectInput.DeviceObjectInstance structure representing it. That means that every axis, every button, every POV hat, and every slider has one of these structures describing it. You're not really going to be concerned with all of the data provided, but in case you ever want it, it's all there for you.

You can use these device object instances to modify the range of each axis. For example, if you want your joystick to range from -10,000 to 10,000 rather than 0 to 65,535, you can set it using the DirectInput.Device.Properties.SetRange function.

The first step is to enumerate all the device object instances to find all the axes:

```
foreach( DirectInput.DeviceObjectInstance inst in gameinput.Objects )
{
```

This enumerates every instance inside of a foreach loop, using inst to represent each instance. The DirectInput.Device.Objects property returns a list of these instances.

For each instance, you need to check to make sure it's an axis:

```
if( (inst.ObjectId & (int)DirectInput.DeviceObjectTypeFlags.Axis) != 0 )
{
```

Using the ObjectId data binary anded with a DirectInput.DeviceObjectTypeFlags value, you can also check to see other properties, like if it's a Button, or a Pov, or any number of other things that you probably don't care about.

Once you know you've got an axis, you can set the range of the axis:

```
gameinput.Properties.SetRange(
    DirectInput.ParameterHow.ById,
    inst.ObjectId,
    new DirectInput.InputRange( -10000, 10000 ) );
```

This is kind of convoluted because you're not allowed to just change the object instance yourself. Instead, you have to access the DirectInput.Device.Properties.SetRange function to set a new range using the object instance's ObjectId property. You can see that the code sets the input range to -10,000 to 10,000, meaning that every axis will now have that range, with the center being 0, which makes a whole lot more sense than the default range.

note

Using a range like this makes sense for traditional axes of a joystick, but there's one exception to the rule: throttle sliders. Typically you want throttle sliders to range from 0 to some large number (10,000 perhaps? It's up to you), rather than some large negative number to another large number, because there's no such thing as a "negative throttle" in the real world. The choice, as always, is yours.

The Dead Zone

You should also be concerned with is the *dead zone*. No, I'm not talking about a Stephen King book; I'm talking about an actual property of an axis. A dead zone is a zone in which a particular axis will return a zero-value, even when it's not actually zero.

If you know how a joystick works, then the device usually has the stick in a center position; if you move it anywhere and then let go, a spring will make the stick go back to the center position automatically. Ideally, you want the center position to be exactly 0 when the joystick is not moved, but in reality, this is rarely the case. Imperfections in the materials and other factors cause the joystick to almost always have values other than 0 when you're not touching it. Even though the values are small, they're still non-zero, and therefore the game thinks that the user is moving the joystick. This is rarely a good thing.

That's where the *dead zone* comes in. You can set it to whatever you like; a value of about 15 percent is usually good. Set it just like you set the range of your axis:

```
gameinput.Properties.SetDeadZone(
    DirectInput.ParameterHow.ById,
    inst.ObjectId,
    1500 );
```

The value passed in is a number from 0 to 10,000, where 10,000 represents the entire range of the controller. The previous code segment shows a range of 15 percent. Figure 8.3 shows a diagram of how a dead zone on a vertical axis works.

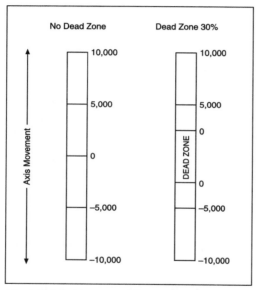

Figure 8.3 How axis values are reported when using a dead zone

More Joystick Data

So far, you only know how to obtain data about the various axes of a joystick, but there are still more input objects on a joystick about which you can get information, including button values and the POV hat values.

POV Hats

POV hats are like buttons, except that they can be moved in different directions; they commonly have four, eight, or even sixteen different values. On a four-value hat, the directions are commonly north, east, south, and west. With an eight-value hat, you get the addition of northeast, northwest, southeast, and southwest, and with a sixteen-value hat you get directions like north-northeast, west-southwest, and so on.

The DirectInput.JoystickState.GetPointOfView function returns an array of integers, each one representing a hat value. DirectInput 9.0 seems to be set at having a maximum of four different hats, but that could change, so your best bet is to determine how many hats are usable by viewing a device's capabilities. I show you how to do this in Demo 8.3.

The value for each POV hat is typically a degree value. If it's -1, then that means the hat is untouched (or doesn't exist). For a four-direction hat, the values are typically 0 (north), 9000 (east), 18000 (south), and 27000 (west). You should notice that those roughly correlate to degree angles multiplied by 100, with some minor differences: they go clockwise, rather than counter-clockwise as degrees usually do, and 0 degrees is north, rather than east.

note

Some joystick drivers use the value 65,535 rather than –1 to indicate that a hat is not pressed. Be on the lookout for that.

Buttons

Buttons on a joystick are very simple, and accessing them is just like accessing mouse buttons. The DirectInput.JoystickState.GetButtons function returns an array of bytes, wherein each byte can be 0 or 128, with 128 meaning the button is pressed and 0 meaning it is not.

Demo 8.3: Joysticks

Demo 8.3 is the most complex out of all the demos in this chapter so far, simply because joysticks are the most complex devices. I'm going to show you the ProcessInput function that retrieves all the available joystick data and prints out text telling you exactly what is going on.

The very first thing the function does is retrieve the device state and capabilities:

```
protected virtual void ProcessInput()
{
    // get device state
    DirectInput.JoystickState state = gameinput.CurrentJoystickState;

    DirectInput.DeviceCaps caps = gameinput.Caps;
    gameinputinfo = "Device Information:\n";
    gameinputinfo += "  Type: " + caps.DeviceType.ToString() + "\n";
    gameinputinfo += "  Axes: " + caps.NumberAxes.ToString() + "\n";
    gameinputinfo += "  Buttons: " + caps.NumberButtons.ToString() + "\n";
```

```
gameinputinfo += "  POVs: " + caps.NumberPointOfViews.ToString() + "\n";
gameinputinfo += "  Force Feedback: " + caps.ForceFeedback.ToString()
                 + "\n\n";
```

The gameinput variable is a DirectInput.Device that represents your joystick.

Using a device capabilities structure, you can obtain the type of the device (Keyboard, Mouse, Joystick, Gamepad, Driving, or any number of other values). Then you can retrieve the number of axes on the stick. There can be up to five axes on one device; typically, the first three are the X, Y, and Z axes; and the last two are the U and V axes.

Next the demo retrieves how many buttons there are, how many POV hats there are, and whether the device supports force feedback.

Once you show all the capabilities, you can get the device state:

```
gameinputinfo += "X: " +      state.X.ToString() + " ";
gameinputinfo += "Rx: " +     state.Rx.ToString() + " ";
gameinputinfo += "ARx: " +    state.ARx.ToString() + " ";
gameinputinfo += "AX: " +     state.AX.ToString() + " ";
gameinputinfo += "FRx: " +    state.FRx.ToString() + " ";
gameinputinfo += "FX: " +     state.FX.ToString() + " ";
gameinputinfo += "VRx: " +    state.VRx.ToString() + " ";
gameinputinfo += "VX: " +     state.VX.ToString() + "\n";
```

Most of the time, most of those variables will end up being 0, as I've mentioned before. The first variable, X, is the most important. The code is duplicated two more times, once for the Y axis and once for the Z axis, so there's no need to show you that code.

The next part of the code gets the U and V axis information:

```
int[] sliders = state.GetSlider();
int[] sa = state.GetASlider();
int[] sf = state.GetFSlider();
int[] sv = state.GetVSlider();
for( int i = 0; i < sliders.Length; i++ )
{
    gameinputinfo += "Slider " + i.ToString() + ": ";
    gameinputinfo += "Position: " + sliders[i].ToString();
    gameinputinfo += " Acceleration: " + sa[i].ToString();
    gameinputinfo += " Force: " + sf[i].ToString();
    gameinputinfo += " Velocity: " + sv[i].ToString() + "\n";
}
```

In my experience, the first array (sliders) is the only one you'll be concerned with; typically, the rest are empty. But for demonstration purposes, I've retrieved all of the arrays and I loop through each array, showing each slider value.

Now get the POV hat information:

```
int[] POV = state.GetPointOfView();
for( int i = 0; i < POV.Length; i++ )
{
    gameinputinfo += "POV " + i.ToString() + ": " +
                        POV[i].ToString() + "\n";
}
```

This simply loops through the array of POV values and prints out each one.

Finally, show the button information:

```
byte[] buttons = state.GetButtons();
gameinputinfo += "Buttons: ";
for( int i = 0; i < buttons.Length; i++ )
{
    if( buttons[i] == 128 )
        gameinputinfo += " Button " + i.ToString();
}
```

If a button is pressed, then "Button X" is printed out (where X is the number of the button); otherwise, nothing is printed.

The output for this program is shown in Figure 8.4.

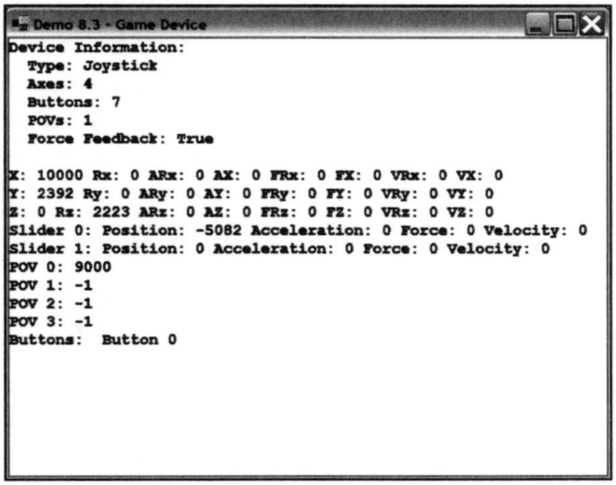

Figure 8.4 Output from Demo 8.3

Force Feedback

When I was a kid, there was an arcade game named *After Burner*. It was this really cool machine that you could sit in, and when you moved the controller around, the whole machine would move around, making you feel like you were actually flying the plane. Sort of. It may not have exactly replicated the 6Gs you'd get by pulling up as hard as you could while flying at a thousand miles an hour in a fighter jet, but even the limited movement was far more realistic than anything I'd ever felt or seen before. When you got hit by missiles or bullets, the whole machine would rumble and you really felt like you just hit something. This was why arcades were so much better than going home and playing the game on the Sega Genesis—you got that whole immersion experience.

Games you played at home on your computer and video game consoles didn't have anything like this full experience until years later, when Nintendo made the Rumble Pak, a little device that would sit in your N64 controller and vibrate whenever certain events occurred, like collisions. Nintendo made the N64 able to send data back to the controller, so that it became more than just an input device.

This rumble effect was the beginning of a whole revolution in game input technology, called *force feedback*. The idea of force feedback is to make the controller interactive—to send data back to the user. If you're flying a jet and your rudders are damaged, then the joystick may give you some resistance when you are trying to pull it up. If you're flying in a turbulent patch of air, the controls will shake; or if you're driving on a bumpy road, your steering wheel will pop up and down.

Force feedback makes your computer games much more realistic, and DirectInput makes it incredibly easy to use.

The Effect Editor

The DirectX SDK comes with a program called fedit.exe, which allows you to create various force feedback effects and save them to disk. It's really a simple program, and it makes your life easier; it even comes with a whole bunch of built-in effects, as well. The effects are stored in files called FFE files, for *force feedback effects*.

Figure 8.5 is a screenshot of the program in action.

The editor supports a number of different kinds of effects, the simplest of which is the *constant force* effect, which will apply a single constant force in the direction of your choosing.

If you insert one of these effects, it will point north by default and use the maximum power. If you press the Play button, you'll see the stick of your device move backward immediately and stay there until the effect ends. You can change the direction of the effect by going into its properties and messing around with the options in there.

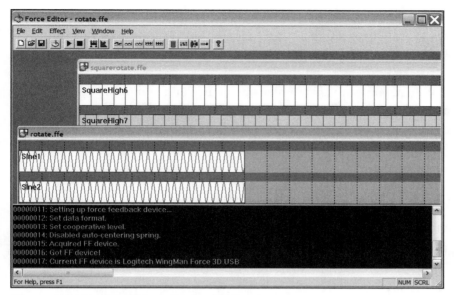

Figure 8.5 The DXSDK Force Feedback Editor program

There are a bunch of other effect types as well, such as a ramp effect that will linearly move the stick from one direction to another based on time, or various repeating patterns (sine, sawtooth, square) that move the stick back and forth according to a particular algorithm.

Then there are effects that make it hard for you to move the handle around, like friction, damper, and so on. Just play around with them and see what you can do.

Loading Effects

DirectInput allows you to load in effects from a file and play them, but the process is somewhat difficult, so I've created a helper class to help you along. The class is called AdvancedFramework.ForceEffect, and it can be found in the directory of Demo 8.4.

Essentially, an FFE file contains a list of effects, where each effect can be any of the effects I mentioned previously, like a sine wave effect, or a constant force effect. So the ForceEffect class will store an array of these effects, as well as the name of the effect:

```
public class ForceEffect
{

    System.Collections.ArrayList effectlist;
    string name;
    public string Name
    {
```

```
        get { return name; }
    }
    <code snipped>
}
```

Once you have all that, you can pass the filename of an FFE file into the constructor, as well as the name of the effect, and the device that you're going to be using it on:

```
public ForceEffect( string filename, string name, Device device )
{
    // save the name
    this.name = name;
    effectlist = new System.Collections.ArrayList();
```

This just initializes the name and the list of effects.

Next, you load a list of EffectFiles from disk:

```
    EffectList effects;
    effects = device.GetEffects( filename, FileEffectsFlags.ModifyIfNeeded );
```

An EffectList is just a list of EffectFiles, which are structures that describe an effect inside an FFE file. Once you have that list, you need to look at each one and load it into an EffectObject object:

```
    foreach( FileEffect e in effects )
    {
        EffectObject effect = new EffectObject(
            e.EffectGuid, e.EffectStruct, device );

        effectlist.Add( effect );
    }
}
```

Now effectlist has a bunch of EffectObjects in it, and that represents the entire FFE file.

Playing Effects

Once you have an effect list loaded, you need some way to actually play the effects; you do so with the Play function:

```
public void Start( int iterations, bool restart )
{
    foreach( EffectObject effect in effectlist )
    {
        if( !effect.EffectStatus.Playing || restart )
        {
```

```
        effect.Start( iterations, 0 );
    }
  }
}
```

The function takes two parameters: the number of iterations to make, and whether or not the effect should be restarted. For each EffectObject inside the list, the function checks to see if the effect is already playing. If it is, and you don't want it reset, then the effect isn't played; otherwise it is. Calling the Start function on an effect automatically resets it, so that's why you need to check it.

The Start function takes the number of times you want to repeat the effect as its first parameter, and a flag as its second. There are only two valid flags: EffectStartFlags.NoDownload, which disables auto-downloading of effects into the device (I'm not sure why anyone would want that), and EffectStartFlags.Solo, which stops everything the device is playing and starts the new effect. You probably won't want to use either of those flags, but it's good to know that they exist.

Stopping Effects

The next thing the class manages is the ability to stop playing an effect; this is an extremely simple process:

```
public void Stop()
{
    foreach( EffectObject effect in effectlist )
    {
        effect.Stop();
    }
}
```

Demo 8.4

Demo 8.4 is designed to show you how to use force feedback effects. It's pretty simple, as most of the hard work is already done within the ForceEffect class.

The first thing the demo does is declare some new variables:

```
ForceEffect[] effects;
string instructions;
int currenteffect;
bool lastfiring = false;
bool lastchanging = false;
```

The first is an array of effects, which will store the effects. Next are the instructions, which tell the user how to use the demo.

The currenteffect variable stores the index of the current effect that is being used, and the last two Booleans are used to determine whether a button state has changed since the last frame. You'll see how these work in just a bit.

Setting Up the Device

There are two changes you need to make to your code that sets up a DirectInput device: you must make it search for force-feedback devices, and make it acquire the device in exclusive mode. This should probably be obvious to you, but I'll say it anyway: trying to run force feedback effects on a non-force feedback device will cause errors.

DirectInput requires that force feedback effects be used only on exclusive devices—two programs can't be using a device at the same time if you're using feedback effects. So here's the new setup code:

```
foreach( DirectInput.DeviceInstance i in
    DirectInput.Manager.GetDevices(
    DirectInput.DeviceClass.GameControl,
    DirectInput.EnumDevicesFlags.AttachedOnly |
    DirectInput.EnumDevicesFlags.ForceFeeback ) )
{
    gameinput = new DirectInput.Device( i.InstanceGuid );
    gameinput.SetCooperativeLevel(
        this,
        DirectInput.CooperativeLevelFlags.Background |
        DirectInput.CooperativeLevelFlags.Exclusive );
    gameinput.SetDataFormat( DirectInput.DeviceDataFormat.Joystick );
<code snipped>
}
```

The two important changes from Demo 8.3 are in bold.

Initializing the Effects

Thanks to the handy-dandy ForceEffect class, loading FFE files is a snap!

```
effects = new ForceEffect[3];
effects[0] = new ForceEffect( "gatling.ffe", "Gatling Gun", gameinput );
effects[1] = new ForceEffect( "pistol.ffe", "Pistol", gameinput );
effects[2] = new ForceEffect( "shotgun3.ffe", "Shotgun", gameinput );
```

That loads three FFE files meant to emulate Gatling gun fire, pistol fire, and shotgun fire. All three of these came with the DXSDK, and there are plenty more where they came from.

Gathering Input and Playing Output

The final step is to actually gather input and play the feedback out to the device, which is accomplished inside ProcessInput:

```
DirectInput.JoystickState state = gameinput.CurrentJoystickState;

if( state.GetButtons()[0] != 0 )
{
    if( lastfiring == false )
        effects[currenteffect].Start( 1, true );
    lastfiring = true;
}
else
{
    if( lastfiring == true )
        effects[currenteffect].Stop();
    lastfiring = false;
}
```

This first chunk of code returns the joystick state and checks to see whether button 0 is pressed. If it is, then it checks to see if lastfiring is false. If lastfiring is false, that means that the last time input was gathered, button 0 was up and this time it is down—meaning the button was just pressed. Therefore, the program tells the current effect to start playing.

The reason for the lastfiring Boolean is to tell exactly when a button is pressed down. Chances are, if you quickly press a button down, about 10–20 frames will be processed before you let go, and without that check you'd end up starting the current effect 10–20 times instead of just once. Likewise, the function figures out when you've stopped pressing the button and stops the effect.

The second joystick button is used in a similar manner to change the current effect:

```
if( state.GetButtons()[1] != 0 )
{
    if( lastchanging == false )
    {
        currenteffect++;
        if( currenteffect >= effects.Length )
            currenteffect = 0;
    }
    lastchanging = true;
}
else
{
```

```
    lastchanging = false;
}
```

And finally, the instructions string is constructed:

```
instructions = "Press Button 0 to play an effect\n";
instructions += "Press Button 1 to change the effect\n";
instructions += "Current effect: " + effects[currenteffect].Name;
```

This demo produces the output shown in Figure 8.6.

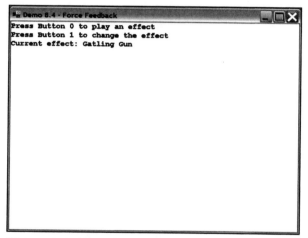

Figure 8.6 The output from Demo 8.4

Summary

Who would have thought there was so much to be learned about input programming? It's certainly gotten a lot more complex than the olden days, when you simply just asked the keyboard what keys were pressed down. And I've got some news for you, too: DirectInput is even more complex than what you've seen here. DirectInput supports event-based input gathering, which I didn't show you because it requires knowledge of threading, which is a topic I didn't have room to get to in this book. But you should now know enough about DirectInput to be able to write code for almost any input device you want to use.

What You Learned

The main concepts that you should have picked up from this chapter are:

- How to get information from keyboards.
- How to get information from mice.

- How to get information from game devices like joysticks and steering wheels.
- How to use force feedback to send data back to a game device.

Review Questions

These review questions test your knowledge on the important concepts exposed to you in this chapter. The answers can be found in Appendix A.

8.1. DirectInput supports two methods of input gathering. What method was shown in this chapter?

8.2. True or False: A keyboard will tell you about every key that is pressed down when you poll it.

8.3. What is the third axis typically used for on a mouse?

8.4. Name the four different types of input objects that a game device can have.

8.5. Can force feedback devices be created non-exclusively?

On Your Own

There were a few major topics that I didn't get to in this chapter. One of them is *action mapping*. Action mapping is an advanced concept that allows you to associate certain events on a device to actions in your game, and it makes re-mapping input keys in your game extremely easy to do. You should look into this concept on your own, and play around with it.

You might also want to look into multithreading and using event-based input handling, in order to get an idea of how they work.

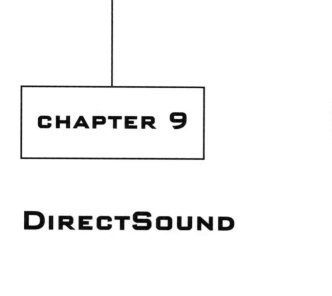

CHAPTER 9

DirectSound

You know how to show graphics and how to get user input, but you still haven't learned one major portion of game programming: how to use sound in your games. In this chapter, I'll remedy that situation by teaching you the basics of DirectSound, DirectX's sound API.

In this chapter, you will learn:

- How to create a sound device.
- How to load a wave from disk.
- How to play a sound buffer.
- How to fine-tune your buffers.
- How to process sound effects.
- How to use 3D sound.

The Sound Device

As with Direct3D and DirectInput, the fundamental class in DirectSound is Device, which represents your sound card.

Creating a sound device is really quite simple:

```
DirectInput.Device sound;
sound = new DirectSound.Device();
sound.SetCooperativeLevel( this, DirectSound.CooperativeLevel.Priority );
```

Just create a sound device and set the cooperation level. Remember that the sound device is shared across the entire operating system, so you have to tell it how you want to cooperate with other programs. For a game, you're going to want to use the Priority level because it gives you a decent level of access to the sound card.

Sound Buffers

The basic unit of sound in DirectSound is a buffer. A *sound buffer* is an object that holds wave data, which the sound card uses to play out to the speakers. There are two kinds of sound buffers: primary buffers and secondary buffers.

Every program has one primary buffer, which is created by DirectSound and managed automatically for you. This buffer is represented by the Buffer class, and it will perform mixing of secondary buffers.

Secondary buffers will hold individual sounds that you want to play; they are represented by the SecondaryBuffer class. You're going to be working with secondary buffers most of the time.

Loading a WAV file into a secondary buffer and playing it is amazingly simple:

```
DirectSound.SecondaryBuffer wave;
wave = new DirectSound.SecondaryBuffer( "laser1.wav", sound );
wave.Play( 0, DirectSound.BufferPlayFlags.Default );
```

The secondary buffer constructor takes the name of the wave file you want to load and a reference to the sound device, which I named sound.

Playing Buffers

The Play function takes two parameters: a priority value (you're safe using 0, which is the highest priority) and a flag that represents how the buffer should be played. Table 9.1 lists the available flags.

Table 9.1 BufferPlayFlags **Values**

Value	Meaning
Default	Use default settings
Looping	The sound is played repeatedly until it is stopped manually
LocateInHardware	Play this sound in a hardware buffer
LocateInSoftware	Play this sound in a software buffer
TerminateByTime	If the hardware is full, the sound with the least time left is stopped, and this sound starts playing
TerminateByDistance	If the hardware is full, then the sound furthest away from the user is stopped
TerminateByPriority	If the hardware is full, then the sound with the lowest priority (highest number) is stopped

You'll probably just end up using the default value for everything. A hardware device can mix only a certain number of sounds at any given time. Most sound cards can handle around 32 different sounds. If, however, you end up needing more than 32 buffers, the default flag will automatically begin mixing the rest of the sounds in software, which takes extra processing time. It's not that big of a deal, though, because sound processing is relatively cheap nowadays. But you'll rarely need to have more than 32 sounds playing at once.

Buffer Descriptions

Creating a buffer using the method I showed you is okay for simple stuff, but it doesn't allow for much customization. In order to customize your buffers, you need to fill out a BufferDescription object. These objects have lots of variables; the important ones are listed in Table 9.2.

Table 9.2 Important BufferDescription **Values**

Value	Meaning
BufferBytes	Size of the buffer in bytes. Can be left to 0 when loading a wave file.
Control3D	Can be manipulated in 3D
ControlEffects	Can be manipulated with effects processing
ControlPan	Can be panned left or right. Can't be used with 3D processing.
ControlVolume	Controls buffer's volume
DeferLocation	Places buffer in either hardware or software when being played
GlobalFocus	If true, will play even when your window is minimized. (By default, buffers don't play when your window has no focus.)
StickyFocus	If true, will play when your window is not in focus, but only if the currently focused window isn't using DirectSound.

Many more values exist than what's listed in the table, but you probably won't be concerned with them.

Here's how to create a sound buffer that supports sound effects:

```
DirectSound.BufferDescription desc = new DirectSound.BufferDescription();
desc.ControlEffects = true;
```

Once you set up your description, you can use it to create a sound buffer:

```
wave = new DirectSound.SecondaryBuffer( "laser1.wav", desc, sound );
```

Demo 9.1

Demo 9.1 doesn't really need a lot of explanation; in fact, loading and playing a sound is so incredibly easy that I'm not going to show you any of the code. The demo simply loads a wave file from disk and then plays it every two seconds. As usual, you can find it on the CD.

Sound Effects

Effects processing is a very neat thing. It used to be that you would just load wave files and play them, no matter what the environment of the game was. But doing that often gives an unrealistic effect. If a sound occurs in a closed sewer, then the sound should ricochet off of the walls and echo, whereas the same sound made outside in the open won't have any echo at all.

With effects processing, you can change how the sounds sound! You can edit a whole mess of different parameters to customize exactly how you want things to sound. These effect flags are located within the DSoundHelper class, and are listed in Table 9.3.

Table 9.3 DSoundHelper **Effect Values**

Value	Effect
StandardChorusGuid	Chorus effect; causes a "doubling" of the sound
StandardCompressorGuid	Compression effect; strips off certain amplitudes
StandardDistortionGuid	Distorts sounds by clipping tops of waveforms
StandardEchoGuid	Echo effect; causes sound repetition
StandardFlangerGuid	Similar to an echo sound
StandardGargleGuid	Causes a gargle-like sound
StandardParamEqGuid	Parametric equalizer; allows you to modify certain frequencies
StandardWavesReverbGuid	Causes the sound to reverberate

It's very easy to set an effect or any number of effects:

```
DirectSound.EffectDescription[] e = new DirectSound.EffectDescription[1];
e[0].GuidEffectClass = DirectSound.DSoundHelper.StandardFlangerGuid;
wave.SetEffects( e );
```

The first line creates a new array of effect descriptions. As I'm only using one effect, I only need one index.

The next line sets the class of the effect to a flanger, and the final line sets the effects of the wave.

note

Effects can only be applied to buffers that are not being played at the moment, so make sure you call the Stop function on a buffer before changing its effects.

Demo 9.2 is similar to Demo 9.1, except that it adds a flange effect to the sound and plays it repeatedly.

Sound in 3D

One of the newest sound technologies is that of 3D sound processing, and DirectSound makes it incredibly easy to manage.

3D Buffers

The key component of 3D sound is the Buffer3D class, which simply wraps around an existing SecondaryBuffer:

```
// create a secondary buffer first
DirectSound.BufferDescription desc = new DirectSound.BufferDescription();
desc.Control3D = true;
wave = new DirectSound.SecondaryBuffer( "explosion1.wav", desc, sound );

// create the 3D buffer
wave3D = new DirectSound.Buffer3D( wave );
```

First, you need to create the secondary buffer with the Control3D flag set. If you don't, then your 3D buffer won't be created properly. Once you do that, you can simply create a new Buffer3D object encapsulating your sound, and you're all set.

Now all you have to do is play the secondary buffer, and it will be processed in 3D automatically.

You can move the buffer around by changing its Position property:

```
wave3D.Position = new Vector3( 1, 0, 0 );
```

That sets the buffer one unit to the right, so that it will play out of the right speakers. Demo 9.3 basically moves the position of the buffer around using the movement of the mouse so that you can see how 3D sound works.

Additional 3D Topics

This is just a very basic introduction to the 3D component of DirectSound. There's actually a lot more to it than what I've shown you, but this is enough to get you started.

There are some additional points you should keep in mind when using 3D sound buffers, though. First, 3D sounds must be monaural, not stereo, so make sure the waves you load are in mono format. 3D sound is processed as a single source, and stereo sound is an artificial creation designed to simulate 2D sound, not 3D sound.

Another thing to keep in mind is that each secondary buffer can only be associated with one 3D buffer; in order to have multiple 3D sounds, each sound will require its own secondary buffer and its own 3D buffer.

Finally, it's very expensive to keep moving all the buffers around, so you may want to look into the Listener3D class, which allows you to move a listener and your buffers around at the same time, simulating a true 3D environment. Setting up a listener requires playing around with the primary buffer.

Summary

DirectSound makes sound even easier to use than it ever was before. I was amazed that I was able to piece together a simple 3D sound program without even breaking a figurative sweat!

Sound is a topic that many people tend to overlook, as it's so simple. Sound is a very important part of your games—it can really set the mood of your game.

What You Learned

The main concepts that you should have picked up from this chapter are:

- How to create a sound device.
- How to load a wave from disk.
- How to play a sound buffer.
- How to fine-tune your buffers.
- How to process sound effects.
- How to use 3D sound.

Review Questions

These review questions test your knowledge on the important concepts in this chapter. The answers can be found in Appendix A.

9.1. By default, do sounds play when your program is not in focus?

9.2. What is the difference between hardware mixing and software mixing?

9.3. True or False: You put your individual sounds into a Buffer class.

9.4. What do you put into a secondary buffer?

9.5. True or False: You are only limited to one sound effect per secondary buffer.

9.6. Can you use more than one 3D buffer per secondary buffer?

On Your Own

Look into using *Doppler effects* in conjunction with the `Listener3D` class. These are the effects that you experience when you're at a racetrack and you hear a car speed toward you and then speed away. As the car gets closer, the pitch of the sound gets higher because the sound waves are getting compressed; the pitch gets lower as the car speeds away because the sound waves are decompressed. Using Doppler effects can make your programs really neat.

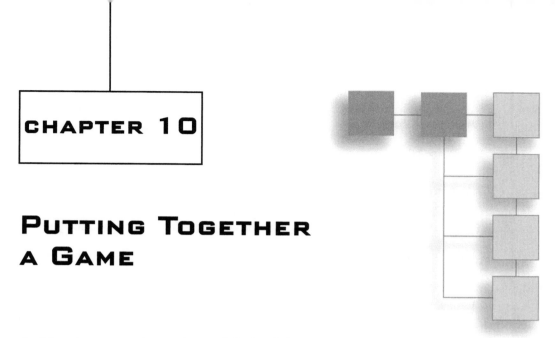

CHAPTER 10

PUTTING TOGETHER
A GAME

At this point—assuming you've read the book first and aren't some weirdo who starts at the last chapter—you should know enough about C# and DirectX to start piecing together your own game. There are literally millions of different kinds of games you can make, and I can't show you all of them; instead, I'll just show you how to make one simple little game.

This chapter will teach you:

- How to think about your design.
- How to visualize your universe.
- How to start small, and not bite off more than you can chew.
- How to think about how your actors are going to interact with each other.
- How to figure out what kind of data you need before you write any code.
- How *Generic Space Shooter 3000*'s data and game rules are arranged.
- How to build a better framework to suit your game programming needs.
- How to encapsulate game states into classes to make your programs more modular.
- How to use a stack to store game states.
- How to build your own arcade space shooter game!

Setting Up a Design

Many people, when they first start writing games, make the mistake of just sitting down at the computer and pounding out code as fast as they can. You could have gotten away with this approach back in the early days of game programming, but you really can't do that anymore. Sooner or later, you're going to get hit with a problem, and you're going to have to go back to the start of the code and figure out how to fix it. That is not fun, believe me.

To enjoy stress-free game creation, what you need to do is set up a general idea of what kind of game you want to write, what it's going to have, who is going to play it, and so on.

The Game Genre

The first question you need to ask yourself when setting out to plan your game is "What kind of game do I want to make?" Will it be a first-person shooter? An arcade game? A role-playing game? A puzzle game, or even a sports game? Maybe you're enterprising enough to think of a genre that no one has ever thought of before; if so, good for you!

One of the biggest mistakes a beginning game programmer can make is to bite off more than he can chew. It's easy to look at the new, top-of-the-line games and say, "Oh my god, I want to make something like that!" Everyone wants to be able to make his own *Doom III*. But a game like *Doom III* takes years of effort, dozens of people, and millions of dollars to make. As a beginning programmer, you probably don't have access to those resources. (If you do, drop me an e-mail—maybe we can work something out.)

But games can be fun without being megamaniacal monstrosities. A few years ago, people had the attitude that if a game wasn't bleeding-edge 3D, then it wasn't worth playing. Lately, companies like Popcap have shown that even small, simple games can be extremely fun.

Graphics alone don't make a game. Hell, games don't even need to have graphics. A game is defined by its gameplay, not how pretty it looks, and that's the first thing you should consider.

I suggest choosing something simple to start out with. The most important factor is that you choose a game simple enough that you can complete it. The number one cause of "de-inspiration" for game programmers is not being able to finish a game because it's too large. Think about it: You start trying to make some huge RPG, and you get a few weeks into it and realize you really haven't done anything spectacular—all of a sudden you've completely lost inspiration for completing the project, and it never gets completed.

If you need an idea of where to begin, go back to the old Atari, NES, and SNES games. Tons of fun games were made back in the days of those consoles, and most of those games are really simple to make. I've always been fond of the space shooter games, so that's the kind of game I'm going to design. It's called *Generic Space Shooter 3000*.

Deciding How the Game Works

You can say you want to make a space shooter or an RPG or whatever, but it won't do you much good until you figure out exactly what you're going to put into it and how everything is going to interact.

The Universe

Once you have decided on your genre, you need to think about the universe that your game is set in. If you're making a game that models some real-world concept (running around shooting things, flying airplanes, and so on), then this concept is pretty easy. In an RPG or action game, the universe is defined as everywhere the characters can go.

But things get a little different when you move into an abstract genre like puzzle games—you can't easily describe a universe in real-world terms. The universe, in that case, is simply the board/screen that the player will play on.

The idea for *Generic Space Shooter 3000* is pretty simple. The player is a spaceship flying around outer space, shooting things. The universe is simply outer space. There's really nothing elaborate going on, so I have a pretty open universe to make the game in.

The Actors

The next thing you need to consider are *the actors*—anything in the game that exists within the universe. Actors don't have to be actual animate objects, by the way; they're simply anything worth interacting with. If you can move rocks around on the ground in your game, then a rock is an actor.

For *Generic Space Shooter 3000*, there will be three major types of actors:

- **Spaceships** are the ships flying around, being controlled by the player or by the computer.
- **Projectiles** are defined as objects that cause damage to other objects, such as missiles or laser beams
- **Powerups** are simply objects that power up the player's vehicle.

The Data

Once you have an idea of the general layout of the game, you need to pound out exactly what kind of data your actors are going to have. I'll take you through the process of figuring out what data goes into *Generic Space Shooter 3000*.

Spaceships

This is going to be a simple shooter game, so spaceships won't need that much information. They're going to have *energy*, which indicates how strong the ship is. If the energy level ever drops to 0, then the player dies.

A common concept in games is flexibility—the more flexible everything is, the more you can change while the game is running, and you can give your players extra goals to reach.

Instead of saying, "All spaceships move at 200 pixels per second," you can say, "Spaceships can move at 200 pixels per second, but if they get a speed powerup, they can move faster!" In the interest of flexibility, spaceships in *GSS3K* will contain a speed variable.

Just to spice things up, I've added the concept of *shields* to the spaceships. A shield will diminish or erase damage—say, if the ship gets hit by a laser beam, the damage will be reduced so that it doesn't hurt the ship so much. Shield values will range from 0.0 to 1.0, where 0 will deflect no damage at all, and 1.0 will deflect all damage. To further spice things up, every time the player's shields get hit by something, they will be reduced by 0.02 (2 percent), meaning a ship can get hit 50 times before its shields are completely depleted. If the shields are at 0.5 (50 percent), then a 10-damage laserbeam will take off 5 energy points and 2 percent of your shields.

Spaceships will also have an array of weapons that the player can use, a variable containing the next time at which the player can fire his weapons, and a score variable.

Weapons

Weapons are simple objects that describe how projectiles are generated. Weapons simply have a sound that is played when they are fired, a delay time telling the player how much time the weapon needs to recharge itself, and a name. When weapons are fired, they are asked to return an array of projectiles.

Projectiles

Projectiles are the actual objects in the game that inflict damage; they're extremely simple objects. Projectiles simply store how much damage they inflict, and they have a reference to the spaceship that fired the projectile so that you can award points if the projectile happens to destroy anything.

Powerups

Powerups are the most abstract object in the game; they don't actually store any special data at all. Powerups simply have an abstract function that they apply to a spaceship whenever the player gets them.

Common Attributes

The three tangible object types in *GSS3K*—spaceships, projectiles, and powerups—all share some common attributes. First of all, they're all sprites, so they must have texture information as well as positions, scaling, angles, and so on.

Where have you seen these attributes before? The Sprite class from Chapter 7, of course! That's right, my custom Sprite class has all of those attributes, so all game objects will inherit from the sprite.

Game objects need more than just the attributes provided from the Sprite class, however. For the physics of the game, all game objects will store additional vector data representing the current x and y velocities of the objects, as well as the current x and y accelerations.

Other attributes are the collision rectangle and the destroyed Boolean. The collision rectangle is used to tell whether the object has collided with another object, and the destroyed Boolean is used to tell the game that the object has been killed, and therefore should not be used in any further calculations. You'll see why this is later on.

That pretty much sums up the objects of GSS3K, so now on to a new framework!

A Short Physics Lesson

Velocity and *acceleration* are very simple concepts. If you have an object whose velocity is defined as 10 meters per second in the X axis, then the object will be moved forward by 10 meters in the X axis every second. This is a simple calculation:

```
new position x = old position x + (10 ■ time elapsed)
```

If 0.3 seconds have elapsed, then three units are added to the object's x position.

Acceleration is a more advanced concept, but it's also easy to understand. Acceleration simply defines the speed at which an object's velocity changes. If you have an acceleration of one meter per second squared, it means that the velocity of an object will be increased by one meter per second every second. This is also a simple calculation:

```
new velocity x = old velocity x + (1 ■ time elapsed)
```

If you start off with a velocity of 10, then after one second the velocity will be 11, then 12 the next second, and so on.

A New Framework

The simple frameworks generated by most compilers achieve their purposes: to provide you with a simple place from which to build your program. Such frameworks are not terribly complex, and they're not really expandable, either—they're just something quick-and-dirty.

But a framework can be much more advanced and flexible. For example, almost every game out there uses the concept of a *game state*. A game can be in "Introduction" mode, "Playing" mode, "Show High Scores" mode, or any of a million other modes. The simple frameworks you've seen so far haven't made use of the game state concept.

I've gone ahead and designed a brand-new framework for you to use. It's not that complex, but it involves a fair amount of code, a lot of which I won't be showing you. All of the code is on the CD in Demo 10.1. The framework uses the new concept of states.

Setting Up

In previous demos, I've always just assumed that the resolution 640×480 is available. While there's a 99.999 percent chance that the resolution is available, that's still an assumption, and that's dangerous. I guarantee you that some player won't have that resolution on his system, and he'll track you down, demanding to know why your game won't run. So it's always a good idea to let the game check capabilities and let the user pick some options as well.

In the file Setup.cs on the CD, there's a form class that loads user preferences. The form lets the user select the resolution he wants to run in and the input device he wants to use. The code basically goes into Direct3D and DirectInput and asks them to list all the available devices. The setup form takes a DeviceOptions class when it's created, and fills the class out with the appropriate parameters, depending on what the user wants to use.

Device Options

The DeviceOptions class is simple (in Device.cs):

```
public class DeviceOptions
{
    // graphics
    public bool Windowed;
    public D3D.DisplayMode GraphicsMode;

    // joystick
    public bool UseJoystick = false;
    public Guid Joystick;
    public int JoystickDeadzone = 1500;
    public DI.InputRange JoystickRange = new DI.InputRange( -10000, 10000 );
}
```

The options allow you to define some configurable options for each device on the system. The graphics part, for example, determines whether the user wants windowed mode, and what display mode to use. The setup form allows both of these to be filled out.

The joystick part has a bit more information; it determines whether the user wants to use a joystick, and if so, it determines the GUID of the joystick. Remember the demos from Chapter 8? They simply picked off the first attached joystick; that was kind of stupid because a user may have more than one joystick installed. The DeviceOptions class (used in conjunction with the setup form I'll get to later on) allows the user to pick what he wants.

The deadzone and range are hard-coded to certain values, and the setup form doesn't allow you to change them. There's really no reason to, though. This class is simply a convenient place to put the device values.

Device Blocks

I've found that it's helpful to encapsulate all of the game devices into one class. I've done so, and I call it the DeviceBlock class.

```
public class DeviceBlock
{
    public D3D.Device Graphics   = null;
    public DS.Device Sound       = null;
    public DI.Device Keyboard    = null;
    public DI.Device Mouse       = null;
    public DI.Device Joystick    = null;
    public D3D.Sprite Sprite     = null;

    public void Initialize( DeviceOptions options, Game game )
    void InitGraphics( DeviceOptions options, Game game )
    void InitSound( Game game )
    void InitKeyboard( Game game )
    void InitMouse( Game game )
    void InitJoystick( DeviceOptions options, Game game )
}
```

I've cut out all of the code for the functions because you've seen 99 percent of it already, in Chapters 6, 7, 8, and 9. The functions simply initialize the devices using the given options.

note

Feel free to add more device options to the DeviceOptions class in order to make it more flexible. This simple version suits my needs, so I saw no point in going all-out and making the class ultra-configurable.

Input Checkers

Remember how Demo 8.4 used Booleans to determine exactly when a joystick button was pressed or released, transforming the "polling" input gathering process into a pseudo "event notification" system? That was kind of a pain in the butt, wasn't it? You had to have a Boolean variable for each button, and you had to check whether the Boolean changed.

I decided to encapsulate that behavior into classes called KeyboardChecker, MouseChecker, and JoystickChecker. Each class is different, and each handles a different kind of device. I'm willing to bet you can figure out which class handles which device. These classes are in Input.cs.

The code for the classes is long and boring and doesn't really show you anything that you haven't seen before, so I'll skip it and jump right into explaining how the classes work.

Keyboard Checking

The keyboard is a simple device, consisting only of buttons. Whenever a button is pressed or released, a message should be sent to an event handler.

The keyboard checker must be polled; you do this by calling KeyboardChecker.ProcessInput. This function gets an array of the buttons that are pressed down and compares this array with the buttons that were pressed down the last time ProcessInput was called. If any of the buttons changed, then the function sends out the button event.

Set up button events using delegates, like this:

```
KeyboardChecker checker = new KeyboardChecker( keyboard );
checker.PressEvent = new KeyboardChecker.KeyFunction( KeyDown );
checker.ReleaseEvent = new KeyboardChecker.KeyFunction( KeyUp );
```

KeyboardChecker.KeyFunction is a delegate for a function that takes one DirectInput.Key structure as its input. The previous code would then call this function whenever a key was pressed down:

```
public void KeyDown( DirectInput.Key k )
{
    // code to handle key press
}
```

Mouse Checking

Mice are more complicated than keyboards because they have buttons and axes, and you need to handle both. Buttons are handled in a similar manner to keyboard keys, except that instead of DirectInput.Key values, they use ints. For example:

```
MouseChecker checker = new MouseChecker( mouse )
checker.PressEvent = new MouseChecker.ButtonFunction( MouseDown );
// later:
public void MouseDown( int button )
{
    // handle button press
}
```

The checker also checks axis movement:

```
checker.MoveEventX = new MouseChecker.MovementFunction( MouseMoveX );
checker.MoveEventY = new MouseChecker.MovementFunction( MouseMoveY );
checker.MoveEventZ = new MouseChecker.MovementFunction( MouseMoveZ );
// later:
public void MouseMoveX( int delta )
{
    // x moved by "delta" units, handle that here
}
```

Whenever a mouse moves, the move events are triggered. However, if a mouse doesn't move, then the delta value is 0, and the events don't get triggered at all.

As with the keyboard, mouse checkers must be polled using the ProcessInput function:

```
checker.ProcessInput();    // call any events if they occur
```

Joysticks

The last class, the JoystickChecker, is very similar to the mouse checker, with one difference in behavior: The Joystick axis events are called every time the ProcessInput function is called. This is because joystick devices use absolute positioning—it's more useful to know *where* the joystick is positioned at all times than simply *if* it moved.

Joysticks have two button delegates and five axis delegates:

```
public ButtonFunction PressEvent;
public ButtonFunction ReleaseEvent;
public MovementFunction MoveEventX;
public MovementFunction MoveEventY;
public MovementFunction MoveEventZ;
public MovementFunction MoveEventU;
public MovementFunction MoveEventV;
```

These are used just like the mouse functions.

Game States

Games are *state machines*, meaning their states, or modes, are always changing. When you start up a game, it shows you the title screen and maybe the name of the company that designed it. This is the Introduction state. When you're actually playing the game, you're in the Game state. If you're playing around with options, you're in the Configuration state. Some games may even have many different kinds of playing states, as when the player must change user interfaces to go from different modes of gameplay.

Each state handles things differently. In the Introduction state, you might want all input to just exit and move on to a Menu state. In the Game state, when a button is pressed a gun is fired, but obviously you don't want that to happen in any other state. The Help state will show you a help menu explaining the game, so you don't want all the objects in the game being drawn; you only want to see a Help menu.

Having different states allows you to separate all of this kind of stuff into discrete chunks. A state object will handle input, process events, and draw the game screen, essentially encapsulating the ProcessInput, ProcessFrame, and Render functions from the earlier frameworks.

Let me show you the base GameState class, *sans* code:

```
public abstract class GameState
{
    protected bool graphicslost = false;
    protected KeyboardChecker keychecker = null;
    protected MouseChecker mousechecker = null;
    protected JoystickChecker joystickchecker = null;

    public GameState()
    public virtual void ProcessInput()

    protected virtual void KeyboardDown( DI.Key key )    {}
    protected virtual void KeyboardUp( DI.Key key )      {}

    protected virtual void MouseButtonDown( int button ){}
    protected virtual void MouseButtonUp( int button )   {}
    protected virtual void MouseMoveX( int delta )   {}
    protected virtual void MouseMoveY( int delta )   {}
    protected virtual void MouseMoveZ( int delta )   {}

    protected virtual void JoyButtonDown( int button )   {}
    protected virtual void JoyButtonUp( int button )     {}
    protected virtual void JoyMoveX( int delta )   {}
    protected virtual void JoyMoveY( int delta )   {}
    protected virtual void JoyMoveZ( int delta )   {}
    protected virtual void JoyMoveU( int delta )   {}
    protected virtual void JoyMoveV( int delta )   {}

    public virtual void LostFocus() {}
    public virtual void GotFocus() {}
```

```
    public abstract GameStateChange ProcessFrame();

    protected abstract void CustomRender();
    public void Render()
}
```

There is, obviously, a lot more to the class than just those three functions. Input processing is a major component of this class—it defines three input checkers and the functions to use with those input checkers. You'll note that all the input event functions are empty and virtual, allowing you to just override whichever ones are important to you later on and not have to code any of the others. If you don't care to read the V axis of a joystick (really, who does?), then you don't have to declare your own custom JoyMoveV function because the base GameState class already has one that does nothing.

Rendering is a little streamlined; there are two rendering functions: Render and CustomRender. Render is implemented in this class; it takes care of losing the device and all that other cool stuff so that you don't have to. Render calls the CustomRender function, which is up to you to define.

State Changes

The state system for this framework is *stack-based*, meaning that all states are stored on a stack. This is quite handy, and let me explain why. First, imagine a non-stack system: You start off the game with an introduction state—it shows the title screen and maybe an introduction movie or something—then the game switches to the Menu state, which allows you to start a new game, after which the game switches to the Game state. Figure 10.1 shows this.

When the Menu state is exited, the game destroys it and creates a Game state.

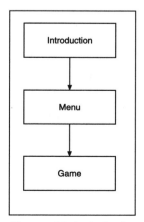

Figure 10.1 A simple state system

Now what happens when the user quits the game? In a non-stack-based system, the Game state is destroyed and the Menu state is created again. That seems like kind of a waste; the Menu state was already created at one time, so why destroy the Menu state if the game is just going to go back to it later on?

This is where a stack system comes into play: Instead of destroying the Menu state, you can keep it and put a new state on top of it—the Game state. Once the Game state is done, pop it off the stack and go back to the Menu state. Figure 10.2 shows this new method in a theoretical game.

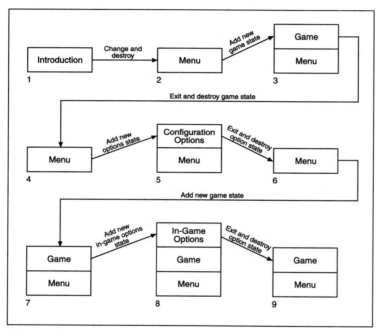

Figure 10.2 A stack-based state system

The stack allows you to suspend a state and then return to it at a later time without destroying anything.

The ProcessFrame function returns a GameStateChange class, which tells the game how the state should change. It has two variables:

```
public class GameStateChange
{
    public bool Terminated = false;
    public GameState NextState = null;
}
```

The Terminated Boolean tells the game whether the current state has been terminated or not. If so, the state is popped off the stack. The NextState variable holds a reference to the next state; if it's null, then the game should fall back to the state that is before it on the stack. Table 10.1 lists the behaviors.

Table 10.1 State Change Behaviors

Terminated	NextState	Behavior
false	null	Essentially does nothing because the state isn't terminated and there's no new state. There's no reason to use these parameters.
true	null	Current state is terminated, so the game should go back to the previous state. See transitions 3 to 4, 5 to 6, and 8 to 9 from Figure 10.2.
false	non-null	Suspend the current state and add a new state on top of the existing state. See transitions 2 to 3, 4 to 5, 6 to 7, and 7 to 8 from Figure 10.2.
true	non-null	Terminate the current state and go to a new state. See transition 1 to 2 from Figure 10.2.

A Sample State

I've provided a sample state in the State.cs file for you to examine. Here it is:

```
public class SampleState : GameState
{
    bool done = false;
    bool focused = true;

    public override GameStateChange ProcessFrame()
    {
        if( done == true )
            return new GameStateChange( true, null );

        if( focused )
        {
            // do processing here
        }
        else
        {
            // else sleep the thread to prevent eating processor cycles
            System.Threading.Thread.Sleep( 1 );
        }
```

```
            return null;
        }


    public override void LostFocus() { focused = false; }
    public override void GotFocus() { focused = true; }

    protected override void CustomRender()
    {
        Game.devices.Graphics.Clear(
            D3D.ClearFlags.Target, System.Drawing.Color.White,
            1.0f, 0 );
        Game.devices.Graphics.BeginScene();
        // do drawing here
        Game.devices.Graphics.EndScene();
        Game.devices.Graphics.Present();
    }


    protected override void KeyboardDown( DI.Key key )
    {
        if( key == DI.Key.Escape )
            done = true;
    }

}
```

This state simply draws a white screen and exits out when the user presses Escape. This is pretty much the same behavior you saw from the very first framework, except now it's encapsulated into its very own state object instead of being inside the Game class.

The Game Class

Finally, there's the old Game class, which provides the entry point for your program. Some parts of it have been changed a lot, and others not at all. First there's the data:

```
public class Game : Form
{
    static string gametitle = "Demo 10.1 - Framework V3";

    public static DeviceOptions options = new DeviceOptions();
    public static DeviceBlock devices = new DeviceBlock();

    static System.Collections.Stack states = new System.Collections.Stack();
```

```
    static GameState state = null;
<snip>
}
```

The game title is there again, but everything else is different.

Game options and a device block (which hold all of your device options and devices) are in there as well. The devices and device options are public-static so that everything in your game can access them; so if any part of your program needs a graphics device, it can get it by accessing Game.devices.Graphics. While it's generally bad practice to have global objects, it's not a big deal in this case because there are not a lot of real-world situations in which a player will need to access different sets of devices on the same machine.

There are also state objects: a stack of states and state, which stores the current state. state is just a helper that makes it easier to get the current state. Instead of constantly coding (GameState)states.Peek(), you can just write state instead.

Changing States

There are two functions that govern the changing of states: StateChange and AddState. StateChange takes a GameStateChange object and changes the state using that object; and AddState simply takes a new GameState object and switches to it.

Here's StateChange:

```
void StateChange( GameStateChange change )
{
    // current state is terminated, pop it off
    if( change.Terminated )
        states.Pop();

    // push on the new state, if any
    if( change.NextState != null )
        states.Push( change.NextState );

    // if any states in stack, set to top
    if( states.Count != 0 )
        state = (GameState)states.Peek();
    else
        state = null;
}
```

The code is pretty self-explanatory. The only part you might be concerned with is the last one. If there are no more states in the stack, then state is set to null. This means that the game is over, and that the game loop will check to see if state is null. You'll see this behavior later on.

The other function:

```
void AddState( GameState newstate )
{
    states.Push( newstate );
    state = newstate;
}
```

The Game Loop

The game loop is very similar to the loop from the old framework you've seen previously, except that it uses states instead of hard-coded functions. Take a look at it:

```
public void Run()
{
    // define a state change so we're not constantly creating
    // one on the stack
    GameStateChange result = null;

    // loop while state is valid
    while( state != null )
    {
        // render the current scene
        state.Render();

        // only process input while focused
        if( this.Focused == true )
            state.ProcessInput();

        // process a frame of animation
        result = state.ProcessFrame();

        // change the state if a state change is requested
        if( result != null )
            StateChange( result );

        // handle all events
        Application.DoEvents();
    }
}
```

In overall form, this game loop very similar to the old framework's Run function. The main difference is that instead of calling global Render, ProcessInput, and ProcessFrame functions, you're now calling those functions on the current state object.

The Entry Point

The last part of the framework is the entry point, which loads the game and runs it:

```
static void Main()
{
    Game game;
    try
    {
        // show the setup form to gather device options
        Setup setup = new Setup( options );
        setup.ShowDialog();

        // create a new game form
        game = new Game();

        // initialize the devices
        devices.Initialize( options, game );

        // initialize the game objects
        InitializeGlobalResources();

        // initialize the game state
        game.AddState( new SampleState() );

        // show the form and run it
        game.Show();
        game.Run();
    }
    catch( Exception e )
    {
        MessageBox.Show( "Error: " + e.Message + "\n" + e.ToString());
    }
}
```

This is very similar to the old version of the framework, with a few key changes. The first change is that the `Setup` form is created in order to gather user preferences. Once that is done, the game is created, the devices are initialized, the global resources are initialized, and the demo starts running a `SampleState`. That's pretty much all there is to it!

Generic Space Shooter 3000

Generic Space Shooter 3000 is based on the new framework you just learned about, which makes it pretty easy to design a game.

Game Objects

In the next subsections, I'll describe all of the various game objects that are created and used throughout *GSS3K*.

The Loader

The very first object I created for *GSS3K* was a game object loader, which loads all of the game resources. In *GSS3K*, the game loader is all hard-coded, which is actually not the best way to go about it, but will work for the purposes of this book.

> **tip**
>
> Instead of hard-coding your game resources, it's better to have *resource file lists,* which are simply files that tell the game which resources it should load. Better yet, you could create your own archive file, which would store everything you needed into one large file and tell the game how to load it all. Most modern games use this approach.

This loader contains helper functions and static variables that will be used as templates in the game.

Here's part of the class with all of the code cut out:

```
public class GameObjectLoader
{
    // define all the textures
    public static D3D.Texture[] ShipTextures;
    public static D3D.Texture[] ProjectileTextures;
    public static D3D.Texture[] PowerupTextures;
    public static D3D.Texture[] PowerBars;

    public static DS.SecondaryBuffer[] Bloops;
    public static DS.SecondaryBuffer[] FiringSounds;
    public static DS.SecondaryBuffer[] Explosions;
```

The class has numerous arrays of textures and sound buffers. These contain, as you would imagine, textures and sound buffers for all of the objects in the game. All of these objects are loaded using the following functions:

```
    // load all the objects
    public static void LoadObjects()
```

```
static void LoadTextures()
static void LoadSounds()

// helpers:
public static D3D.Texture LoadTexture( string filename )
public static DS.SecondaryBuffer LoadSound( string filename )
```

The last two functions contain code you've seen before; they exist only to simplify the loading of textures and sounds, so you don't have to mess up your code trying to remember a million different parameters. I'm going to show you a bit of the LoadObjects function later on; for now, let me show you the rest of the class:

```
public static Powerup RandomPowerup()

// static templates:
public static Spaceship Player = new Spaceship( 100, 200.0f, 0.5f, 0 );
public static Spaceship Enemy0 = new Spaceship( 5, 0, 0.0f, 10 );
public static Spaceship Enemy1 = new Spaceship( 10, 0, 0.0f, 15 );
public static Spaceship Enemy2 = new Spaceship( 15, 0, 0.0f, 20 );
public static Spaceship[] Enemies =
    new Spaceship[3] { Enemy0, Enemy1, Enemy2 };

public static Projectile Laser = new Projectile();
public static Projectile Plasma = new Projectile();
public static Projectile Missile = new Projectile();
}
```

RandomPowerup returns a new random PowerUp object, which I will get to later on. The rest of the objects listed are all templates, static Spaceships and Projectiles that will be used to generate actual game objects.

As you can see in the code, there are four different kinds of spaceships and three different kinds of projectiles. The values used for the spaceships will become apparent later on, when I show you the Spaceship class.

For now, I'll show you a bit of the LoadObjects function:

```
public static void LoadObjects()
{
    LoadTextures();
    LoadSounds();

    // set player textures and sizing
    Player.Texture = ShipTextures[1];
    Player.Scale = 0.25f; Player.Center();
```

```
        Player.AddWeapon( new LaserWeapon() );
<snip>
}
```

The static Player object is created at load-time, when your program runs. As Player is a static, it is created and its constructor is called even before your program runs the Main function.

Keep in mind that a Player is a Spaceship, which is a GameObject, which in turn is a Sprite, which contains a Texture object. You can't create a texture without a graphics device, and you don't want to create a graphics device before you get options from the user, which means that the Player object is created before the textures are even loaded into the game. This has the unfortunate result of requiring the game to go back and set the Player texture later on, which is precisely what the LoadObjects function does.

When you create the Player object with

```
    public static Spaceship Player = new Spaceship( 100, 200.0f, 0.5f, 0 );
```

you can only set options like its energy, speed, shields, and score. You can't set its texture because the textures haven't even been loaded yet.

This is where the LoadObjects function comes in. It loads all of the textures and sounds, and then sets the texture of the Player and the scale, then tells Player to center itself, and adds a LaserWeapon.

note

Ship textures are at 256×256, which are huge for sprites. For *GSS3K*, they've been scaled to 25 percent of the size, making them 64×64. This is the kind of data that you should be storing on disk, however, and not hard-coding into the game. This is just a quick-and-dirty solution.

The rest of the function is similar; it loads the other ships and the projectile templates.

The Base Game Object Class

I touched on this earlier: Most of the game objects (the Spaceships, Projectiles, and PowerUps, in particular) share many common attributes, such as physics data and sprite data. Therefore, it's logical to create a base class for all of these objects. Here it is, with the code cut out of it:

```
public class GameObject : Sprite, System.ICloneable
{
    // data:
    bool destroyed = false;
    float vx, vy, ax, ay;
    System.Drawing.Rectangle bounding;
```

```
    // properties:
    public float VX
    public float VY
    public float AX
    public float AY
    public bool Destroyed

    // functions:
    public bool Collide( GameObject other )
    public void CalculateBounding()
    public void Move( float timedelta )
    public object Clone()
}
```

As I stated before, the class has velocity and acceleration data, as well as a Boolean denoting whether it has been destroyed or not. All of these values have accessor properties as well.

Each game object also has a System.Drawing.Rectangle, which will hold a rectangle representing the object in *world space*. The reason they all have a rectangle is that the Rectangle class has *bounds checking*—you can call a function to see if one rectangle intersects with another. If it does, then you know the objects have collided; this knowledge becomes particularly useful later, when you want to determine if a laser has hit a ship, or a ship has picked up a powerup, and so on.

The Collide function checks the rectangles to see whether they collided, but there's one catch: the function does not recalculate the rectangles for you. You must do this on your own, using the CalculateBounding function. I'll go into detail on this when I show you the collision system.

The Move function performs the simple physics calculations on the object, based on a time value:

```
public void Move( float timedelta )
{
    VX += AX ■ timedelta;
    VY += AY ■ timedelta;
    X += VX ■ timedelta;
    Y += VY ■ timedelta;
}
```

The new velocity is calculated and then the new position is calculated, both based on the time delta value passed in. The time value passed in should represent the time (in seconds) since the last time the object was moved.

The final function is the `Clone` function, which you get from inheriting the `ICloneable` interface. You have to implement it yourself, however:

```
public object Clone( )
{
    return MemberwiseClone();
}
```

This simply calls the `MemberwiseClone` function, which you get from the `Object` class. `MemberwiseClone` simply copies all of the references of the object and places them into a new object and returns it.

note

The process of copying the references into a new object and returning it is known as a *shallow copy* because everything is only copied on one level. Let me give you an example: As the `GameObject` class inherits from `Sprite`, it has a `Direct3D.Texture` reference in it. This shallow copy will create a brand-new `GameObject`, but that new object will point to the same texture object as the original does. The opposite of the shallow copy process is a *deep copy*. A deep copy of a game object would actually create a brand-new texture identical to the original texture, and the new object will point to the new texture instead of having two objects pointing at the same texture. You must implement deep copies yourself because C# doesn't provide an automatic method for doing so.

The Spaceship Class

Spaceships are the most complex of the game objects and have the most data in them. Here's a listing of the data:

```
public class Spaceship : GameObject
{
    float energy;
    float speed;
    float shields;
    float nextfire = 0;
    System.Collections.ArrayList weapons = new System.Collections.ArrayList();
    int currentweapon = 0;
    int score;
<snip>
}
```

All of the data has been described before, when I went over what data the game objects will have. Some of the variables that ships have are energy, speed, shields, the next firing time, an array-list of weapons, the index of the current weapon, and the score of the ship.

None of these variables is public, and for a very good reason: The spaceships use properties to enforce that certain values don't go above or below given values. For example, the energy of a ship can't go above 100, and if it goes to 0 or below, the ship is destroyed. Furthermore, whenever the energy of a ship is decreased, the damage amount needs to be scaled based on the current shield value.

That's a lot of extra processing; I take care of it all using the Energy property:

```
public float Energy
{
    get { return energy; }
    set
    {
        // figure out how much energy is changing
        float delta = value - energy;

        // energy drain, calculate shield absorption
        if( delta < 0 )
        {
            delta *= (1.0f - Shields);
            Shields -= 0.02f;
        }

        energy += delta;

        // make sure energy doesn't go below 0 or above 100
        if( energy <= 0 )
        {
            Destroyed = true;
            energy = 0;
        }
        if( energy > 100.0f )
            energy = 100.0f;
    }
}
```

That's a lot of code, but it makes absolutely certain that the rules are always enforced. The get code is pretty simple; it just returns the raw energy value.

The set code is where all the magic is done. First it figures out the *delta* value, or how much the energy is changing. This is particularly important because if the energy is being drained, then the shields should take some of that damage. If the shields are taking the damage, the delta value is multiplied by the shields' absorption rate. If the shields are at 1.0, for example, then the delta is multiplied by 0, meaning exactly 0 damage is done to the energy; then the shields are decreased in power by 2 percent. After that, the delta is added to the raw energy value, and the function checks to see if the energy went below 0 or above 100, in which case more operations must be performed. If the energy went below 0, then the ship is destroyed and the energy is reset to 0 (for cleanliness' sake). If the energy went above 100, then it is set back to 100.

note

You could find a way to use the extra energy, rather than letting it go to waste. Perhaps you could have a special "reserve tank" add-on to the ship, into which all extra energy would be tossed. The possibilities are really endless. Always think about expansion.

The Shields property is simpler; it just makes sure the energy can't go below 0 or above 1. The CurrentWeapon property is get only (no set function); it simply goes into the weapons array and returns a reference to the current weapon.

Here's the rest of the functions in the class, with code removed:

```
public void NextWeapon()
public void PreviousWeapon()
public void AddWeapon( Weapon weapon )
public Projectile[] Fire( float time )
```

The first two functions change the current weapon to the previous or next weapon. AddWeapon simply adds a new Weapon object to the weapons, and Fire asks the current weapon for an array of projectiles—but only if the ship can fire. If the ship can't fire, then null is returned. Here's the code for the function that checks for that:

```
public Projectile[] Fire( float time )
{
    // no weapons
    if( weapons.Count == 0 )
        return null;

    // check the time
    if( time >= NextFire )
    {
        // get the weapon
        Weapon w = CurrentWeapon;

        // reset the firing delay
        NextFire = time + w.Delay;

        // tell the weapon to fire
        return w.Fire( this );
    }
```

```
    // can't fire yet
    return null;
}
```

The most important part of the code is the part where it checks the time. Weapons can only be fired at certain intervals, so if your code tells the ship to fire before it can fire again, then the ship needs to put its foot down and say, "No how, no way!" The weapon class needs a reference to a Spaceship when it fires because it needs certain information, such as current speed and velocity, in order to create its projectiles. Also, projectiles need to know about who fired them so that they can award points to whomever did so when something is destroyed. That's why a this reference is passed into the firing function.

Projectiles

Projectiles are really simple objects:

```
public class Projectile : GameObject
{
    int damage;
    Spaceship owner = null;
<snip>
}
```

I snipped out two properties, Damage and Owner, which simply get and set the values of damage and owner. Everything else a projectile needs is inherited from GameObject.

Powerups

Powerups are even simpler than projectiles:

```
abstract public class Powerup : GameObject
{
    public Powerup()
    {
        this.VY = 50;
    }
    public abstract void DoPowerup( Spaceship s );
}
```

Powerups set their default Y velocity to 50, meaning they'll scroll downwards at 50 pixels per second, just slow enough to let the player catch most of them. They also define an abstract DoPowerup function, which performs a powerup on a spaceship. Following are two powerup examples.

Energy Powerups

The first example is an energy powerup, which adds energy to a ship:

```
public class EnergyPowerup : Powerup
{
    public EnergyPowerup()
    {
        this.Texture = GameObjectLoader.PowerupTextures[0];
        this.Scale = 0.5f;
        this.Center();
    }

    public override void DoPowerup( Spaceship s )
    {
        s.Energy += 20.0f;
    }
}
```

An energy powerup uses powerup texture 0, and is scaled to 50 percent of the size of the texture (the textures are 64×64, so powerups end up being 32×32).

The DoPowerup function simply adds 20 energy to a ship, and that's it.

Shield powerups and speed powerups are almost identical to energy powerups; they just add shields or speed to a ship.

Weapon Powerups

The second example—and the fourth powerup type—is the WeaponPowerup, which adds a new weapon to a ship:

```
public class WeaponPowerup : Powerup
{
<snip>
    public override void DoPowerup( Spaceship s )
    {
        // find out how many weapons the ship has
        switch( s.Weapons )
        {
            case 1:
                s.AddWeapon( new DoubleLaserWeapon() );
                break;
            case 2:
                s.AddWeapon( new PlasmaWeapon() );
                break;
```

```
        case 3:
            s.AddWeapon( new DoublePlasmaWeapon() );
            break;
        case 4:
            s.AddWeapon( new MissileWeapon() );
            break;
        case 5:
            s.AddWeapon( new DoubleMissileWeapon() );
            break;
        case 6:
            s.AddWeapon( new LaserSpreadWeapon() );
            break;
        case 7:
            s.AddWeapon( new AnihilatorWeapon() );
            break;
    }
  }
}
```

I cut out the constructor; it was simply rehashing the same code you've seen before. The weapon powerup checks how many weapons a ship already has, and depending on how many weapons there are, adds a new weapon of a different type. So if a ship only has one weapon, then WeaponPowerup adds a double-laser weapon, and if the ship has two weapons, then WeaponPowerup adds a plasma weapon, and so on.

note

This is all hard-coded in, which, as I've said before, is inflexible. A better way to do this would be to have an advancement list for each kind of spaceship, or even have different powerups for each weapon type. For example, a laser powerup could add a double laser weapon, then a triple laser weapon, then a laser spread weapon, and so on. You're free to do whatever you want.

Weapons

The weapon system of *GSS3K* is pretty flexible because each weapon has been abstracted into its own class. You can program each class to do anything you want.

Here's the base Weapon class with the code cut out of it:

```
public abstract class Weapon
{
    // data
    float delay = 0;
    DS.SecondaryBuffer sound;
```

```
    string name;

    // properties
    public float Delay
    public DS.SecondaryBuffer Sound
    public string Name

    // constructor
    public Weapon( float delay, string name )

    public Projectile[] Fire( Spaceship owner )
    protected abstract Projectile[] CustomFire( Spaceship owner );
    protected void SetupProjectile(
        Projectile p,
        float vx, float vy,
        float ax, float ay,
        float offsetx,
        int damage,
        Spaceship owner )
}
```

Each weapon knows how long it takes to recharge, hence the delay variable. Weapons also make a sound when fired—that's why they have a DirectSound secondary buffer.

The interesting parts are the Fire, CustomFire, and SetupProjectile functions. Fire is a function that takes care of some housekeeping details:

```
public Projectile[] Fire( Spaceship owner )
{
    // play the sound
    Sound.Stop();
    Sound.Play( 0, DS.BufferPlayFlags.Default );

    // return a custom firing action
    return CustomFire( owner );
}
```

It plays the sound (stopping it first, in case it's already playing), and then calls CustomFire to actually return a list of projectiles. This is done so that your CustomFire function (which is abstract here) doesn't have to remember to play the firing sound. You can make your own weapon objects play additional sounds if you like.

SetupProjectile is a helper function that automatically sets up a bunch of information, such as velocity, acceleration, damage, and so on, for a projectile object. It's not really that important, but you can look at it on the CD if you want; it's in the Weapons.cs file.

Your Own Weapons

I've defined a bunch of custom weapons for you to use, but feel free to make your own. Here's an example of the simplest one:

```
public class LaserWeapon : Weapon
{
    // fire every 1/2 second, name "Lasers", and use firing sound 0.
    public LaserWeapon()
        : base( 0.5f, "Lasers" )
    {
        Sound = GameObjectLoader.FiringSounds[0].Clone( Game.devices.Sound );
    }

    protected override Projectile[] CustomFire( Spaceship owner )
    {
        Projectile[] values = new Projectile[1];

        values[0] = (Projectile)GameObjectLoader.Laser.Clone();
        SetupProjectile( values[0], 0, 400, 0, 0, 0, 5, owner );
        return values;
    }
}
```

This code needs a little explaining. The constructor creates a new sound buffer by cloning the existing FiringSound[0] buffer object; this is done because any given sound buffer can only make one sound at any given time. If you have two weapons using the same sound buffer and firing at almost the same time, then only one of them is going to make a sound. In order to duplicate the sound so that both weapons sound as if they're firing, the buffer must be cloned.

The CustomFire function creates a new array of projectiles that contains only one projectile, which is cloned from the Laser object. Now that you have a base laser projectile, all you need to do is set up the other values on it; this is done using SetupProjectile. In this particular case, SetupProjectile is making a laser that is traveling 0 pixels per second in the x direction and 400 pixels per second in the y direction, has 0 acceleration for x and y and an 0 x offset (you'll see what this is used for in a bit), and does 5 damage.

Finally, the projectile array is returned.

Here's a more complicated example:

```
public class DoubleLaserWeapon : Weapon
{
<snip>
    protected override Projectile[] CustomFire( Spaceship owner )
```

```
    {
        Projectile[] values = new Projectile[2];

        values[0] = (Projectile)GameObjectLoader.Laser.Clone();
        values[1] = (Projectile)GameObjectLoader.Laser.Clone();
        SetupProjectile( values[0], 0, 400, 0, 0, 28, 5, owner );
        SetupProjectile( values[1], 0, 400, 0, 0, -28, 5, owner );

        return values;
    }
}
```

This creates a "double laser," which is two projectiles. The main difference is the x offset parameters, which are set to 28 and -28, meaning the first projectile is moved 28 pixels to the right and the second is moved 28 pixels to the left.

There are other weapons defined, such as plasma, double plasma, missiles, double missiles, laser spread, and the annihilator weapon, as well. You can play the game or look at the code to see how these work out.

The States for *GSS3K*

The game will have four different states in it. The first state is the startup state, which shows the title screen. The next state is the obligatory "cheesy arcade shooter storyline" state, which opens up the game with a very vague background story. The most important state is the actual game state, which manages all the objects and physics and pretty much everything else. A final state takes care of the help menu, showing the user what keys to use to accomplish different tasks.

All of the states are stored within the GSS3KStates.cs file.

The Startup State

The startup state is very simple; all it does is load a texture from disk and display it for a few seconds. The state should also quit out if the user presses a certain key—you don't want to lock the user into looking at a title screen for longer than he wants to. (I just hate it when a game does that to me!)

The state will need a timer, a Boolean denoting whether the user wants to quit out, a texture, and a few vertices used to display the texture:

```
public class GSS3KStartup : GameState
{
    Timer timer;
    bool done = false;
    D3D.Texture loadscreen;
```

```
        D3D.CustomVertex.TransformedTextured[] vertexes = null;
<snip>
}
```

As you can see, this inherits right from the GameState class, gaining all of its wonderful built-in utilities. The only things this class needs to define are the following:

```
public GSS3KStartup()
public override GameStateChange ProcessFrame()
protected override void CustomRender()
protected override void KeyboardUp( DI.Key key )
protected override void MouseButtonUp( int button )
protected override void JoyButtonUp( int button )
```

I cut out the code for the functions. The constructor, GSS3KStartup, doesn't do anything spectacular; it simply loads a texture from disk and sets up the vertices to show it on the screen.

ProcessFrame is quite simple:

```
public override GameStateChange ProcessFrame()
{
    // return after 10 seconds or key pressed
    if( timer.Time() >= 10.0f || done )
        return new GameStateChange( true, new GSS3KIntro() );

    // sleep the thread to prevent eating processor cycles
    System.Threading.Thread.Sleep( 1 );

    return null;
}
```

Basically, ProcessFrame just waits for the timer to pass 10 seconds or until the player presses a key (which sets done to true, as you'll see in a moment). If either of those conditions apply, then a new game state is returned, telling the game to destroy this state and switch to the GSS3KIntro state.

You don't really need to see the CustomRender function—all it does is draw the texture on the screen the way you saw it done in Demo 7.4.

The input functions are quite simple:

```
protected override void KeyboardUp( DI.Key key )
{
    done = true;
}
protected override void MouseButtonUp( int button )
```

```
{
    done = true;
}
protected override void JoyButtonUp( int button )
{
    done = true;
}
```

Whenever a keyboard button, mouse button, or joystick button is released, the `done` Boolean is set to `true` so the state knows that it needs to exit when it gets to the `ProcessFrame` function. Wasn't that simple?

> **note**
>
> When you're changing states, it's generally a better idea to check if a button is released than if it's pressed. Whenever you switch to a brand-new state, new input handler objects are created. They're going to think that you just pressed down a key as well, as they have no previous state data to compare to, and the state will change much faster than you can release the key. The only way around this is to make the input checkers transfer key states from one state to the next; the framework doesn't handle this in its current state.

The Introduction State

I'm not going to spend much time going over the Introduction state, as it's just something really cheesy and simple I threw together to give the game an authentic 1980s arcade machine feel. It simply prints out a text string onto the screen, asking the player for assistance in defending a space outpost against space raiders.

Here's the data:

```
public class GSS3KIntro : GameState
{
    Timer timer;
    float next;
    bool done = false;

    D3D.Font typefont = null;
    DS.SecondaryBuffer beep = null;

    string fullmessage = @"... INCOMING TRANSMISSION ...\n
... CAPTAIN TYRAZIEL... PLEASE COME IN...\n
... OUTPOST GSK53-ALPHA IS UNDER ATTACK ... \n
... WE NEED YOU ...";
```

```
    string message = "";
    int stage = 0;
<snip>
}
```

The `fullmessage` contains the whole message, and `message` will contain a partial string. The idea is that you're receiving a text transmission over subspace communications (or something, it doesn't matter); you receive the transmission character by character, so it's printed out as you get the message. That's what `stage` is for—it keeps track of where the message is in terms of being received. If `stage` is 0, then you haven't received any part of the message yet, and if it's 10, then you've received "... INCOM," so that's what's going to be inside of `message`. The `beep` buffer contains the beeping sound, played for each character printed out.

note

> The @ symbol in the code may be new to you. It simply states that everything in between the double quotation marks following the @ sign should be read in literally from the file. This is an easy way to allow you to split up long strings onto multiple lines.

Here's the `ProcessFrame` function:

```
public override GameStateChange ProcessFrame()
{
    // exit when user presses a key, go to game
    if( done == true )
        return new GameStateChange( true, new GSS3KGame() );

    // add a new character if it's time and there are characters
    // left to add
    if( timer.Time() >= next && stage < fullmessage.Length )
    {
        stage++;
        message = fullmessage.Substring( 0, stage );
        next += 0.10f;
        beep.Stop();
        beep.Play( 0, DS.BufferPlayFlags.Default );
    }

    // sleep the thread to prevent eating processor cycles
    System.Threading.Thread.Sleep( 1 );

    return null;
}
```

The code basically adds a new character to message every 1/10th of a second, until there are no more characters left. Then the code sits there and waits for the player to press a key or a button, and then it switches to the Game state.

The Help State

The Help state is almost identical to the Startup state, except that it doesn't have a timer—it just sits there showing the help screen until the player presses a key or a button, at which point it destroys itself. The Help state sits on top of the Game state, so when it's destroyed, it doesn't start up a new state; instead, it goes back to the Game state.

The Game State

The Game state is by far the most complex state in the game, for obvious reasons. There are a lot of things that need to be taken care of; I'll start off by explaining the data.

```
public class GSS3KGame : GameState
{
    Timer timer;
    bool done = false;
    bool help = false;
    bool paused = false;
    System.Random random = new System.Random();
    float nextwave = 0;

    Camera camera = new Camera( GSS3KConstants.Width,
                                GSS3KConstants.Height );
    Camera UIcamera = new Camera( GSS3KConstants.Width,
                                  GSS3KConstants.Height,
                                  GSS3KConstants.Width / 2,
                                  GSS3KConstants.Height / 2 );

    Spaceship player;
    System.Collections.ArrayList ships =
        new System.Collections.ArrayList();
    System.Collections.ArrayList projectiles =
        new System.Collections.ArrayList();
    System.Collections.ArrayList powerups =
        new System.Collections.ArrayList();

    // are any of the key directions down? Joystick moved?
    // player firing?
    bool kl, kr, ku, kd;
```

```
    float jx, jy;
    bool firing = false;

    Sprite EnergyBar;
    Sprite ShieldBar;
<snip>
}
```

The timer and the done Boolean aren't new to you, but the help Boolean is. help is simply a flag that tells the state that the user requested to see the help menu.

The paused Boolean lets the state know if it's paused or not, and the random variable simply holds a random number generator. The nextwave variable holds the time at which the next wave of enemies will be generated. (I'll get into this in much more detail later on.)

Two cameras are created; one for the game and one for the user interface. The UI camera simply makes the coordinates 0,0 appear at the upper-left-hand corner of the screen rather than at the center.

note

You may have noticed the usage of a class called GSS3KConstants. This is a simple class that holds a bunch of constants, such as the playing field width and height, among other things. It makes your programs cleaner than does tossing in values of 640 and 480 everywhere.

There's a Spaceship representing the player, and then three ArrayLists in which to store all the spaceships, projectiles, and powerups.

The next block of code holds Booleans that determine which arrow keys are being held down, the last joystick values, and whether the player ship is firing. You'll see how all of this works when I show you the input section and the processing section.

Finally, there are two sprites, one representing the energy bar and the other representing shield bar, which will be used to draw the user interface.

Miscellaneous Functions

The class contains a lot of functions and properties that aren't very complicated; I'll just briefly cover what they do without showing the code.

The Paused property toggles the paused Boolean and starts or stops the timer, depending on what value you're changing the property to. This is very similar to what you've seen in the earlier frameworks.

The constructor, GSS3KGame, creates a player object and adds it to the ships list, and then goes ahead and creates the two UI bar sprites.

The LostFocus function (overridden from the GameState class) simply pauses the game. You want the game to be paused whenever the player switches the window.

NextWeapon and PreviousWeapon are called when the player wants to switch weapons. To switch weapons, the game simply plays an interface beep sound and then tells the player object to switch its current weapon.

Game Processing

The ProcessFrame function for the game state does a lot of work. That's not surprising, as it's where all of the game processing is done. Go figure!

I'll take you through the code step-by-step, starting with the state changes:

```
public override GameStateChange ProcessFrame()
{
    if( done )
        return new GameStateChange( true, null );

    if( help )
    {
        Paused = true;
        help = false;
        return new GameStateChange( false, new GSS3KHelp() );
    }
```

If the done Boolean is set, then the state should simply exit out without setting a new state. In this simple demo, the entire program will simply exit out. In a more complicated system, you may want to have a menu system underneath to fall back on.

If the help Boolean is set, then the game is paused, the Boolean is reset to false, and the state is changed to the GSS3KHelp state.

Continuing on, the game checks to see if it's paused and then performs the processing:

```
    if( !Paused )
    {
        // get amount of elapsed time
        float time = timer.Elapsed();

        // generate a new wave of enemies if it's time
        if( timer.Time() >= nextwave )
            GenerateEnemyWave();

        // game processing
        foreach( GameObject o in ships )
```

```
        o.Move( time );
foreach( GameObject o in projectiles )
        o.Move( time );
foreach( GameObject o in powerups )
        o.Move( time );
```

The amount of time that has passed since the last frame was processed is retrieved and stored into time. The next part of the code checks to see whether a new wave of enemies should be generated, and if so, it generates them.

Next, every object is processed using the Move function of the GameObject class, which performs the physics calculations.

In the next step, the game checks to make sure the player doesn't stray outside of the screen, and if so, it corrects the position:

```
// now correct the players position
if( player.X < GSS3KConstants.LeftBound )
    player.X = GSS3KConstants.LeftBound;
if( player.X > GSS3KConstants.RightBound )
    player.X = GSS3KConstants.RightBound;
if( player.Y > GSS3KConstants.BottomBound )
    player.Y = GSS3KConstants.BottomBound;
if( player.Y < GSS3KConstants.TopBound )
    player.Y = GSS3KConstants.TopBound;
```

note

A more efficient method of making sure the player doesn't stray outside the screen would be to only check these values when you know they change, rather than on every iteration of the game loop. For this simple game, you can spare the minor performance loss, but keep in mind that if you start doing bounds checking on many game objects instead of just on the player, you ought to find a better method.

And finally, the last part of the processing:

```
// perform the firing
DoFire();

// perform collision checking
DoCollisions();

// check to see if the validity of all the objects is ok
CheckValidity( ships );
CheckValidity( projectiles );
```

```
        CheckValidity( powerups );
    }
    else
        System.Threading.Thread.Sleep( 1 );

    return null;
}
```

DoFire performs all firing calculations, DoCollisions performs collision detection, and CheckValidity goes through all of the objects to see whether they've been destroyed. If so, the game goes ahead and destroys them.

If the game is paused, then the thread is told to sleep, so that you don't eat up all the processor cycles. Finally, null is returned, signifying that the state has not changed.

Performing Firing Calculations

As you saw before, the game encapsulates all of the firing calculations into one function: DoFire. The game is very simple and doesn't have any AI to speak of; in fact, the enemy ships simply move forward and continuously fire. It's pretty silly, but it works.

This function will go through every ship and tell it to fire:

```
void DoFire()
{
    Projectile[] plist;
    float time = timer.Time();

    foreach( Spaceship s in ships )
    {
```

At this point, the code will loop through all of the spaceships in the game and perform a simple check:

```
        // only firing if it's a non-player
        // or "firing" Boolean is true
        if( firing || (s != player) )
        {
```

Basically, the only time a ship *won't* fire is when the ship is the player and the firing Boolean is false. All other ships will fire, as they are computer ships. Then the function tells the ship to return a list of its projectiles, and if the list isn't null, it adds all the projectiles to the projectiles list:

```
        plist = s.Fire( time );

        if( plist != null )
```

```
        {
            foreach( Projectile p in plist )
                projectiles.Add( p );
        }
    }
  }
}
```

That's all there is to it!

tip

A more complex system would determine whether ships were firing on a case-by-case basis and wouldn't be checking every single frame, as it's not very often that a ship will fire anywhere close to once per frame. For this simple game, the system in place is not that inefficient, but for a larger game you would want to explore an event system, wherein the game waits until a ship *can* fire to see if it wants to or not, rather than constantly asking it "Can you fire yet?"

Object Validity Checking

When an object is "destroyed" in this game—whether it gets hit by a laser and dies, gets picked up by a spaceship, or whatever—the object isn't actually destroyed immediately. That would only cause a huge, ugly mess to untangle. Instead, the destroyed Boolean of the object is set to true, and the game will then remove the destroyed objects at a later time. The function that does this is the CheckValidity function, which takes an ArrayList of GameObjects and removes each one if it's destroyed:

```
void CheckValidity( System.Collections.ArrayList list )
{
    for( int i = 0; i < list.Count; i++ )
    {
        GameObject o = (GameObject)list[i];
```

Here you have a loop that goes through each object in the list, checking to see whether it's been destroyed:

```
        // only perform these actions on objects that are
        // explicitly destroyed by the game
        if( o.Destroyed )
            PerformDestroyActions( o );
```

There are two ways for an object to be destroyed in this game. The first way is to be explicitly destroyed (the ship is damaged by lasers, a powerup is picked up by ship, and so on), in which case the object's Destroyed flag is set. If this is the case, the game calls the PerformDestroyActions function on that object. The other way is to simply scroll off of the playfield, in which case the object isn't really "destroyed"—you just remove it from the gameplay.

The next part of the code simply removes all of the objects that fit the parameters:

```
if( o.Destroyed ||
    o.Y < GSS3KConstants.KillZoneBottom ||
    o.Y > GSS3KConstants.KillZoneTop )
{
    list.RemoveAt( i );
    i--;    // move back an index, everything is moved down
}
    }
}
```

Destroying Objects

If an object has been physically destroyed, then the PerformDestroyActions function is called on it. PerformDestroyActions does some extra processing on the object before it's finally discarded. For spaceships, the game figures out if a random powerup should be created and plays a random explosion sound:

```
void PerformDestroyActions( GameObject o )
{
    if( o is Spaceship )
    {
        GameObjectLoader.Explosions[random.Next(3)].Play(
            0, DS.BufferPlayFlags.Default );

        // 1/2 chance of powerup
        if( random.Next( 2 ) != 0 )
        {
            Powerup p = GameObjectLoader.RandomPowerup();
            p.X = o.X;
            p.Y = o.Y;
            powerups.Add( p );
        }
    }
```

For powerups, a powerup sound is played:

```
    if( o is Powerup )
    {
        GameObjectLoader.Bloops[0].Play(
            0, DS.BufferPlayFlags.Default );
    }
}
```

No action is required when a projectile is destroyed; however, you may want to think about adding force feedback effects in the future. If a projectile is destroyed, and it was the player's ship that was hit, then you might consider making the game play a force feedback effect on the player's joystick

Generating Waves

"Waves" of enemy ships are generated using the GenerateEnemyWave function. I'm not going to cover this in depth because it's not really that important as far as concepts you should be learning.

Basically, GenerateEnemyWave picks out a random integer and then generates a list of new ships based on that number:

```
Spaceship[] newships = null;

// choose a pattern
int pattern = random.Next( 0, 5 );

switch( pattern )
{
    case 0:     // one random ship
        newships = new Spaceship[1];

        newships[0] =
            (Spaceship)GameObjectLoader.Enemies[random.Next(3)].Clone();
        newships[0].X =
            random.Next( GSS3KConstants.LeftBound,
                            GSS3KConstants.RightBound );
        newships[0].Y = GSS3KConstants.SpawnZone;
        newships[0].VY = 200;
        break;
<snip>
// add the wave to the ships
foreach( Spaceship s in newships )
    ships.Add( s );
}
```

I only showed one pattern, because the code for each pattern is generally similar. The code picks out a pattern number, and then uses a switch statement to go to the appropriate code. The pattern I've shown here generates one random ship with a velocity of 200 pixels per second.

tip

You might want to consider making a file format that describes patterns and then generate ships using that file format, instead of hard-coding everything. The possibilities are endless that way, and you can easily add new patterns. Each pattern would indicate how many ships to generate, their relative positions, and so on.

Checking Collisions

Collision checking is one of the most complex parts of this game. There are generally only a few cases in which you're going to be concerned with checking, which are all handled inside of one function. First, you need to check ship-to-ship collisions to see if your ship runs into another. Then you want to check ship-to-projectile collisions, to see if any projectiles hit any ships. Finally, you want to check player-to-powerup collisions.

Note that I didn't say ship-to-powerup collisions—the game doesn't really care if an enemy ship collides with a powerup; enemy ships shouldn't be getting powerups anyway. Powerups are bonuses for the player and the player only, so you don't bother checking powerup collisions with every ship—just the player's ship.

Note also that there are no powerup-to-projectile collisions; this is just a personal preference of mine. If you want to be devious, you can add those in and allow the ability to destroy powerups by accidentally shooting them.

Here's the code:

```
void DoCollisions()
{

    // first calculate all the bounding rectangles
    foreach( GameObject o in ships )
        o.CalculateBounding();
    foreach( GameObject o in projectiles )
        o.CalculateBounding();
    foreach( GameObject o in powerups )
        o.CalculateBounding();
```

The first step is to calculate the bounding rectangles of every object. As the DoCollisions function is called once per frame after every object has been moved, you need to update the bounding rectangles of each game object, as the old rectangles for each object are no longer valid.

Now you can check ship-to-projectile collisions:

```
    // now see if any projectiles have hit any ships
    foreach( Spaceship s in ships )
```

```
{
    // only check non-destroyed ships
    if( !s.Destroyed )
    {
        // check all projectiles
        foreach( Projectile p in projectiles )
        {
            // only check non-destroyed projectiles
            // and make sure projectile isn't owned by the ship
            // either
            if( !p.Destroyed && p.Owner != s )
            {
                if( s.Collide( p ) )
                {
                    // we have a collision!
                    Collide( s, p );
                }
            }
        }
    } // end projectile checking
```

You don't want the function to look at any destroyed ships or destroyed projectiles because for all intents and purposes, those objects aren't part of the game anymore (even though they might still be in the arrays). Anything that has its Destroyed property set will be ignored, and removed from the game at a later time (it's a bad idea to remove objects from arrays that are currently being used).

You also want to check to make sure that a projectile can't hit the ship that fired it. If you do have a collision, then you should call the Collide function (which I'll get to in a bit).

Next, check ship-to-ship collisions:

```
foreach( Spaceship s2 in ships )
{
    // only check non-destroyed ships
    // and make sure ship isn't itself
    // either
    if( !s2.Destroyed && s != s2 )
    {
        if( s.Collide( s2 ) )
        {
            // we have a collision!
            Collide( s, s2 );
        }
    }
```

```
    }    // end ship collisions
}    // end ship/projectile, ship/ship collisions
```

The previous code segment is mostly the same as the ship-to-projectile collision checking code, except that the code checks each ship with other ships this time, rather than projectiles.

Finally, the last piece of code checks to see if the player collides with any powerups:

```
// check powerups
if( s == player )
{
    foreach( Powerup p in powerups )
    {
        // only check non-destroyed powerups
        if( !p.Destroyed )
        {
            if( s.Collide( p ) )
            {
                // we have a collision!
                Collide( s, p );
            }
        }
    }
}    // end powerup checking
    }
}
```

That's an awful lot of code, actually; the reason for this is all the special case checking. In a truly flexible collision system no special cases would exist, and things would know how to collide with one another, so you could simply have one loop that checked every object with every other object. Instead, you have three loops for each of the special cases. The choice of system is really up to you; I think for this game, a special-case system is better than handling collisions between objects that don't need to collide.

Colliding Ships and Projectiles

If a collision *does* occur, one of three Collision functions is called. The first is the ship-to-projectile collision function:

```
void Collide( Spaceship s, Projectile p )
{
    // hit the ship
    s.Energy -= p.Damage;
```

```
    // destroy the projectile; it can only hit one ship
    p.Destroyed = true;

    // if ship is destroyed, add points to whoever fired projectile
    if( s.Destroyed )
        p.Owner.Score += s.Score;
}
```

The ship's energy is reduced by the amount of damage the projectile can deal out, and the projectile is destroyed.

If the ship is destroyed, then the score of the ship that fired the projectile (p.Owner) is increased by the score of the destroyed ship.

Colliding Ships

Ship-to-ship collisions add an element of strategy to the game. Rather than killing ships by staying back and shooting lasers at them, you could instead become a *kamikaze* and ram into ships if you have enough energy.

This is the function that is called when two ships collide:

```
void Collide( Spaceship s1, Spaceship s2 )
{
    // the amount of damage done is the same as the amount of
    // energy a ship has left times 2.
    float e1 = s1.Energy * 2;
    float e2 = s2.Energy * 2;
    s2.Energy -= e1;
    s1.Energy -= e2;

    // modify points if either ship is destroyed.
    int score1 = s1.Score;
    int score2 = s2.Score;
    if( s1.Destroyed )
        s2.Score += score1;
    if( s2.Destroyed )
        s1.Score += score2;
}
```

The general rule for colliding ships is that the damage done to one is twice the current energy level of the other. So if I have 100 energy and I hit a ship with 10 energy, I'll whack him for 200 energy points, and he'll whack me for 20. If either ship dies, the score of the surviving ship is increased by the score of the dead ship.

Colliding Ships and Powerups

This collision function that allows for ships to collide with powerups is the easiest:

```
void Collide( Spaceship s, Powerup p )
{
    // powerup the spaceship
    p.DoPowerup( s );

    // destroy the powerup
    p.Destroyed = true;
}
```

The powerup is told to power up the spaceship and is then destroyed.

Need Input!

Johnny 5 is alive! Er...

Okay, the next part of the game state handles gathering input. Luckily for you, it's not all that hard.

The Keyboard

The keyboard is the default control of the game. I actually prefer using a joystick for this game, but alas, you can't expect your players to have a joystick, so you need to support the keyboard. Here's the KeyboardDown function:

```
protected override void KeyboardDown( DI.Key key )
{
    switch( key )
    {
        case DI.Key.Left:
            kl = true; break;
        case DI.Key.Right:
            kr = true; break;
        case DI.Key.Up:
            ku = true; break;
        case DI.Key.Down:
            kd = true; break;
        case DI.Key.Space:
            firing = true; break;
        case DI.Key.LeftControl:
            PreviousWeapon(); break;
        case DI.Key.RightControl:
            NextWeapon(); break;
    }
}
```

For the arrow keys, the kl, kr, ku, and kd variables are set to true when those keys are pressed down. You'll see how this works a bit later; for now, all you need to know is that those Booleans are true when a key is down, and false when the key is up.

Pressing the left Ctrl or right Ctrl keys switches the current weapon of the player.

Next is the complement of KeyboardDown, KeyboardUp:

```
protected override void KeyboardUp( DI.Key key )
{
    switch( key )
    {
        case DI.Key.Escape:
            done = true; break;
        case DI.Key.P:
            Paused = !Paused; break;
        case DI.Key.F1:
            help = true; break;
        case DI.Key.Left:
            kl = false; break;
        case DI.Key.Right:
            kr = false; break;
        case DI.Key.Up:
            ku = false; break;
        case DI.Key.Down:
            kd = false; break;
        case DI.Key.Space:
            firing = false; break;
    }
}
```

In addition to setting the arrow Booleans to false when the arrow keys are released, this also takes care of the Escape key, P key, and F1 key. Escape causes the game to exit by setting done to true, P toggles the pause status, and F1 turns on the help mode.

The Joystick

Joystick input is simple, as well:

```
protected override void JoyMoveX( int delta )
{
    jx = delta;
}
protected override void JoyMoveY( int delta )
{
    jy = delta;
}
```

The axis movement functions simply tell the jx and jy variables the current value of the joystick position. I'll get to this in just a bit.

The next piece of code handles button presses:

```
protected override void JoyButtonDown( int button )
{
    switch( button )
    {
        case 0:
            firing = true; break;
        case 1:
            NextWeapon(); break;
        case 2:
            PreviousWeapon(); break;
    }
}

protected override void JoyButtonUp( int button )
{
    if( button == 0 )
        firing = false;
}
```

The joystick buttons simply toggle firing (Button 0), and switching weapons (Buttons 1 and 2).

Processing Input

In the previous game state classes, there was no need to alter the GameState.ProcessInput function. The function simply called the input checkers, which in turn directly handled the input by way of the keyboard/mouse/joystick up/down/axis functions. You can't do that in this case, however, because the input hasn't really been handled. For example, when the user presses the Left Arrow key, the ship is supposed to move left, but that doesn't happen. Instead, a Boolean kl is set to true, and nothing else happens. The game is supposed to handle the player movement calculations later on.

The ProcessInput function, once it has gathered all the input, must actually process the input, which is why I override it:

```
public override void ProcessInput()
{
    // do the default input processing
    base.ProcessInput();
```

The first thing I do is call the base ProcessInput function, which simply tells the mouse, keyboard, and joystick input handlers to gather input. At this point, the kl, kr, ku, kd, jx, and jy variables will hold the states of the arrow keys and the joystick axis. Now it's time to actually do something with those values, such as calculate the X and Y velocity of the player's ship:

```
float vx = 0;
float vy = 0;

if( kl )
    vx -= player.Speed;
if( kr )
    vx += player.Speed;
if( ku )
    vy -= player.Speed;
if( kd )
    vy += player.Speed;

// now add joystick values
vx += (jx/10000.0f) *         player.Speed;
vy += (jy/10000.0f) *         player.Speed;
```

If the Left Arrow key is held down, then the player's speed is subtracted from the player's X velocity. This means that if only the Left Arrow key is down and the ship can move 200 pixels per second, then vx will be -200. The same thing is done with the other three arrow keys.

The next step is to calculate the joystick input. The function takes jx and jy and divides them by 10,000 (the range of the joystick). If jx is at 5000, then you'll end up with 0.5, which means that the stick is halfway to the right. In this case, you multiply that value with the player's speed, and if you use the example from above, you'll end up with a vx component of +100 pixels per second. Same goes for the Y axis.

So now you've calculated the speed of the ship in the X and Y axes, but there's a problem: As it stands now, the player can "cheat" and make his ship go up to twice as fast as it should go! If the player is holding down the Left Arrow key and has the joystick at the -10,000 x position, this will calculate a speed of -400 pixels per second, which is twice as fast as the 200 pixels per second ship should be moving! Oops! (Yes, it's difficult to actually play using the arrow keys and a joystick at the same time, but someone will manage it eventually.)

So the last step is to make sure the values never exceed the ship's speed, and then adjust the speed accordingly:

```
// make sure player isn't getting a speed boost
// by using keyboard and joystick at the same time
```

```
    if( vx > player.Speed )
        vx = player.Speed;
    if( vx < -player.Speed )
        vx = -player.Speed;
    if( vy > player.Speed )
        vy = player.Speed;
    if( vy < -player.Speed )
        vy = -player.Speed;

    player.VX = vx;
    player.VY = vy;
}
```

Now your players can't cheat!

Rendering

Rendering is fairly simple. First let me show you the `CustomRender` function:

```
protected override void CustomRender()
{
    Game.devices.Graphics.Clear( D3D.ClearFlags.Target,
        System.Drawing.Color.Black, 1.0f, 0 );
    Game.devices.Graphics.BeginScene();
    Game.devices.Sprite.Begin();

    foreach( Sprite s in ships )
        s.Draw( Game.devices.Sprite, camera );
    foreach( Sprite s in projectiles )
        s.Draw( Game.devices.Sprite, camera );
    foreach( Sprite s in powerups )
        s.Draw( Game.devices.Sprite, camera );
```

The same old D3D initialization code makes up the first three lines of the function, and then the sprite drawing kicks in. The game simply loops through all three object arrays and draws them. Remember that as `GameObjects` are `Sprites`, you can draw them quite easily.

The next step is to draw the user interface (UI) and some miscellaneous text strings:

```
    DrawUI();

    if( paused )
    {
        Game.bigfont.DrawText(
            "PAUSED",
```

```
          new System.Drawing.Rectangle(
              0, 0,
              GSS3KConstants.Width, GSS3KConstants.Height ),
          D3D.DrawTextFormat.Center |
          D3D.DrawTextFormat.VerticalCenter,
          System.Drawing.Color.White );
    }


Game.smallfont.DrawText(
    "Press F1 for help",
    new System.Drawing.Rectangle(
        0, 0,
        GSS3KConstants.Width, GSS3KConstants.Height ),
    0, System.Drawing.Color.FromArgb( 127, 255, 255, 255 ) );


Game.devices.Sprite.End();
Game.devices.Graphics.EndScene();
Game.devices.Graphics.Present();
}
```

If the game is paused, then PAUSED is printed out to the screen, and a string telling the user "Press F1 for help" is printed at the upper-left of the screen. I made the text half-translucent so it's not a big nuisance.

The user interface is drawn inside the DrawUI function, but I'm not going to show that to you. You're probably sick of all this graphics code by now anyway. If you're interested, check it out on the CD, as usual.

Playing *GSS3K*

Playing the game is pretty simple, as you've already seen all the control code. The Arrow keys move your ship, Spacebar fires, the Control keys switch weapons, P pauses the game, F1 takes you to the Help screen, and Escape quits. In addition to that, you can choose to use a joystick (make sure you select it from the setup screen), in which case Button 0 fires, and Buttons 1 and 2 are used to switch weapons.

Figures 10.3 and 10.4 show screenshots of the game in action.

The game is very simple, as you'll see after about, say, 10 seconds of playing it. But it's a start! Besides, this simple game is already 10 times more complex than most of the original space shooters.

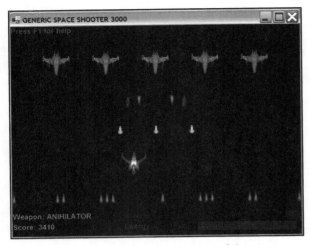

Figure 10.3 Oh no! There's too many of them!

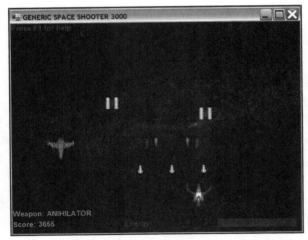

Figure 10.4 Hah! The Annihilator got most of them! Suckers!

You'll notice some quirks in the game—things I didn't have time to get to. For starters, the game just continues playing after you die. This is probably a bad idea, but the code is structured enough so that nothing fails, and it continues running with no problem. In the future, you may consider adding a "YOU LOSE!" screen to the game.

As it stands now, the game is endless; there is no final boss, there are no levels. You have an endless array of ships swarming around you. This is another situation that you may want to address in a real version of the game.

Another major problem is the lack of detail—this is a space game, yet there are no space objects, such as stars, asteroids, and so on. Including such details would make the game much more immersive. As it stands now, the game actually looks kind of boring—just a black screen with spaceships on it.

Anyway, Demo 10.2 is a decent demonstration of something that could go on to become a great arcade-style game. Feel free to modify it for your own purposes.

The Future

Writing a book on general game programming is a very difficult thing to do. The problem is that there are literally thousands of different game genres out there, and one book cannot possibly cover a substantial amount of information even on just one of them!

This book covers a lot of topics that are seen in almost every game out there, so this should have given you a good start. Most games use graphics, sound, input, sprites, collision detection, and so on. There's also a ton of other concepts that games use, but I just didn't have room to get to them.

3D Worlds

Most games these days are 3D, and for a good reason! 3D games look so much more realistic than 2D, and have much more flexibility. Not only that, but 3D hardware is dirt-cheap. You should be able to find a video card that has coloring hardware for less than $20, and a card that supports hardware vertex transformations and lighting for less than $50.

Advanced Collision Detection

Obviously, the collision detection in *GSS3K* is simplistic; it basically puts a theoretical square around your objects and checks to see if those squares intersect. But not everything in the real world is square-shaped! The problem gets even worse in 3D because not everything is cube-shaped; so there are tons of different ways to check if objects collide in a game world.

Artificial Intelligence

GSS3K had no artificial intelligence of any kind in it. The enemy ships simply flew forward and shot at you. Pretty silly, if you ask me. Game companies put lots and lots of research put into AI topics because the more advanced your AI is, the more realistic the game is. Nothing ruins the element of reality worse than having a computer-controlled object do something really stupid, like get stuck in a wall or something. Entire books can are written on the topic of AI. It's that complex.

Networking

Networking is another huge topic in game programming. When's the last time you played a big game that didn't support multiplayer online game play? Probably a long time ago, right?

Advanced Storage

The storage for *GSS3K* is amazingly simple: three arrays of objects. This is about as simple as it gets because it doesn't get any easier. In larger games, you have to figure out how to store all kinds of data—entire *worlds* worth of data, sometimes! How are you going to do that? Well, that's where data structure theory comes into play. There's more to data structures than just arrays, and you need to research what kind of structure is best suited to storing your virtual worlds.

You may even look into having a database to store your data, but that's usually only done with huge, massively-multiplayer online games.

Summary

Well, now that you've assembled a whole game, what are you going to do? Go to Disney World? You *should* be thinking about building onto your first game, or building something better. By now, you should know enough to get started on your own projects.

What You Learned

The main concepts that you should have picked up from this chapter are:

- How to think about your design.
- How to visualize your universe.
- How to start small, and not bite off more than you can chew.
- How to think about how your actors are going to interact with each other.
- How to figure out what kind of data you need before you write any code.
- How *Generic Space Shooter 3000*'s data and game rules are arranged.
- How to build a better framework to suit your game programming needs.
- How to encapsulate game states into classes to make your programs more modular.
- How to use a stack to store game states.
- How to build your own arcade space shooter game!

Review Questions

These review questions test your knowledge on the important concepts exposed to you in this chapter. The answers can be found in Appendix A.

10.1. Why is it important to think about your design before you start writing any code?

10.2. What parts of your game should you think about while designing it?

10.3. Why is it a bad idea to start a huge game project on your own, especially if it's your first game?

10.4. How can using game states make your programs more modular?

10.5. Why is it a good idea to use a stack to store game states?

10.6. You should always be thinking about ways to improve your game, and should plan accordingly. Why?

On Your Own

There's quite a bit you can do on your own with the knowledge that you have now. Some features of *GSS3K* were cut out due to time and space restraints, so the game isn't quite complete in its current form. Among those features were:

- A scrolling star field
- Force feedback effects
- Enemy waves generated from files on disk
- Enemy and weapon data stored on disk in a flexible format

Pick some of these features and add them to the game. Or, make up your own features and add them.

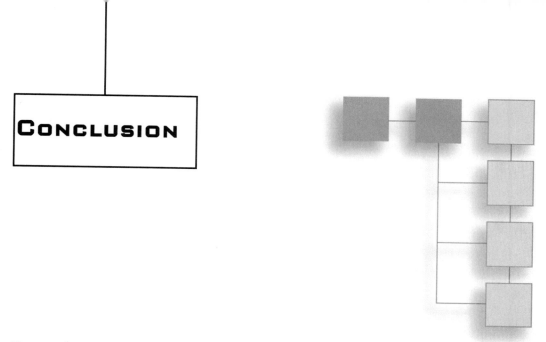

Conclusion

You now know everything there is to know about game programming in C#! Okay, no, I'm just kidding. I really hate to be the one to break it to you, but you've barely just scratched the surface. But you're off to a great start! Game programming is one of the most complex areas of study in the entire world, and you should be proud that you're part of this elite community.

You will always be learning. No one can possibly know everything there is to know about game programming, ever. It's simply not possible. But this is a good thing. I find that most people get into game programming in the first place because they are on a never-ending quest to learn. If that describes you, then boy, have you found the right niche!

Chapters 5 and 10 gave you some ideas about where to continue your knowledge in the areas of C# and Game Programming in general. Luckily for you, there are tons of books that can help you out in this quest. In particular, you're probably going to want to continue reading on about DirectX and Direct3D. *Beginning DirectX 9*, by Wendy Jones, and *Beginning Direct3D Game Programming (2nd Edition)*, by Wolfgang Engel, will be particularly useful to you.

And now, pupils, I'm afraid it is time for me to go, and it's time for you to spread your wings and explore the vast world of game programming.

If you have any questions or comments about the book, feel free to drop me a line at CSBook@ronpenton.net, or visit my public forum discussing this book at http://ronpenton.net/forum.

Thank you for reading this book—it has been a pleasure teaching you game programming in C#. Fare thee well!

PART III

APPENDIXES

APPENDIX A

Answers to Review Questions 287

APPENDIX B

Setting Up DirectX and .NET 303

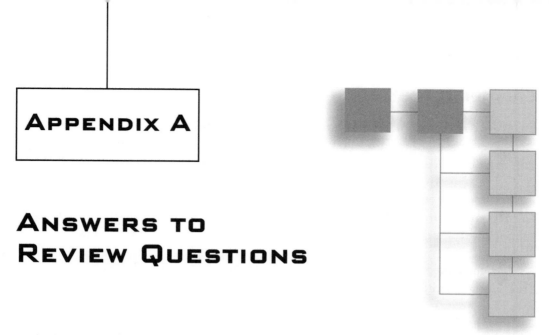

APPENDIX A

ANSWERS TO REVIEW QUESTIONS

Each chapter in this book includes review questions about some of the important concepts covered in the chapter. Here are the answers to those questions.

Chapter 1: The History of C#

1.1. Why does a virtual machine slow down programs?

A virtual machine needs to translate virtual machine code into real machine code, which takes time and adds a significant amount of overhead to your program.

1.2. How does JIT compilation speed up VM execution?

JIT (Just In Time) compilation speeds up the execution of virtual machines by converting the VM code into real machine code when the program is first loaded, so that the conversion doesn't occur while the program is running.

1.3 What languages does Microsoft officially support for .NET?

Microsoft officially supports four languages on .NET:

- Managed C++
- C#
- Visual Basic.NET
- J#

1.4. Can other languages support .NET as well?

Yes. Since the .NET platform runs virtual machine code in the form of MSIL (Microsoft Intermediate Language), any program in any language can be converted into MSIL code and run on the .NET framework.

Chapter 2: The Basics

2.1. Every C# program requires at least one main static class. (True/False)
False. Every program must contain at least one static *function*, not class. This static function must be called `Main` and will be the entry point of the program.

2.2. Booleans are only one bit in size. (True/False)
False. Booleans are one *byte* in size. Storing bits is inefficient in speed, as a computer cannot address memory that small.

2.3. Unsigned integers can hold numbers up to around 4 billion. (True/False)
True. Unsigned integers can hold values from 0 to 4,294,967,295, which is one less than 2^{32}.

2.4. Floating-point numbers hold exact representations of numbers. (True/False)
False. Floating-point numbers hold approximations of decimal numbers.

2.5. Why can't you use variables before they have been assigned a value?
In older languages, whenever you created a new variable and didn't assign anything to it, the variable would contain whatever data was previously in that address, which could be anything. This would end up causing many hard-to-detect errors because the variable would hold seemingly valid data. In C#, the compiler detects if you haven't assigned anything to the variable and gives you a compiler error if you try using it.

2.6. Why do constants make your programs easier to read?
Constant values, such as *pi* and *e*, are very recognizable, and if you used 3.14159 in your program, most people would probably recognize it. But if you wanted all spaceships in your game to move at 200 pixels per second, then putting the value 200 in your program might not be so obvious. A constant called `Shipspeed`, however, makes your programs much more readable.

If you need to change how fast spaceships travel later on, it's much easier to change the value of the constant in one place than to search your code for the value 200 and change it multiple times—this can lead to big bugs.

2.7. Is the following code valid?
```
int x = 10;
float y = 20;
x = y;
```
No. You cannot convert a float to an int like this (implicitly). To fix this code, you would replace the last line with:

```
x = (int)y;
```

2.8. What is the value of x after this code is done?

```
int x = 10;
if( x == 10 )
    x = 20;
```

The value is 20.

2.9. Assume that c is 0. What are the values of the variables after this code is done, and why?

```
int w = 0, x = 0, y = 0, z = 0;
switch( c )
{
case 0:
    w = 10;
case 1:
    x = 10;
case 2:
    y = 10;
    break;
case 3:
    z = 10;
    break;
}
```

w is 10, x is 10, y is 10, z is 0. The case statements 0, 1, and 2 are all executed because they do not break out of the switch statement. Case 3 isn't executed because case 2 breaks out.

2.10. Now assume c is 2 and the code from question 2.9 is run again. What are the values of the variables w, x, y, and z?

w is 0, x is 0, y is 10, z is 0.

2.11. Does the computer compare the value of x and 10 in this example?

```
int x = 10, y = 20;
if( y == 20 && x == 10 )
    x = 20;
```

Yes. As this is an *and* comparison, the only way the second comparison will be executed is if the first comparison is false, which it is not in this case.

2.12. Does the computer compare the value of x and 10 in this example?

```
int x = 10, y = 20;
if( y == 20 || x == 10 )
    x = 20;
```

No. As the first comparison passed, and this is an *or* comparison, there's no need to check the second part.

2.13. When this code is completed, what is the value of x?

```
int x = 0;
while( x < 10 )
    x++;
```

x is 10 after this code completes.

2.14. For each loop, does the value of x increase before FunctionA executes, or after?

```
for( int x = 0; x < 10; x++ )
{
    FunctionA();
}
```

The value of x executes *after* the function is called. The third part of a for loop is always executed after the actual code.

2.15. Rewrite the code in question 2.14 using a while loop instead.

Your answer should look somewhat like this:

```
int x = 0;
while( x < 10 )
{
    FunctionA();
    x++;
}
```

2.16. How many times is FunctionA executed?

```
int x = 0;
do
{
    FunctionA();
} while( x == 1 );
```

FunctionA is executed exactly once, because the loop executes the code before it checks the condition (x == 1). Once the condition is checked, the loop sees that the condition is false, and exits.

2.17. What is the value of x after this code is done?

```
int x = 0;
for( int y = 0; y < 10; y += 2 )
{
    if( y == 4 )
        break;
    x++;
}
```

The value of x is 2 because the loop exits after two iterations.

2.18. What is the value of x after this code is done?
```
int x = 0;
for( int y = 0; y < 10; y += 2 )
{
    if( y == 4 )
        continue;
    x++;
}
```
The value of x is 4. When y is 4, the loop skips back to the beginning without incrementing x.

2.19. Is this code valid? (Assume FunctionA exists.)
```
for( int y = 0; y < 10; y++ )
{
    FunctionA();
}
y = 0;
```
No, this code is not valid. The variable y is only *in scope* inside of the for loop, not outside of it.

Chapter 3: A Brief Introduction to Classes

3.1. Are basic types created as values or as references?
Basic types (int, float, char, etc.) are always created as values. Creating them as references takes too much overhead and would make your programs much slower.

3.2. Are classes created as values or references?
Classes are always created as references.

3.3. Are structures created as values or references?
Structures are always created as values; this allows you to create efficient programs when you don't want to deal with the memory allocation issues of using references.

3.4. What is the value of x after this code is executed?
```
int x = 10;
int y = x;
y = 20;
```
The value of x is 10 because there are no references involved here. The variable y exists completely independent of x in memory.

3.5. Is the data in x and y the same after this code is executed? (Assume class Foo exists and has a function named change which changes data.)

```
Foo x = new Foo();
Foo y = new Foo();
y = x;
y.change();
```

Yes. After the code y = x; is executed, both y and x point to the very same object (the original y is discarded).

3.6. Where does the old data of y go when you execute this line of code?

```
Foo x = new Foo();
Foo y = new Foo();
y = x;
```

The old data of y is kept around in memory for an undetermined amount of time. When the garbage collector notices that nothing points to the old y any more, it frees up the memory for something else.

3.7. What parts of this function definition are "the signature?"

```
int function1( int x, int y )
```

The name and the two parameters.

3.8. Can a class have these two functions at the same time?

```
int function1( int x, int y )
float function1( int x, int y )
```

No, it cannot. These functions have the same signatures and only differ by return type, and the compiler cannot tell what function to use based on the return type.

3.9. Why is it a good idea to create constructors?

Constructors allow you to automatically set values of a class object, so that you can make sure no objects with invalid data exist.

3.10. Are destructors really needed in C#? Why or why not?

Generally, destructors aren't needed. The garbage collector does most of the work that destructors were needed for in older languages.

3.11. When a class contains data, it is called a has-a relationship—a class has a float, and so on. When a class inherits from another class, what is the relationship called?

The *is-a* relationship. When class A inherits from class B, A is-a B.

3.12. What is the primary reason for using inheritance?

The primary reason for inheritance is code-reuse—inheritance allows you to use the same code in many different classes without having to rewrite it all.

3.13. Why would you want to hide your data?

Hiding your data protects it. When you hide data, you make sure it can only be accessed in ways that you control.

3.14. What can access x from the following class?

```
class foo {
    public int x;
}
```

Everything can access x.

3.15. What can access x from the following class?

```
class foo {
    protected int x;
}
```

The only things that can access x is the class foo and classes that inherit from foo.

3.16. What can access x from the following class?

```
class foo {
    private int x;
}
```

The only thing that can access x is the class foo.

3.17. When you don't specify an access level (protected, private, or public), what is the default level?

The default protection level is *private*.

3.18. Why are accessors and properties a good thing?

Accessors and properties allow you to control access to your variables without allowing the whole world to mess with your data in ways that you don't like.

3.19. How do enumerations make your code cleaner?

Enumerations allow your code to look cleaner by replacing numeric values with labels that make your code more readable. See Question 2.6 for a similar problem.

Chapter 4: Advanced C#

4.1. Are namespaces a vital part of modern computer programming?

Yes. Modern programs are *huge*, and contain dozens of libraries, some of which may contain classes that have identical names. Namespaces allow you to specify extra levels of organization.

4.2. What can you do to make accessing namespaces like Microsoft.DirectX.Direct3D easier?

You can use the `using` keyword:

```
using D3D = Microsoft.DirectX.Direct3D;
```

And then you can use `D3D` as an alias for `Microsoft.DirectX.Direct3D`.

4.3. Polymorphism literally means what?

Polymorphism means "Many forms."

4.4. How does polymorphism make your programs more flexible?

Polymorphism allows you to use different classes with the same code, if the classes all have the same capabilities. You can have a function that works on `Spaceships`, and it will work on any spaceship that you define from now until eternity.

Questions 4.5 through 4.8 use the following code for reference:

```
abstract class Spaceship
{
    abstract public void MissileHit();
};

class CargoShip : Spaceship
{
    override public void MissileHit()
    {
        // some code here
    }
};

class CombatShip : Spaceship
{
    public void MissileHit()
    {
        // some code here
    }
};
```

4.5. Can you create instances of Spaceship?

No, it is an abstract class and cannot be created.

4.6. Will the CombatShip class compile? Why or why not?

No it will not compile. The `MissileHit` function needs to be declared as *virtual*. Otherwise, the compiler thinks that you have not implemented `Spaceship.MissileHit` (because you actually haven't!).

4.7. Is this code legal?

```
Spaceship s = new CargoShip();
```

Yes it is. Because of polymorphism, you can store `CargoShips` inside of a `SpaceShip` reference.

4.8. Is this code legal?

```
CargoShip s = new CombatShip();
```

No it is not, because a `CombatShip` is not a `CargoShip`, even though they share a common base.

4.9. How would you declare a 4-index integer array containing all 5s?

```
int[] array = new int[4] { 5, 5, 5, 5 };
```

Or alternatively:

```
int[] array = new int[] { 5, 5, 5, 5 };
```

4.10. What's the easiest way to create a 5×5 2D array?

```
int[,] array = new int[5,5];
```

4.11. Why would you ever use the array-of-arrays method to create multidimensional arrays?

You would use this method if you ever needed to create a multi-dimensional array wherein each index in each dimension isn't neccessarily the same size.

4.12. When you create an array designed to hold 10 Spaceships, all 10 ships are automatically created for you (assume Spaceship is a class, not a struct). (True/False)

False. The array will hold `null` references to spaceships, which you need to fill in yourself.

4.13. Is this code legal? If not, why?

```
int[] array = new int[5];
foreach( int i in array )
{
    i = 20;
}
```

No it is not. You cannot modify the physical contents of an array in a `foreach` loop.

4.14. Which lines of the following code are illegal?

```
1. string str = "HELLO";
2. char c = str[0];
3. str[1] = 'e';
4. str = str + " HOW ARE YOU?";
```

Line 3 is illegal, the rest are legal. Line 3 is invalid because you cannot modify characters in a string—you must create a new string instead.

Chapter 5: One More C# Chapter

5.1. Can an interface hold function declarations?

Yes, it can.

5.2. Can an interface hold function definitions?

No, it cannot. Interfaces cannot hold any function code whatsoever, only declarations.

5.3. Can an interface hold variables?

No, it cannot.

5.4. Are interface functions virtual by default?

No, they are not—you must declare them to be virtual explicitly.

5.5. Fill in the blank: Interfaces are C#'s way of supporting a limited form of _____ inheritance.

Interfaces are C#'s way of supporting a limited form of *multiple* inheritance.

5.6. How does using exceptions make your code cleaner?

Using exceptions allows you to separate special-case error-handling code away from your important processing code.

5.7. Which lines of code will not be executed?

```
1:   public void Foo()
2:   {
3:       try
4:       {
5:           int[] array = new int[3];
6:           array[3] = 10;
7:           array[2] = 5;
8:       }
9:       catch
```

```
10:      {
11:           System.Console.WriteLine( "EXCEPTION!" );
12:      }
13:      finally
14:      {
15:           System.Console.WriteLine( "Process Completed" );
16:      }
17: }
```

Line 7 is not executed because it is skipped over when an exception is thrown on line 6. Everything else is executed.

5.8. Using the code from Question 5.7, which lines of code will always be executed?
Line 15 will always be executed, no matter what exceptions are thrown.

5.9. How do you rethrow an exception without modifying it?
You rethrow an exception simply by using throw;.

5.10. A delegate can point to any public function, static or non-static, as long as the signatures are the same. (True/False)
True. This is why delegates are extremely powerful and flexible tools.

Use this code for questions 5.11 and 5.12:
```
class Foo
{
    static public int DoubleMe( int p )
    {
        return p * 2;
    }

    static public int TripleMe( int p )
    {
        return p * 3;
    }

    public delegate int MyDelegate( int p );
}
```

5.11. Assume the following code is run. What is the value of i?
```
Foo.MyDelegate d = new Foo.MyDelegate( Foo.DoubleMe );
int i = d( 10 );
```
The value of i is 20.

5.12. Assume the following code is run. What is the value of i?
```
Foo.MyDelegate d = new Foo.MyDelegate( Foo.DoubleMe );
d += new Foo.MyDelegate( Foo.TripleMe );
int i = d( 10 );
```
The value of i is 60.

5.13. What is the primary difference between an array and an arraylist?
An array cannot be resized and an arraylist can.

5.14. Why is it considered an expensive operation to insert or remove items in the middle of an arraylist?
It is expensive because an insertion or deletion in the middle of an arraylist must move everything past the insertion/deletion point up or down an index.

5.15. Fill in the blanks: Hash tables store ____/____ pairs.
Hash tables store *key/value* pairs.

5.16. Text files are good for storing data that you want people to easily read, but name one reason why you would prefer a binary file instead.
Binary files are typically smaller than text files because they pack data better.

5.17. Are the numbers generated by System.Random truly random numbers?
No, they are not. An algorithm is used to generate them, and therefore they are not truly random. They just seem like it to our simple minds.

5.18. If you give two generators the same seed and then get a number from each of them, will they be the same?
Yes, generators with the same seed will always generate the same sequence of "random" numbers.

5.19. Name one reason why the ability to set your own random seed is a good thing.
The ability to set your own random seed allows you to re-create certain circumstances in a game, which allows you to track down intermittent bugs or create game-replays easily.

Chapter 6: Setting Up a Framework

6.1. Why is it a good idea to use a project wizard to start your projects?
Project wizards take care of a lot of the so-called "grunt work" and allow you to start coding the important stuff without worrying about the silly little details.

6.2. All windowed programs must have a class that inherits from System.Window. (True/False)
False. All windowed programs must have a class that inherits from System.Windows. Forms.Form. There is no System.Window class.

6.3. Default Form event handlers do nothing, so you don't ever have to call the base version of the functions. (True/False)
False. Some of the event handlers (most notably OnKeyPress) take care of extra details for you, so you cannot simply override them without any consequences.

6.4. Why is it a better idea to use the AdvancedFramework.Timer class instead of the DXUtil.Timer function?
It's better because the advanced framework's timer class is object-oriented, and it allows you to create multiple timer instances rather than keeping one global timer.

6.5. What does System.Threading.Thread.Sleep() do?
This function causes the operating system to put your program to sleep for a limited duration and focus on more important tasks before coming back.

Chapter 7: Direct3D

7.1. What's the difference between a hardware device and a software device?
A *hardware device* is a special piece of dedicated hardware in your computer that performs tasks such as coloring and vertex transformation. A *software device* is simply a fancy term for saying that your CPU is going to be doing the calculations.

7.2. Why would you prefer to use a hardware device over a software device?
A hardware device is typically preferred because it frees up the CPU for more other tasks, such as artificial intelligence or network processing.

7.3. Why are back buffers used?
Back buffers prevent flickering effects when drawing.

7.4. Why is 32-bit color preferred to 16-bit color?
32-bit color is very close to the full visible spectrum of colors, and it does not have color-banding effects that 16-bit color has. Even though a 32-bit color is two times as large as a 16-bit color, it can store 256 times more colors.

7.5. What is alpha information?
Alpha information is simply defined as any extra information that is stored along with a color value. It is typically used for translucency effects.

7.6. Why bother handling multitasking?

Multitasking is an unavoidable part of modern operating systems, and if you don't handle it properly, your game players are going to be very angry because your game will crash.

7.7. Why does Direct3D draw primarily triangles?

Direct3D (and almost every other 3D API out there) uses triangles because triangles are the simplest solid geometrical shape that exists, and every other solid geometrical shape can be created or approximated by combining triangles.

7.8. What purpose do textures serve?

Textures allow you to add detail and realism to your 3D scenes.

7.9. How can you optimize your geometry so that you don't waste time and space working on duplicate vertexes?

You can optimize your geometry by using complex primitive structures like *triangle strips* and *triangle fans*.

7.10. Why use the D3DX library?

Because it makes your life easier! D3DX already has functions that take care of a lot of the so-called "grunt work" for you, so you can spend more time programming games, instead of trying to figure out how to load a 24-bit JPEG file from disk (or other mundane tasks).

Chapter 8: DirectInput

8.1. DirectInput supports two methods of input gathering. What method was shown in this chapter?

The method shown is called *polling*, which involves asking the device for its current state. The other method is called *event handling*, which allows the device to notify your program whenever something changes.

8.2. A keyboard will tell you about every key that is pressed down when you poll it. (True/False)

False! Keyboards can only store a limited number of keys, and will not tell you every single key that is pressed down if you go past this number. I've found that most keyboards can only record the states of around five keys at any given time.

8.3. What is the third axis on a mouse typically used for?

The third axis on a mouse is typically used for the scroll wheel, if one exists.

8.4. Name the four different types of input objects that a game device can have.

1. Buttons

2. Axes

3. Sliders (why these are considered separate from axes, we'll never know)

4. POV hats

8.5. Can force feedback devices can be created non-exclusively?

No, they cannot. Your program must have exclusive access to a force feedback device in order to use those features.

Chapter 9: DirectSound

9.1. By default, do sounds play when your program is not in focus?

No, they do not. You must set the `GlobalFocus` flag of a `BufferDescription` to allow this.

9.2. What is the difference between hardware mixing and software mixing?

Hardware mixing uses your sound card to mix sounds into one buffer, and *software mixing* uses your CPU.

9.3. You put your individual sounds into a Buffer class. (True/False)

False. You put your sounds into a `SecondaryBuffer`; the `Buffer` is managed by the system automatically.

9.4. What do you put into a secondary buffer?

You put wave data into a secondary buffer, to be mixed into a primary buffer later on.

9.5. You are only limited to one sound effect per secondary buffer. (True/False)

False.

9.6. Can you use more than one 3D buffer per secondary buffer?

No. You can only have one 3D buffer per secondary buffer.

Chapter 10: Putting Together a Game

10.1. Why is it important to think about your design before you start writing any code?

Because if you don't, your game will turn into spaghetti—you'll have bugs all over the place caused by situations you didn't think about.

10.2. What parts of your game should you think about while designing it?
The genre, the audience, the data, the universe, and the actors.

10.3. Why is it a bad idea to start a huge game project on your own, especially if it's your first game?
Because games are insanely complex projects, and you can easily become demotivated if you try making something that is beyond your capabilities on your first try.

10.4. How can using game states make your programs more modular?
Using game states allows you to separate the different behaviors of your game into separate classes, allowing you to switch them whenever you want.

10.5. Why is it a good idea to use a stack to store game states?
Stacks allow you to retain previous states, so you don't have to re-create them when you return to them later.

10.6. You should always be thinking about how to improve your game, and plan accordingly. Why?
Because you spent a lot of time writing your code, and if you make it so that it's not expandable, you're essentially throwing your code away and forcing yourself to write brand new code when you start a new game. That's a lot of wasted effort.

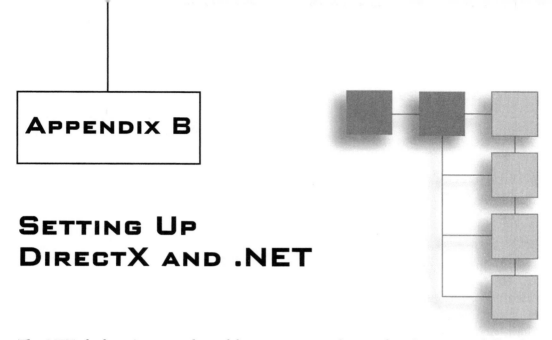

APPENDIX B

SETTING UP DIRECTX AND .NET

The .NET platform is extremely cool for many reasons, but my favorite reason of all is that the SDK and compiler are completely free of charge. You don't need to pay anyone anything to use .NET and DirectX to program C# games.

The .NET Framework

The very first thing you need to do is install the .NET framework, which contains everything you need to run .NET programs. Chances are, if you're running Windows XP, then you already have a .NET framework installed, but it's probably an older version, like 1.0. As of this writing, the current version is 1.1; that's the version you should install. If Microsoft releases a new version in the future, you'll be able to find it at http://microsoft.com as a free download, as well as at the Microsoft Windows Update site, http://windowsupdate.microsoft.com. To use Windows Update, choose the Custom Install option, and then find the .NET framework in the Optional Updates section.

I've included the 1.1 framework installation file on the CD in the directory \extras\ DOTNet1.1Framework\.

The .NET SDK

The framework only allows you to run .NET programs, not create them. In order to create .NET programs, you need to get the .NET 1.1 SDK. It's a free download from Microsoft; you can also find it on the CD in the directory \extras\DOTNet1.1SDK\. The SDK installs everything you need to create your own C# programs, including—and most importantly —the csc command line C# compiler that you saw in Chapter 2.

Integrated Development Environments

Compiling code via a command line is hard. No one does it anymore because no one puts their code into one file anymore, and compiling multifile projects using a command line is a pain in the butt.

This is the future! We use IDEs now! An IDE is a graphical program that keeps track of your projects for you and compiles them automatically. If you've ever used Visual Studio, then you know what an IDE is.

Unfortunately for new game programmers, IDEs are expensive. They fall in the $200–$500 range, and that's a lot of dough for some people to spend. Luckily, there's a better solution: Don't pay anything!

There's an excellent C# IDE out there, called SharpDevelop. All of the examples in this book compile and run with it, as well as Visual C# (a component of Visual Studio). To get SharpDevelop, just head on over to http://icsharpcode.net and download the newest version of the IDE.

Managed DirectX

Microsoft also offers the DirectX SDK free of charge. How nice of them! You can download the newest version of the SDK from http://microsoft.com, or you can install the DX9.0b SDK found on the CD in the directory \extras\DirectX9.0bSDK.

As of this writing, there's a newer version of the DirectX 9 SDK out, version 9.0c, which was released too late for me to switch everything over and test it all out. The major changes with that version of the SDK are all within the D3DX library, which affects texture loading and sprites from Chapter 7 but nothing else.

Setting Up References

C# projects rely on a concept called *references*. A reference is like a library file in C++; it simply defines a library that your program is going to use. For .NET, these references are usually stored in DLL files.

You can find all of the DLLs for the .NET framework and DirectX on your hard drive, typically within the directory C:\Windows\Microsoft.Net.

You need to add references to your project whenever you want to use different namespaces. For example, if you want to use the System namespace, then you need to add a reference to System.dll into your project, and if you want to use System.Windows.Forms, then you need to add System.Windows.Forms.dll to your project.

In Visual C#, you add references by right-clicking on References in your Solution Explorer window and then selecting Add Reference. Once you do that, the Add Reference box shown in Figure B.1 will appear.

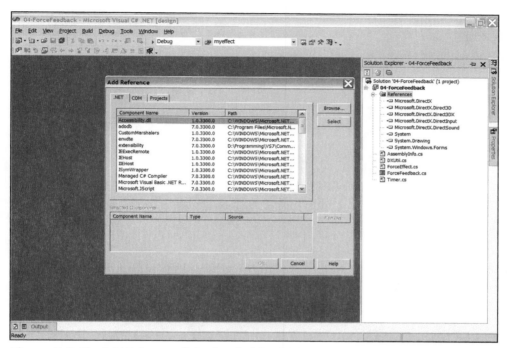

Figure B.1 The Add Reference dialog box for Visual C#

You can double-click on any of the references shown in the dialog box, or click on the Browse button to go into your hard drive and select any references that aren't listed already.

The process is similar for SharpDevelop: You go to the Project tab, right-click on References, and then select Add Reference. A dialog box like the one in Figure B.2 will appear.

You can select any of the installed references in the window, or you can click on the .NET Assembly Browser tab and browse your hard drive for any references you want to add.

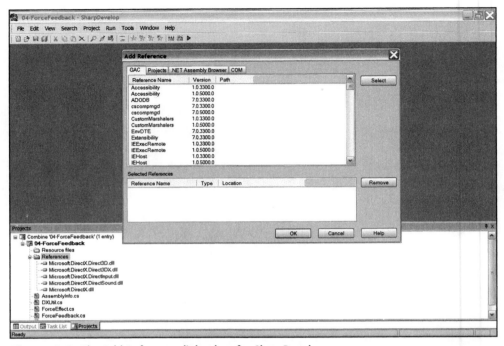

Figure B.2 The Add Reference dialog box for SharpDevelop

INDEX

@ symbol, 259

A

abstract classes, 71–72. *See also* interfaces
    hiding functions in, 91
acceleration, 231
    in *Generic Space Shooter 3000* base class, 247
access levels, defining, 52–53
accessors, 55–56
actors in game, 229
    data for, 229–230
addition operator, 17
AddState function, 241–242
Advanced Framework, 134–142
    entry point in, 142
    events in, 140–141
    function changes in, 139–140
    Game class in, 139
    keyboard, creation of, 197
    namespaces in, 138–139
    Paused property, 141
    ProcessFrame function, 139–140
    timer in, 137–138
After Burner, 210
AI (Artificial Intelligence), 279
aliasing
    in Advanced Framework, 138–139
    namespace aliasing, 66
alpha. *See* Direct3D
alpha blending, 164–167
    for sprites, 179
anchor point for sprites, 180–181, 183
and statements, 26
animating sprites, 187–188

API (Application Programming Interface), 6.
    See also Direct3D
Application class, 130
Arial font, 190
array lists, 103–105
    is operator, 104
    as operator, 104–105
    typeof operator, 104
arrays, 74–82. *See also* strings
    allocating arrays, 79–80
    basic example, 74–75
    changing dimensions of, 78
    defined, 75–76
    in Direct3D, 161–162
    exceptions from, 96
    foreach loop with, 81–82
    indexes in, 80–81
    inheritance, support for, 77
    initializing values of, 76
    multidimensional arrays, 77–81
    sprite array, creating, 186
as operator, 104–105
ASCII files, 109
assemblers, 4
assembly languages, 4
    portability and, 5
Atari games, 228
attributes, designing, 230–231
author's Web site, 283
axes. *See* joysticks

B

back-buffering, 148
backface culling, 162

banding effects, 153
base class
    creating, 49–50
    for *Generic Space Shooter 3000* objects, 246–248
    virtual functions and, 68
BCD calculations, 5
Beginning Direct3D Game Programming, Second Edition (Engel), 160, 263
Beginning DirectX 9 (Jones), 146, 283
behavior flags in Direct3D, 150–151
binary streams, 110–112
    reading, 111–112
binary-coded decimal (BCD) calculations, 5
BinaryReader class, 111
BinaryWriter class, 112
bitshifting, 19
bitwise math operators, 19
blending. *See* alpha blending
.BMP files
    color keys requiring, 186
    for textures, 170
boldfacing text, 190
Boolean values, 19–20
bounds checking, 247
boxing objects, 73–74
branching, 23–27
break keyword, 29
    in switch blocks, 25–26
buffer swapping, 146–149
buffers, 146–149. *See also* sound buffers
    playing buffers, 220–221
Buffer3D class, 223
built-in data types, 16–17
buttons on joysticks, 207
    demo information, 209
by-values, 44

C

C#. *See also* Visual C#
    future of, 10
    Hello C# program, 14–15
    .NET platform and, 8
    2.0 features, 117
C language, 5
    entry point in, 14–15
C++ language, 7, 10
    conditional statements in, 25
    entry point in, 14–15

function pointers, 100
    .NET platform and, 8
    override keyword in, 71
cache, streams using, 108
CalculateBounding function, 247
Camera class for sprites, 184–185
cameras, 181, 184–185
    data for creating, 185–188
    demo for, 185–189
    in *Generic Space Shooter 3000*, 261
cancelable events, 128
catch block, 95–97
    chaining catch blocks, 99
    file-closing code in, 97
    re-throwing exceptions, 99
    specific exceptions and, 98–99
chaining delegates, 102
CheckValidity function, 265–266
child classes
    abstract functions, declaring, 72
    interfaces and, 88
classes, 14, 35–61. *See also* abstract classes; child classes; objects
    accessors, 55–56
    constructors, 45–46
    creating, 40
    destructors, 46–48
    functions in, 41–45
    inheritance, 48–51
    properties, 55–57
    as reference types, 36–39
    static members, 53–54
    structures compared, 40–41
clock operator, 17–18
Clone function, 248
Close function, 108–109
COBOL, 8
collections, 102–107
    array lists, 103–105
    hash tables, 105–106
    is operator, 104
    as operator, 104–105
    queues, 106–107
    stacks, 106–107
    typeof operator, 104
collision checking
    in *Generic Space Shooter 3000*, 268–272
    in 3D worlds, 279

Collision functions, 247, 270–272
collision rectangle, 231
colors. *See also* Direct3D
   display formats, 152–153
   for sprites, 179, 186, 187
combining interfaces, 93
Common Type System, 8
compilers, 5–6
   delegates, creating, 100–102
   for Hello C# program, 15
computers, history of, 3–11
conditional statements, 23–26
   branching, 23–27
   short-circuit evaluation and, 26–27
constant force effect, 210
constants, 21
   in *Generic Space Shooter 3000,* 261
constructors, 45–46
   fir Direct3D, 149–151
   in SharpDevelop, 127
continue keyword, 29–30
conversions, explicit/implicit, 22–23
copying
   buffers, 149
   deep copy, 248
   reference types, 38
   shallow copy, 248

D

dangling pointers, 39
data collections. *See* collections
data hiding, 51–53
Data Structures for Game Programmers, 106
data types, 16–17. *See also* structures
   enumerations, 57–58
   static data, 54
.DDS files for textures, 170
dead zone of joystick, 205–206
   in game state framework, 233
debugging
   short-circuit evaluation and, 27
   truncation and, 22
decimals, conversions with, 23
decrement operator, 17–18
deep copy, 248
default constructors, 45–46
delayed destruction, 47–48

delegates, 100–102
   chaining delegates, 102
   creating, 100–102
   multicasting, 102
   removing, 102
deleting delegates, 102
delta value, 249
demos. *See also* Direct3D
   for cameras, 185–189
   force feedback effects, using, 213–216
   joystick demo, 207–209
   sounds, loading and playing, 222
   for sprites, 185–189
depth buffers, 161
depth information, 161
designing
   actors in game, 229
   flexibility in game, 229–230
   genre of game, deciding on, 228
   for objects in game, 229–230
   setting up, 227–228
   sprites, attributes for, 230–231
destroyed Boolean, 231
destructors, 46–48
   delayed destruction, 47–48
device blocks, 233
DeviceOptions class, 232–233
   adding options to, 233
diamond inheritance, 91–92
.DIB files for textures, 170
DirectInput, 197–217. *See also* force feedback; game devices; joysticks
   input device cooperation flags, 198
   keyboards, 197–200
   mice, 200–201
DirectSound, 219–225. *See also* sound buffers
   demo for, 222
   Device class, 64, 219
   sound effects, 222–223
   3D sound, 223–224
Direct3D, 145–195. *See also* sprites
   alias for namespace, 66
   alpha
      for display formats, 153
      working with, 164–167
   alpha blending, 164–167
   arrays in, 161–162
   availability of device, checking, 151–154

Direct3D *(continued)*
    backface culling, 162
    behavior flags, 150–151
    buffers and buffer swapping, 146–149
    capabilities of device, checking, 154
    colors
        display formats, 152–153
        textures, color key for, 171–172
        vertex colors, 161
        working with, 164
    configurability of devices, 146
    constructor for, 149–151
    copying buffers, 149
    creating devices, 149–151
    current format, using, 154
    demos
        for cameras, 185–189
        font options working with, 191–193
        for sprites, 185–189
        squares, creating, 175–176
        triangles, creating, 167–169
    Device class, 64
    discarding buffers, 149
    display formats, 152–153
    drawing, 159–163
        text, 191
    filters for textures, 171
    flickering effect in, 147
    flipping buffers, 149
    fonts in, 190
    graphics adapter, 150
    hardware devices, 150
    loading textures, 170–172
    lost graphics device, working with, 158
    Manager class with, 151–154
    memory, texture placed in, 171
    mip-mapping, 171
    multi-tasking with, 157–159
    normal data, 161
    performing device checks, 154
    presentation properties, 147
    primitives, 174
    Project for, 124–132
    Render function, 157–158
        triangles, drawing, 162–163
    Reset function, 158
    setting up devices, 155–157

squares
    creating, 173–174
    demo for creating, 175–176
    textures, 169–173
    color key for, 171–172
    coordinates, 172–173
    demo for creating, 175–176
    loading textures, 170–172
    translucency with, 164–167
    triangle fans, 174
    triangle lists, 174
    triangle strips, 174
    triangle-rastering with, 159–160
    triangles
        demo for creating, 167–169
        textures mapped on, 172–173
    updating format, 154–159
    vertexes, 160–162
        for squares, 173–174
DirectX 9.0b, 146
DirectX 9.0c, 146
DirectX SDK
    DLLs, 133, 304
    fedit.exe, 210–211
    free download, 304
    .NET program and, 8
    #3D Framework wizard, 134
    timer in, 135–138
    versions of, 146
dirty rectangles, 147
display
    Direct3D formats, 152
    Generic Space Shooter 3000, staying on screen in, 263
division operator, 17
DLLs
    for DirectX, 133, 304
    for .NET framework, 304
Doom III, 228
doubles, generating, 116
do-while loops, 29
downloading
    DirectX SDK, 304
    .NET SDK, 303
Draw function, 178–179
    for sprites, 181–184
drawing. *See also* Direct3D; sprites
    text, 191

DrawText function, 191
duplicating code, 48

E

EGA format, 152
else clauses, 24
elseif statements, 24
energy. *See Generic Space Shooter 3000*
Engel, Wolfgang, 160, 283
entry point, 14–15
    in Advanced Framework, 142
    in game state framework, 243
    in SharpDevelop, 131–132
enumerations, 57–58
errors. *See* exceptions
event handlers
    in SharpDevelop, 129–131
    Windows event handlers, 130–131
events
    in Advanced Framework, 140–141
    cancelable events, 128
    key press event, 131
    in SharpDevelop, 128
exceptions, 94–100
    catch block, 95–97
    custom exceptions, creating, 100
    example of, 94–95
    finally block, 97–98
    re-throwing exceptions, 99
    specific exceptions, catching, 98–99
    try block, 95–96
explicit conversions, 22–23
extendible languages, 16
extending interfaces, 93

F

fedit.exe, 210–211
FIFO (first-in-first-out) containers, 106
file-closing code, 97
files
    access, 107–114
    resource file lists, 244
    in SharpDevelop, 125–126
    streams, 107–109, 112–114
filters for textures in Direct3D, 171
finally block, 97–98
firing calculations in *Generic Space Shooter 3000*,
    263–265

fixed point numbers, 17
flags
    behavior flags in Direct3D, 150–151
    buffer play flags, 220
    for game devices, 202
    input device cooperation flags, 198
    NonExclusive flag, 198
flexibility in game, 229–230
flipping buffers, 149
floating point numbers, 17
    sprites, rotating, 179
Flush function, 108–109
fonts
    demo for working with, 191–193
    in Direct3D library, 190
    system font, creating, 190
foot pedals, 201
for loops, 28
force feedback, 210–216
    demo for using effects, 213–216
    gathering input for, 215–216
    initializing effects, 214
    loading effects, 211–212
    output, playing, 215–216
    playing effects, 212–213
    setting up device for, 214
    stopping effects, 212–213
Force Feedback Editor program, 210–211
foreach loop, 81–82
    for joysticks, 205
Form class, 130
forms, 127
FrameMove function, 129–130
    in Advanced Framework, 139–140
frameworks, 123. *See also* Advanced Framework;
    game state framework
    Visual C# D3D framework, 133–134
fullscreen applications with Direct3D, 154–159
function pointers, 100
functional programming languages, 7
functions. *See also* delegates; static functions
    in Advanced Framework, 139–140
    in classes, 41–45
    hash functions, 105–106
    interfaces holding declarations, 89
    overloading, 44–45
    parameters with, 43–44
    polymorphism and, 72

functions *(continued)*
 return values with, 41–42
 static functions, 55
 with streams, 107–108
 string functions, 84
 in structures, 41–45
 virtual functions, 68–71

G

Game class
 in Advanced Framework, 139
 in game state framework, 240–243
game devices, 201–209. *See also* joysticks
 axes of data for, 203–204
 creating, 202–203
 finding, 202
 flags for, 202
 modifying axes, 204–206
 range, modifying, 204–205
game pads, 201
game processing
 in *Generic Space Shooter 3000,* 262–265
 in SharpDevelop, 129–130
game state framework, 231–232
 changing states, functions for, 241–242
 Configuration state, 235
 device blocks in, 233
 device options, 232–233
 entry point in, 243
 Game class in, 240–243
 game loop in, 241–242
 Generic Space Shooter 3000 example, 244–279
 Help state, 236
  in *Generic Space Shooter 3000,* 260
 input checkers in, 233–235
 Introduction state, 235–236
  in *Generic Space Shooter 3000,* 258–260
 joysticks in, 232–233, 235
 keyboard checking in, 234
 Menu state, 237–238
 mouse checking in, 234–235
 rendering in, 237
 sample state, code for, 239–240
 setup forms, 232
 stack system in, 237–239
 state changes in, 237–239

garbage collection, 39
 destructors and, 46
GDI components, 123
generating random numbers, 115–116
Generic Space Shooter 3000, 244–279, 257, 258,
 272–273
 base class for objects, 246–248
 cameras in, 261
 changing states in, 258
 collision checking in, 268–272
 Collision functions, 270–272
 constants in, 261
 delta value in, 249
 destroying objects in, 266–267
 energy powerups, 252
 firing calculations in, 263–265
 game objects in, 244–256
 game processing in, 262–265
 Game state in, 260–277
 Help state in, 260
 input
  devices, 257–258
  processing, 274–276
 Introduction state, 258–260
 joysticks, 273–274
  calculating input from, 275
 keyboards in, 257–258, 272–273
 mice, 257–258, 274
 miscellaneous functions class, 261–262
 object validity checking in, 265–266
 paused game, 277
 playing the game, 277–279
 powerups, 251–253
  sounds for, 266–267
 ProcessFrame function in, 259–260
 ProcessInput function in, 274–275
 projectiles in, 251
 rendering in, 276–277
 screen, players staying on, 263
 set code for, 249–250
 sounds
  for powerups, 266–267
  for weapons, 254
 spaceship class, 248–251
 sprites in, 261
 startup state in, 256–258
 states in, 256–261
 waves of ships, generating, 267–268

weapons
  base Weapon class, 253–254
  custom weapons, defining, 255–256
  firing calculations, 263–265
  powerups, 252–253
generics, 117
genre of game, 228
GetMouseButtons function, 201
GetPressedKeys function, 199
global functions, 14–15
graphics. *See also* Direct3D
  in SharpDevelop, 128
graphics adapter, 150
GSS3K. See Generic Space Shooter 3000
GUI (graphical user interface) components, 123
GUID (globally unique identifier)
  for game devices, 202
  for keyboards, 198

H
hard-coded seed, setting, 114
hardware
  devices, 150
  vertex processing, 151
hash tables, 105–106
.HDR files for textures, 170
heap, 37
height of sprites, 183
Hello C# program, 14–15
high level programming languages, 5–6
history of C#, 3–11

I
IDEs (Integrated Development Environments),
      123–124, 304. *See also* SharpDevelop; Visual
      C#
if statements, 24–25
implicit conversions, 22–23
importing modules for Visual C#, 133–134
increment operator, 17–18
inheritance, 48–51
  arrays supporting, 77
  diamond inheritance, 91–92
  multiple inheritance, 91–93
  working with, 49–50
InitializeGraphics function, 155–156

initializing
  arrays, 76
  force feedback effects, 214
  graphics in SharpDevelop, 128
  sprites, 186–187
  variables, 20
input devices
  cooperation flags, 198
  in game state framework, 233–235
  in *Generic Space Shooter 3000*, 257–258, 274–276
installing .NET framework, 303
instance counting
  destructors for, 47
  static functions and, 55
instance members, 53–54
integer-based data types, 16
interactivity
  of keyboard, 199
  of sprites, 188–189
interfaces, 88–93
  combining, 93
  compared to abstract classes, 89–91
  extending, 93
  function declarations and, 89
  multiple inheritances and, 91–93
  user interface (UI), 276–277
  virtual functions and, 89–91
internal access, 52
Introduction state. *See* game state framework
is operator, 104
is-a relationship, 49
italicizing text, 190
iterators, 117

J
J# language, 8
Java
  arrays in, 79
  override keyword in, 71
Java Virtual Machine (JVM), 6
Jones, Wendy, 146, 283
joysticks, 201. *See also* force feedback; *Generic Space
      Shooter 3000*
  buttons on, 207, 209
  configuring, 203
  dead zone of, 205–206, 233
  demo for, 207–209

joysticks *(continued)*
    in *Generic Space Shooter 3000*, 257–258, 273–274
    modifying axes, 204–206
    obtaining axis data, 203–204
    POV hats, 206–207
    range, modifying, 204–205
.JPG files
    color keying with, 186
    for textures, 170
Just In Time (JIT) compilation, 8–9

K

key press event, 131
keyboards, 197–200
    in game state framework, 234
    gathering input from, 199–200
    in *Generic Space Shooter 3000*, 257–258, 272–273
    polling, 199–200
key-value pairs, storing, 105

L

languages. *See also* assembly languages; C#
    C language, 5
    C++ language, 7
    functional programming language, 7
    high level programming languages, 5–6
    machine language, 4
    .NET platform and, 8
libraries. *See also* DLLs
    in SharpDevelop, 126
LIFO (last-in-first-out) containers, 106
linear filters, 171
Linux, Java Virtual Machine (JVM) and, 6
LISP, 7
Listener3D class, 224
loading
    force feedback effects, 211–212
    Generic Space Shooter 3000, game object loader in, 244–246
    textures with Direct3D, 170–172
logical operators, 19–20
Logitech Wingman Force 3D, 203
looping, 27–30
    foreach loop, 81–82
    in game state framework, 242–243
lossless graphics format, 186
lossy format graphics, 186

lost graphics device, working with, 158
lowercase characters, 84

M

machine language, 4
Macintosh, Java Virtual Machine (JVM) and, 6
magic numbers, 21
main class in SharpDevelop, 126–127
Main function, 15
Manager class, Direct3D, 151–154
mathematical operators, 17–18
memory. *See also* references
    dangling pointers, 39
    Direct3D memory, 171
    streams, 112
mice, 200–201
    in game state framework, 234–235
    in *Generic Space Shooter 3000*, 257–258, 274
    polling, 200–201
Microsoft. *See also* Direct3D; Visual C#
    .NET platform, 7–11
    timer provided by, 135
mip-mapping, 171
modulus operator, 17–18
monochrome displays, 152
Move function in *Generic Space Shooter 3000*, 247
MSDN, collections in, 107
MSIL code, 8
    Just In Time (JIT) compilation and, 8–9
multidimensional arrays, 77–81
multi-player online game play, 280
multiple inheritance, 91–93
multiplication operator, 17
multi-tasking
    animation, effect on, 189
    with Direct3D, 157–159

N

name overlapping, 64
namespaces, 64–66
    in Advanced Framework, 138–139
    aliasing, 66
    creating, 65
    working with, 66
naming interfaces, 88
NES games, 228
nesting namespaces, 64–65

.NET framework, 7–11. *See also* C#
  array lists in, 103–104
  DLLs for, 304
  downloading .NET SDK, 303
  future of, 10
  installing, 303
  Just In Time (JIT) compilation, 8–9
  namespaces in, 64
network streams, 112
networking, 280
new keyword
  for arrays, 75
  override keyword and, 71
  reference types, creating, 36–37
Nintendo Rumble Pak, 210
non-default constructors, 46
NonExclusive flag, 198
non-static functions, 101
non-virtual functions, 91
normal data, 161
Now function in timer, 138
NP-Complete problems, 10
N64 controller, 210
null value, 39
number generators, 114
NVIDIA GeForce card, 151

O

object-oriented programming (OOP), 114
objects, 14, 73–74. *See also* arrays; delegates; poly-
    morphism
  array lists storing, 104
  common attributes for, 230–231
  deep copy of, 248
  Generic Space Shooter 3000, game object sin,
    244–256
  shallow copy of, 248
Offset property for sprites, 185
one-dimensional arrays, 77
OnGotFocus event, 140–141
OpenRead function, 113
OpenWrite function, 113
operating system with Direct3D, 155
operator overloading, 116–117
operators, 17–20
overloading
  functions, 44–45
  operator overloading, 116–117

override keyword, 70–71
overrides for event handlers, 130

P

palletized color displays, 152
parameters, 43–44
  delegates returning, 101
  of Draw function, 178–179
  multiple parameters, 43
  for texture loading, 170–172
  variable parameter lists, 117
Paused property
  Advanced Framework, 141
  in *Generic Space Shooter 3000,* 261
performance counters, 135
PERL, 8
.PFM files for textures, 170
pixel shaders, 160
pixels
  depth-checking, 161
  in display formats, 152–153
platforms, portability of, 5
Play function, 220–221
playing buffers, 220–221
.PNG files for textures, 170
polling
  keyboards, 199–200
  mice, 200–201
polymorphism, 67–74
  abstraction in, 71–72
  functions and, 72
  virtual functions, 68–71
portability, 4–5
  of Java Virtual Machine (JVM), 6
  with virtual machines (VMs), 6–7
position vertexes, 160
post-version operator, 18
POV hats, 206–207
  demo information, 209
powerups, 230. *See also Generic Space Shooter 3000*
.PPM files for textures, 170
pre-increment operator, 18
preprocessors, 116
private access, 52–53
ProcessFrame function, 139–140
  animation information, storing, 187–188
  in game state framework, 238–239
  in *Generic Space Shooter 3000,* 259–260

ProcessInput function, 274–275
projectiles
  designing, 230
  in *Generic Space Shooter 3000,* 251
properties, 55–57
protected access, 52–53
protected internal access, 52
protected tags, 127
public data, 40
  use of, 55
public keyword, defined, 50–51
Python, 8

Q

queues, 106–107

R

Random class, 115–116
random numbers, 114–116
  generating, 115–116
  seed values, 114–115
range
  in game devices, 204–205
  in game state framework, 233
Read function, 107–108
  from text stream, 109
ReadByte function, 107–108, 113
readers, 109–112
ReadFloat function, 111
reading
  binary streams, 111–112
  strings, 112
ReadLine function, 109
read-only
  foreach loop and arrays as, 82
  strings as, 83
ReadSingle function, 111
ReadToEnd function, 109
recursion detection, 57
reduction theory, 9–10
references, 36–39. *See also* arrays
  copying, 38
  declaring, 36–37
  garbage collection, 39
  null value, 39
  objects and, 73
  parameters, 43–44

setting up, 304–306
  working with, 37–38
remainder operator, 17–18
Render function. *See* Direct3D
rendering
  in game state framework, 237
  in *Generic Space Shooter 3000,* 276–277
  sprites, 188
repetition. *See* looping
Reset function
  in Direct3D, 158
  in timer, 138
resolution of system, 232
resource file lists, 244
re-throwing exceptions, 99
return keyword, 42
review questions, answers to, 287–302
rotating sprites, 178–180
RPGs (role-playing games), 228
  universe for, 229
Rubik's cube, 77

S

scaling object, parameter for, 178
scoping, 30–31
screen. *See* display
seed values, 114–115
Sega Genesis, 210
sequencing, 23
setup form, 232
shading sprites, 179
shallow copy, 248
SharpDevelop, 15, 124–132, 304
  code, explanation of, 126–132
  constructor in, 127
  entry point, 131–132
  event handlers in, 129–131
  events in, 128
  files in, 125–126
  game processing in, 129–130
  graphics, initializing, 128
  libraries, 126
  main class in, 126–127
  references, adding, 305–306
shifting operators, 19
short-circuit evaluation, 26–27
16-bit color displays, 153

SNES games, 228
software
    devices, 150
    virtual machines (VMs), 6–7
sound. *See also* DirectSound; *Generic Space Shooter 3000*
    devices, creating, 219
sound buffers, 220–222
    customizing buffers, 221
    in *Generic Space Shooter 3000*, 244–246
    3D buffers, 223–224
sound cards, 220–221
sound effects, 222–223
    sound buffers supporting, 221
specific exceptions, catching, 98–99
sprites, 177–189. *See also* cameras
    anchor point for, 180–181, 183
    animating, 187–188
    arrays, creating, 186
    attributes for, 230–231
    colors for, 186, 187
    data for creating, 185–188
    data members for, 179–180
    Draw function for, 181–184
    in *Generic Space Shooter 3000*, 246, 261
    initializing, 186–187
    interactivity, adding, 188–189
    parameters for drawing, 178–179
    properties of, 181
    renderer, creating, 186
    rendering, 188
    rotating, 178–180
    texture for, 187
    width and height of, 183
squares. *See* Direct3D
stacks, 106–107
    state system, stack-based, 237–239
    system stack, 36
StateChange function, 241–242
states. *See also* game state framework
    in *Generic Space Shooter 3000*, 256–261
static data, 54
static functions, 15, 55
    delegates pointing to, 101
static members, 53–54
steering wheels, 201
storage issues, 280

streams, 107–109
    binary streams, 110–112
    file streams, 112–114
    text and, 109
StreamWriter object, 113–114
strikeout text, 190
StringBuilders, 83
strings, 82–84
    functions, list of, 84
    reading, 112
struct keyword, 40
structures
    classes compared, 40–41
    constructors, 46
    creating, 40
    functions in, 41–45
subtraction operator, 17
switch statements, 25–26
System DLLs, 133
system font, creating, 190
system stack, 36
System.10.Stream, 107
System.Text.StringBuilder, 83

T

tags, protected, 127
text. *See also* fonts
    binary streams, 110–112
    drawing text, 191
    special effects on, 190
    and streams, 109
    strings for, 82–84
textures. *See also* Direct3D
    coordinates, 172–173
    in *Generic Space Shooter 3000*, 244–246
    mip-mapping, 171
    for sprites, 178, 187
.TGA files
    color keys requiring, 186
    for textures, 170
32-bit display formats, 153
2D arrays, 77–81
3D arrays, 77–81
#3D Framework wizard, 134
3D transformations, 160
3D worlds, 279

timer, 134–138
  in Advanced Framework, 137–138
  in DirectX SDK, 135–138
  function options, 135
  problems with, 137–138
transformed vertexes, 160
translucency with Direct3D, 164–167
triangle fans, 174
triangle lists, 174
triangle strips, 174
triangle-rastering, 159–160
triple-buffering, 148
true color displays, 152–153
truncation, 21–22
try block, 95–96
  in Direct3D, 159
  file-closing code in, 97
typecasts, 21–23
typeof operator, 104
typesize, specifying, 190

U

unboxing objects, 73–74
underlining text, 190
universe for game, 229
unsafe code blocks, 117
uppercase characters, 84
USB ports, 202
user interface (UI), 276–277
using keyword, 66, 132
using-block, 132

V

V axes, 204
validity checking in *Generic Space Shooter 3000*,
    265–266
values
  delegates returning, 101
  parameters, 43–44
  return values, 41–42
value-types, 36
  as operator with, 105
  objects and, 73
variable parameter lists, 117
variables, 20–21
  switch statements, 25–26

VC#. *See* Visual C#
velocity, 231
  in *Generic Space Shooter 3000* base class, 247
vertexes. *See* Direct3D
VGA format, 152
virtual functions, 68–71
  interfaces and, 89–91
virtual machines (VMs), 6–10
virtualism, 70–71
Visual C#, 132–134, 304
  D3D framework, 133–134
  new project, creating, 133
  references, adding, 305

W

.WAV files, 220
  for 3D sound, 224
weapons. *See also Generic Space Shooter 3000*
  designing, 230
Web site of author, 283
while loops, 28
white space, trimming, 84
width of sprites, 183
WIN32 API, 6
windowed applications, 155
Windows, Java Virtual Machine (JVM) and, 6
wizards, 123–124. *See also* SharpDevelop; Visual C#
world space, 247
  for sprites, 181
Write function, 107–108
  with streams, 110
WriteByte function, 107–108, 113
WriteLine function, 110
writers, 109–112
writing binary data, 112

X

XBox 2, 10
x86 code, 9
XYZ axes, 204

Gamedev.net
The most comprehensive game development resource

- The latest news in game development
- The most active forums and chatrooms anywhere, with insights and tips from experienced game developers
- Links to thousands of additional game development resources
- Thorough book and product reviews
- Over 1,000 game development articles!
  Game design
  Graphics
  DirectX
  OpenGL
  AI
  Art
  Music
  Physics
  Source Code
  Sound
  Assembly
  And More!

Gamedev.net

License Agreement/Notice of Limited Warranty

By opening the sealed disc container in this book, you agree to the following terms and conditions. If, upon reading the following license agreement and notice of limited warranty, you cannot agree to the terms and conditions set forth, return the unused book with unopened disc to the place where you purchased it for a refund.

License:

The enclosed software is copyrighted by the copyright holder(s) indicated on the software disc. You are licensed to copy the software onto a single computer for use by a single user and to a backup disc. You may not reproduce, make copies, or distribute copies or rent or lease the software in whole or in part, except with written permission of the copyright holder(s). You may transfer the enclosed disc only together with this license, and only if you destroy all other copies of the software and the transferee agrees to the terms of the license. You may not decompile, reverse assemble, or reverse engineer the software.

Notice of Limited Warranty:

The enclosed disc is warranted by Thomson Course Technology PTR to be free of physical defects in materials and workmanship for a period of sixty (60) days from end user's purchase of the book/disc combination. During the sixty-day term of the limited warranty, Thomson Course Technology PTR will provide a replacement disc upon the return of a defective disc.

Limited Liability:

THE SOLE REMEDY FOR BREACH OF THIS LIMITED WARRANTY SHALL CONSIST ENTIRELY OF REPLACEMENT OF THE DEFECTIVE DISC. IN NO EVENT SHALL THOMSON COURSE TECHNOLOGY PTR OR THE AUTHOR BE LIABLE FOR ANY OTHER DAMAGES, INCLUDING LOSS OR CORRUPTION OF DATA, CHANGES IN THE FUNCTIONAL CHARACTERISTICS OF THE HARDWARE OR OPERATING SYSTEM, DELETERIOUS INTERACTION WITH OTHER SOFTWARE, OR ANY OTHER SPECIAL, INCIDENTAL, OR CONSEQUENTIAL DAMAGES THAT MAY ARISE, EVEN IF THOMSON COURSE TECHNOLOGY PTR AND/OR THE AUTHOR HAS PREVIOUSLY BEEN NOTIFIED THAT THE POSSIBILITY OF SUCH DAMAGES EXISTS.

Disclaimer of Warranties:

THOMSON COURSE TECHNOLOGY PTR AND THE AUTHOR SPECIFICALLY DISCLAIM ANY AND ALL OTHER WARRANTIES, EITHER EXPRESS OR IMPLIED, INCLUDING WARRANTIES OF MERCHANTABILITY, SUITABILITY TO A PARTICULAR TASK OR PURPOSE, OR FREEDOM FROM ERRORS. SOME STATES DO NOT ALLOW FOR EXCLUSION OF IMPLIED WARRANTIES OR LIMITATION OF INCIDENTAL OR CONSEQUENTIAL DAMAGES, SO THESE LIMITATIONS MIGHT NOT APPLY TO YOU.

Other:

This Agreement is governed by the laws of the State of Massachusetts without regard to choice of law principles. The United Convention of Contracts for the International Sale of Goods is specifically disclaimed. This Agreement constitutes the entire agreement between you and Thomson Course Technology PTR regarding use of the software.